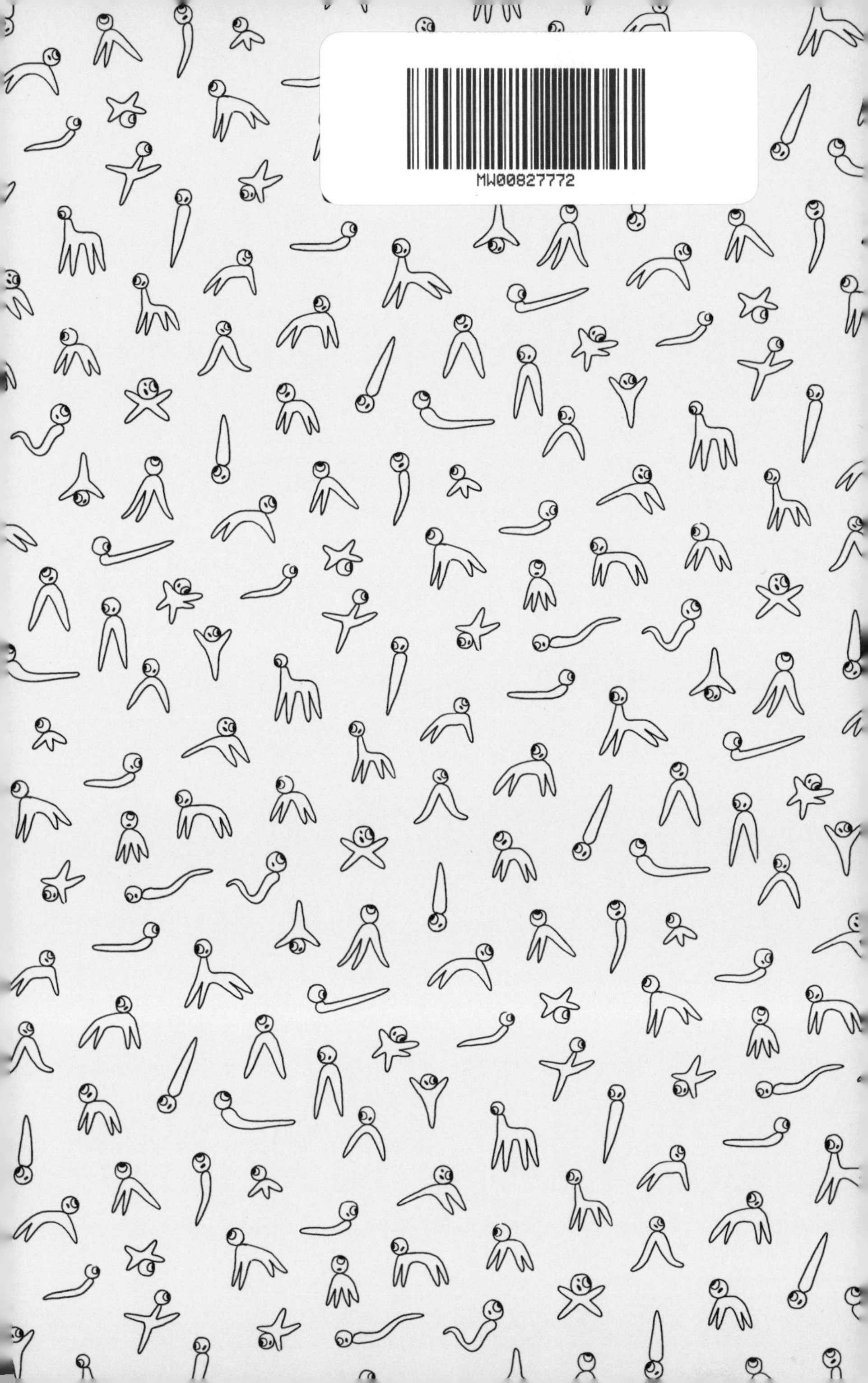

DRESSING

DRESSING

PUBLISHED BY KOYAMA PRESS
KOYAMAPRESS.COM

FIRST EDITION: SEPTEMBER 2015

ISBN: 978-1-927668-22-1

PRINTED IN CHINA

KOYAMA PRESS GRATEFULLY ACKNOWLEDGES THE CANADA COUNCIL
FOR THE ARTS FOR THEIR SUPPORT OF OUR PUBLISHING PROGRAM.

DRESSING

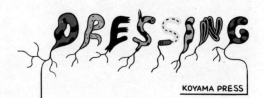

KOYAMA PRESS

We were able to keep living in the apartment because my dad was the building manager. All of our friends got kicked out after the renovations, though.

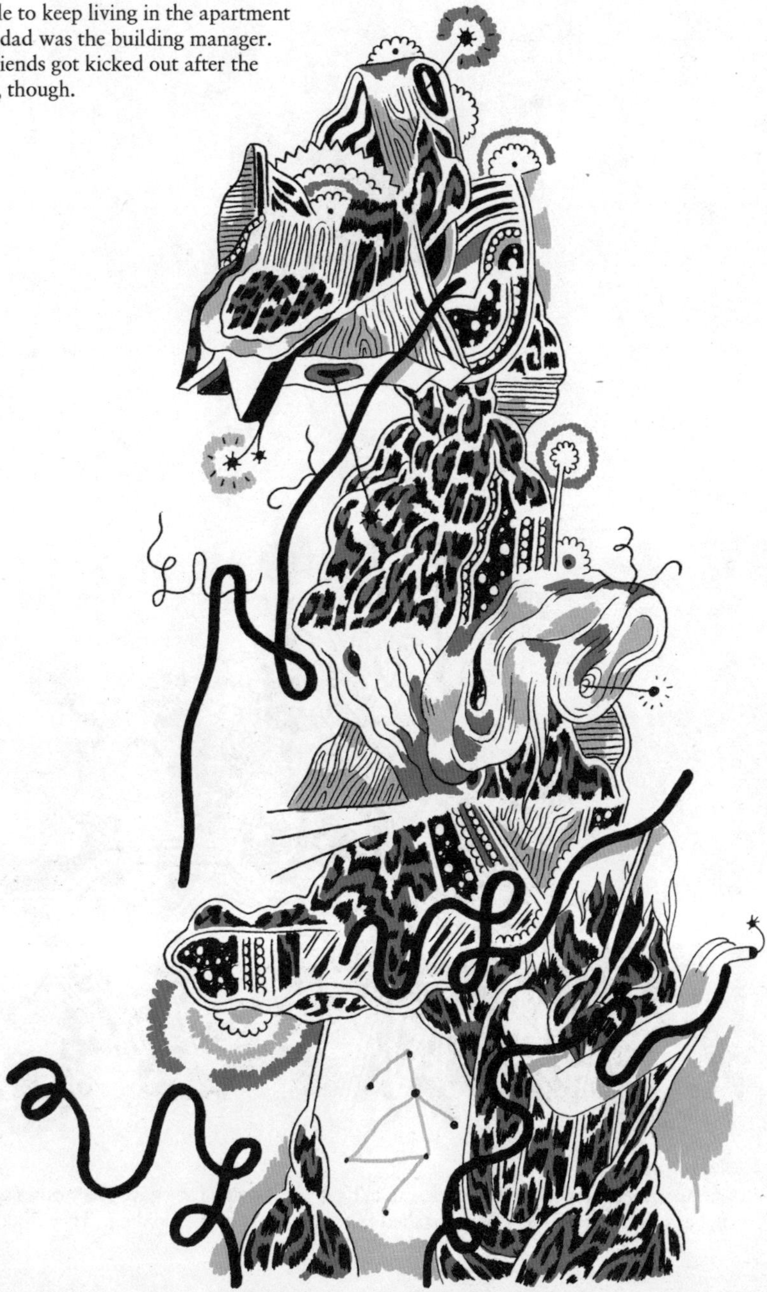

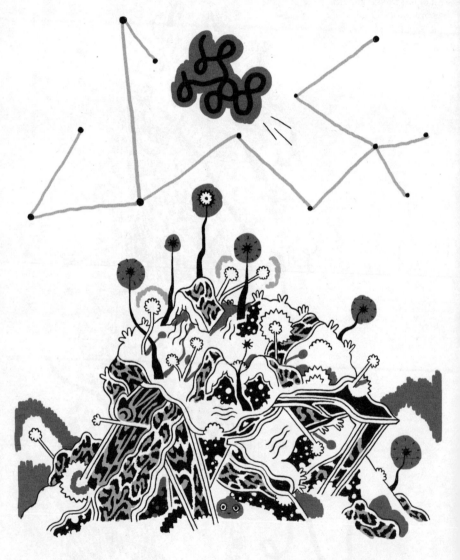

Our apartment was the only one that didn't get renovated. They gave every other space new kitchens, bathrooms, etc. They installed faster elevators in the building. They hired a doorman.

Rich people moved in. My new neighbours had these sorts of outfits that I'd never seen before.

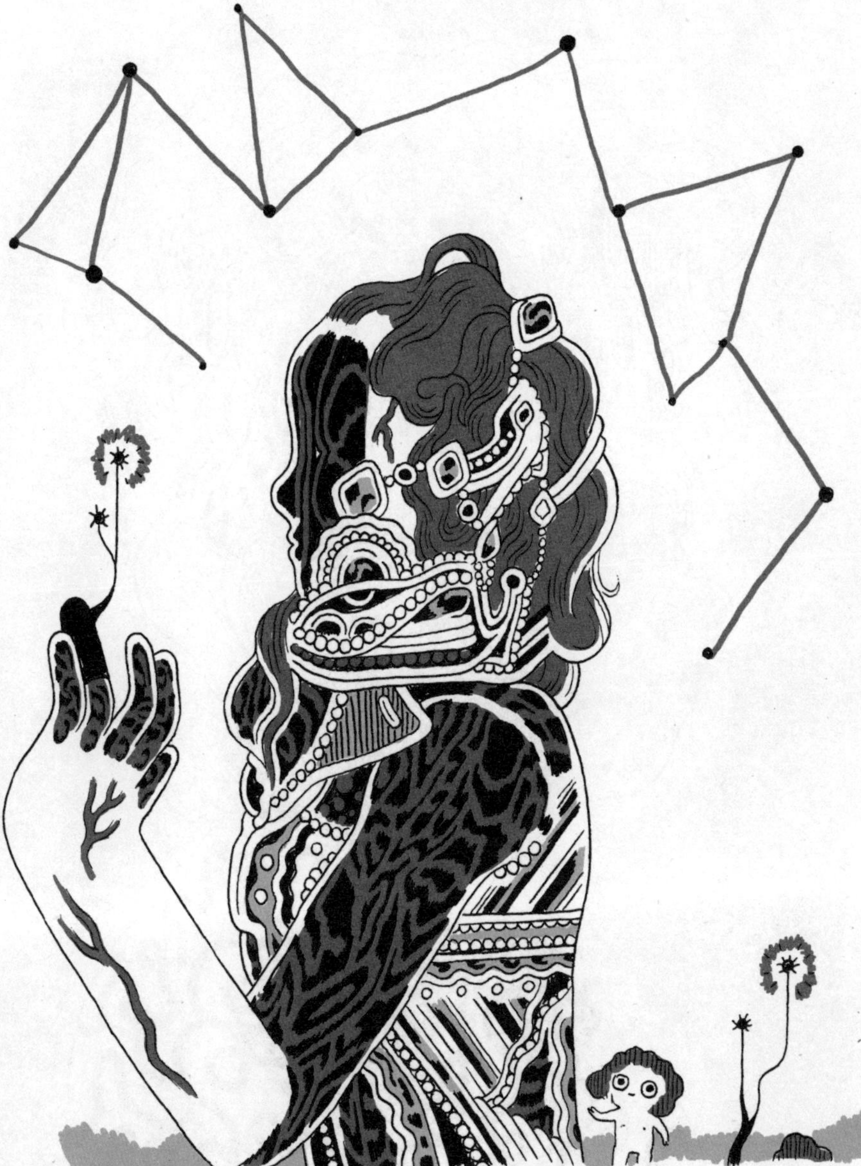

I befriended their eldest daughter. She was about five years older than me. She'd lend me computer stuff I couldn't really afford, let me play with her old toys, stuff like that.

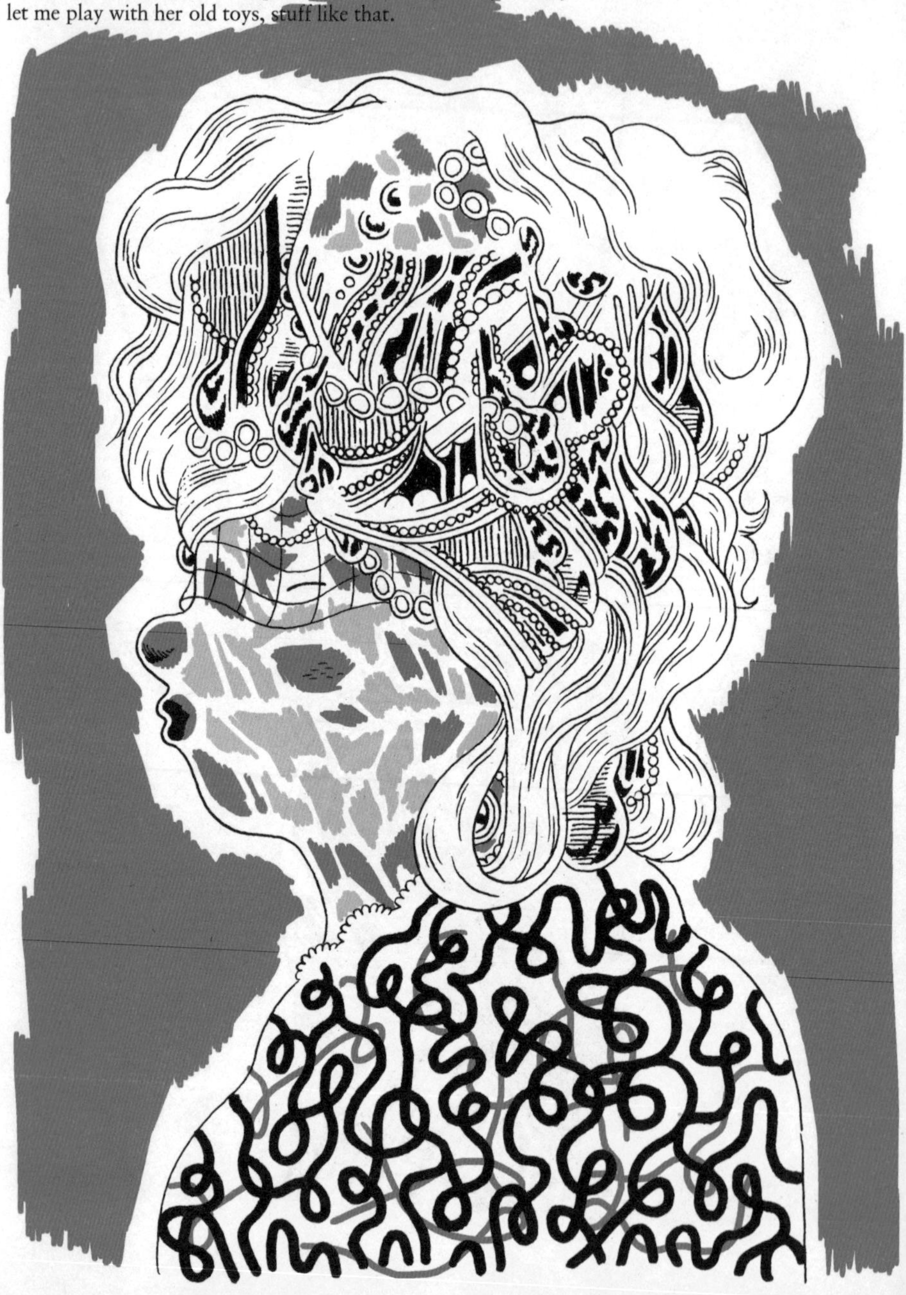

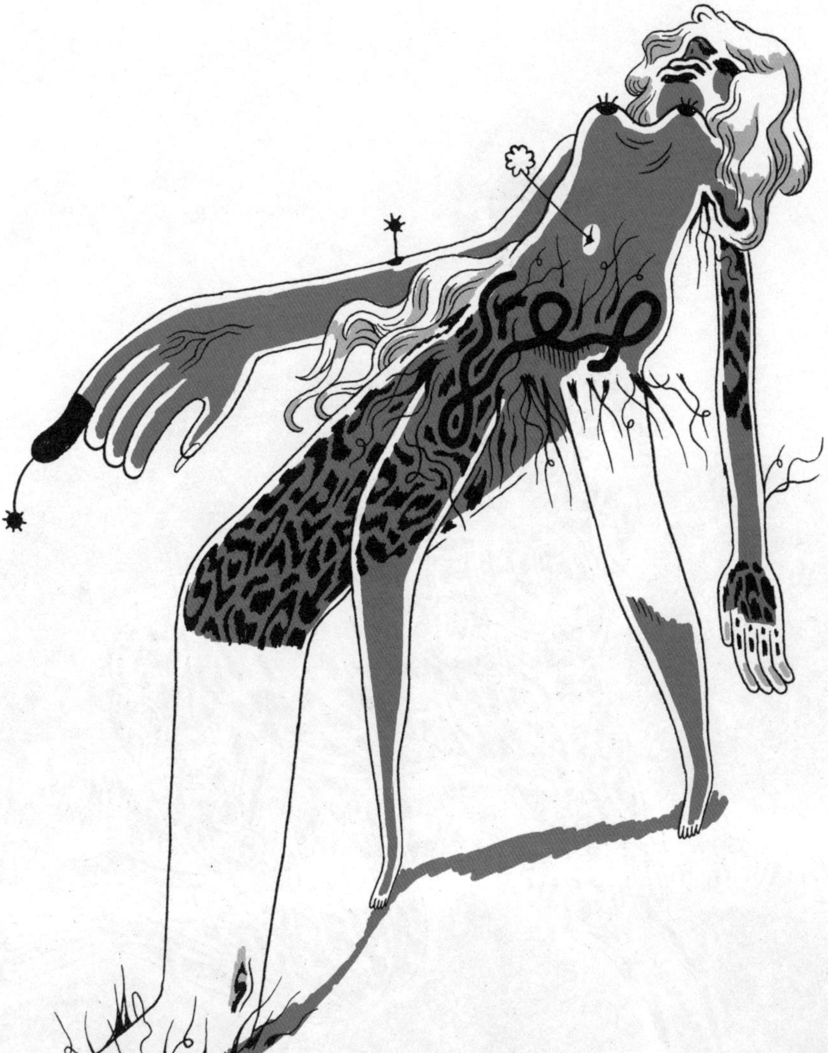

Once, she let me use her laptop while
she took a shower. She came out to greet
me completely naked and sopping wet. She held
a towel out for me to dry her with. Then she let me
watch her while she tried on different outfits.

Then she let me try on outfits.

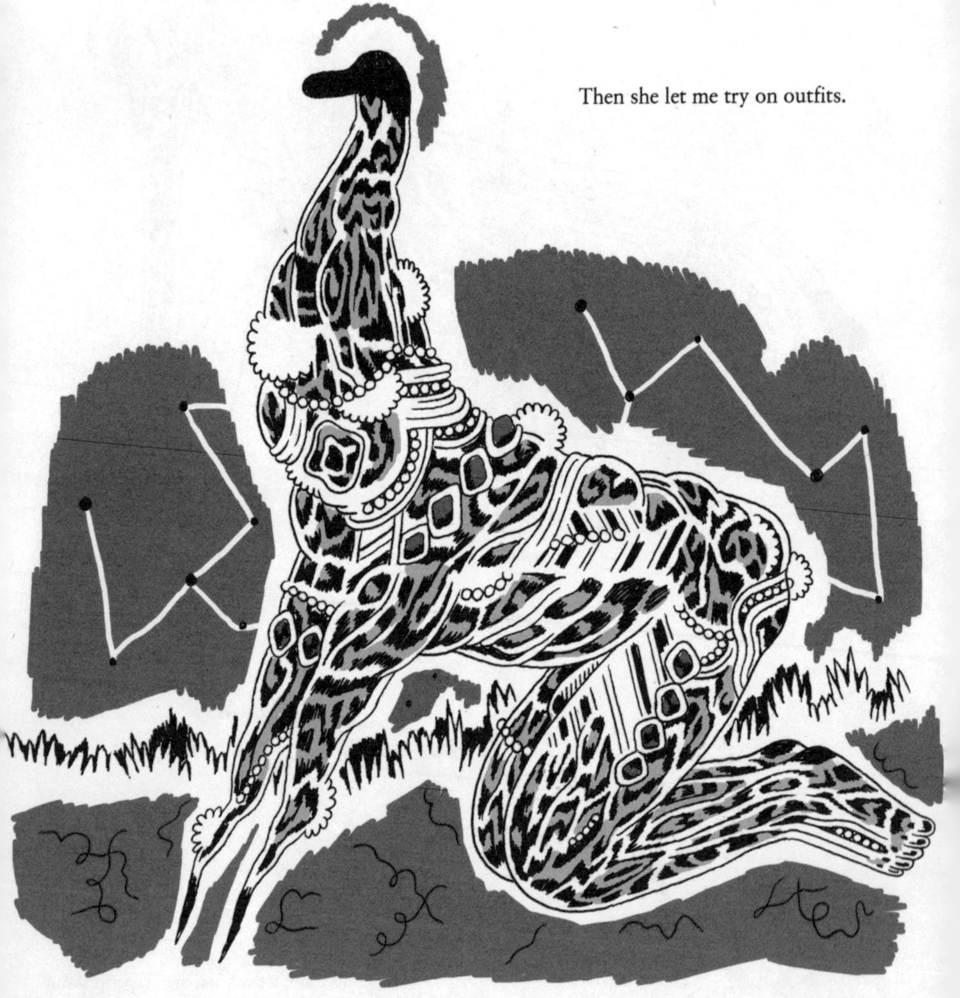

She applied the make-up to my face, since I didn't know how to do it myself. I don't think it actually made me look very feminine. It instead added definition to all of my facial features. The outlines lent my likeness a depth and personality it otherwise lacked. I looked older - like the boy I would grow up to be.

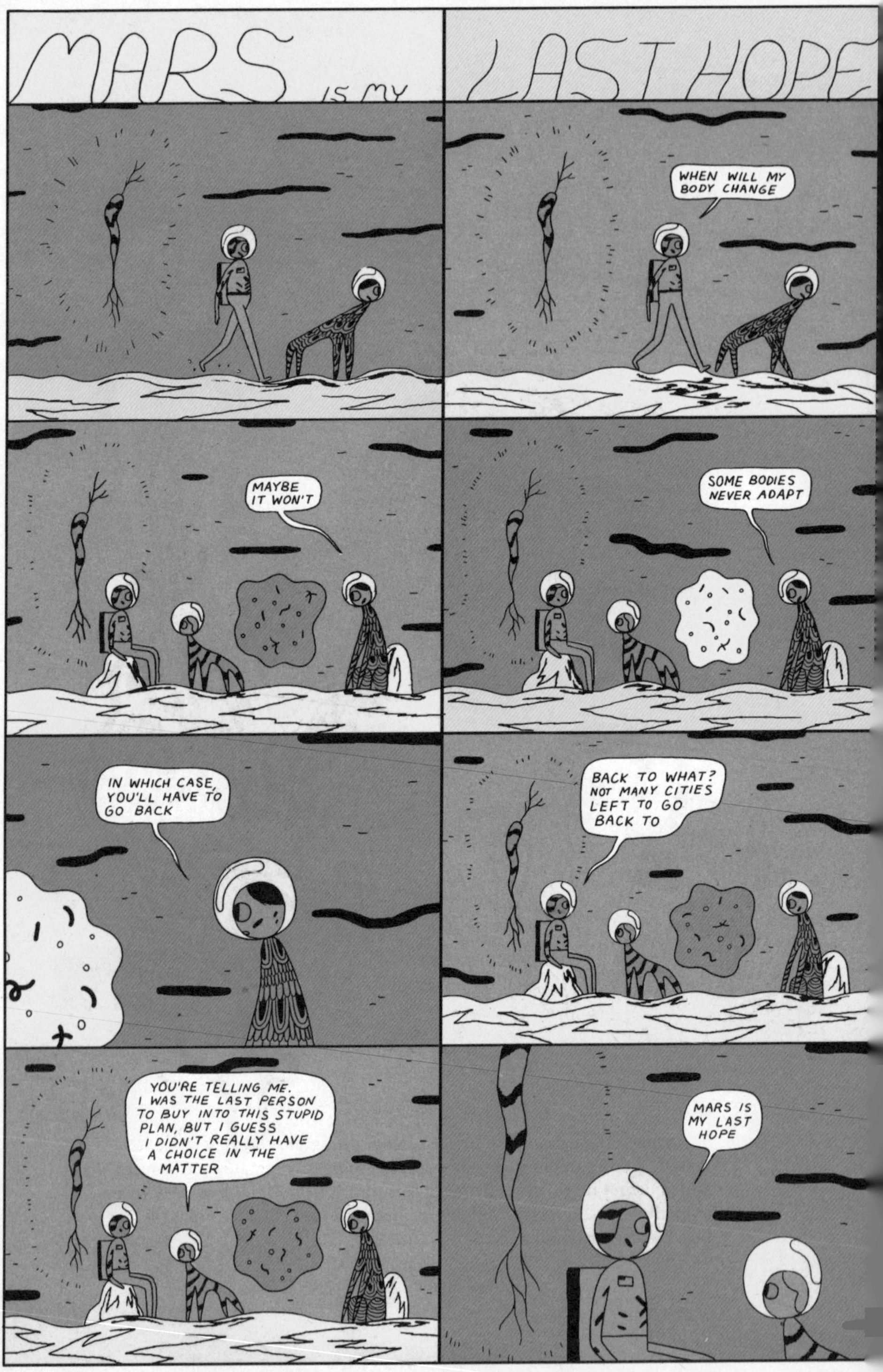
MARS IS MY LAST HOPE
WHEN WILL MY BODY CHANGE
MAYBE IT WON'T
SOME BODIES NEVER ADAPT
IN WHICH CASE, YOU'LL HAVE TO GO BACK
BACK TO WHAT? NOT MANY CITIES LEFT TO GO BACK TO
YOU'RE TELLING ME. I WAS THE LAST PERSON TO BUY INTO THIS STUPID PLAN, BUT I GUESS I DIDN'T REALLY HAVE A CHOICE IN THE MATTER
MARS IS MY LAST HOPE

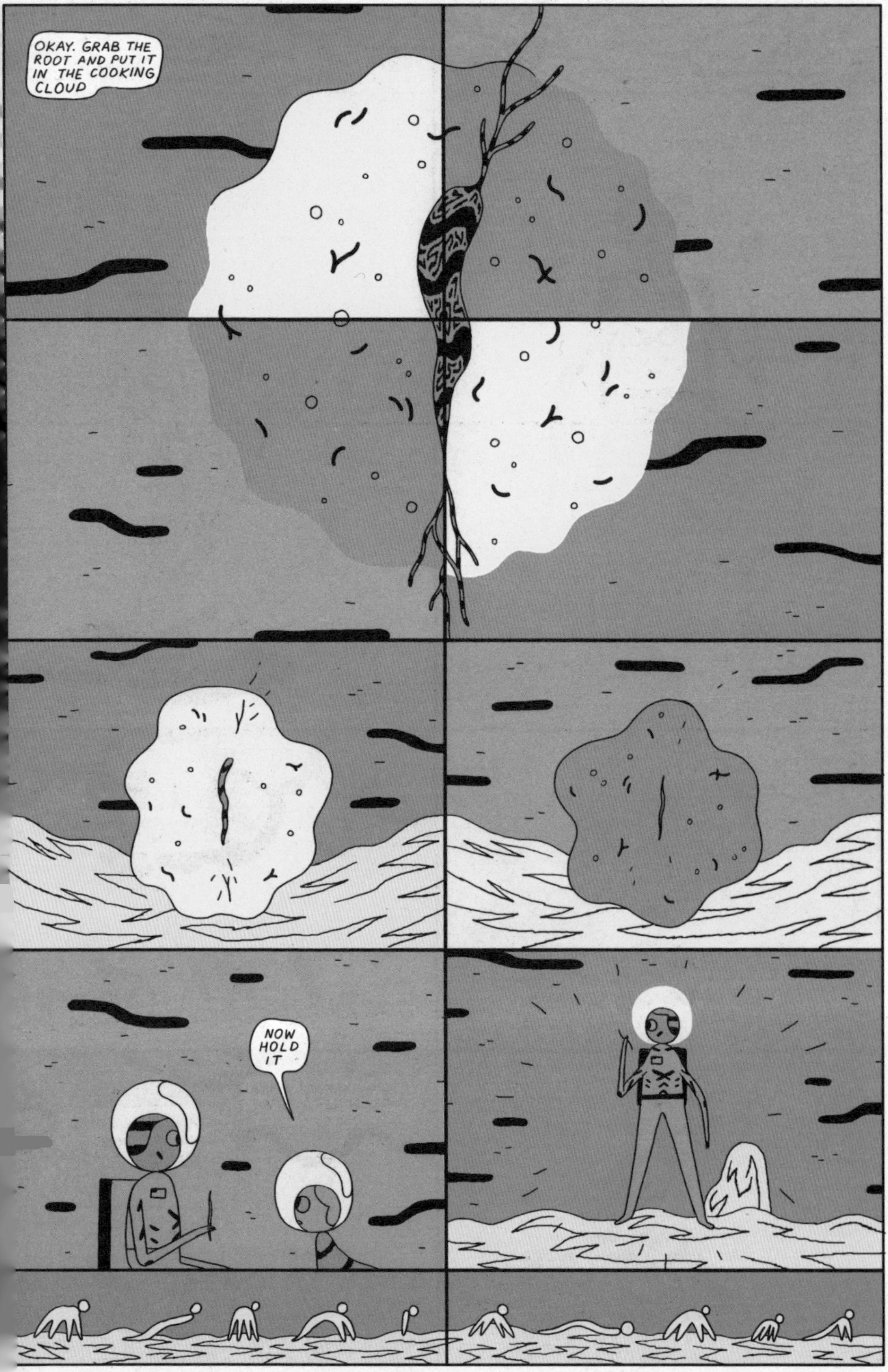
OKAY. GRAB THE ROOT AND PUT IT IN THE COOKING CLOUD
NOW HOLD IT

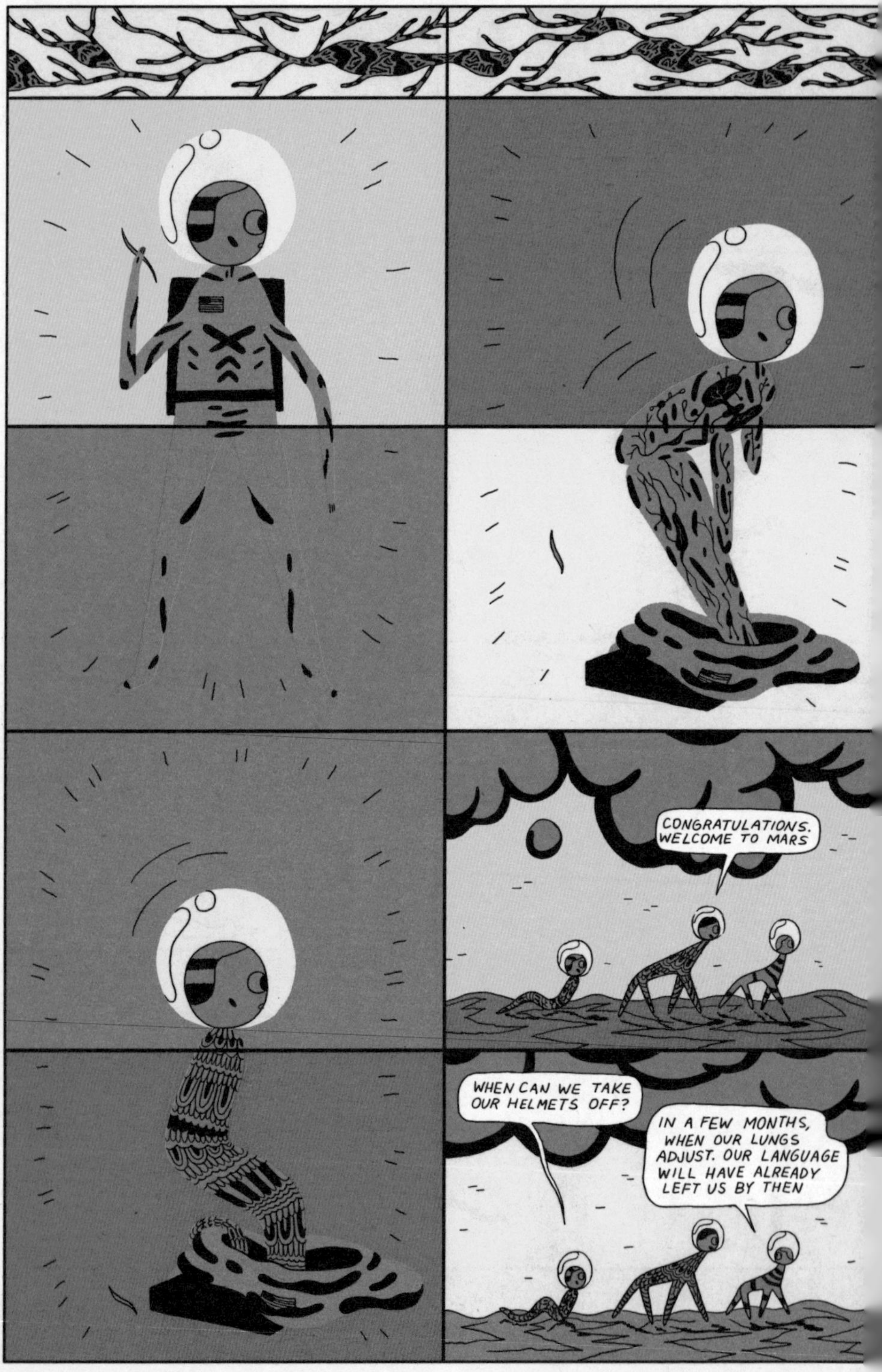
CONGRATULATIONS. WELCOME TO MARS
WHEN CAN WE TAKE OUR HELMETS OFF?
IN A FEW MONTHS, WHEN OUR LUNGS ADJUST. OUR LANGUAGE WILL HAVE ALREADY LEFT US BY THEN

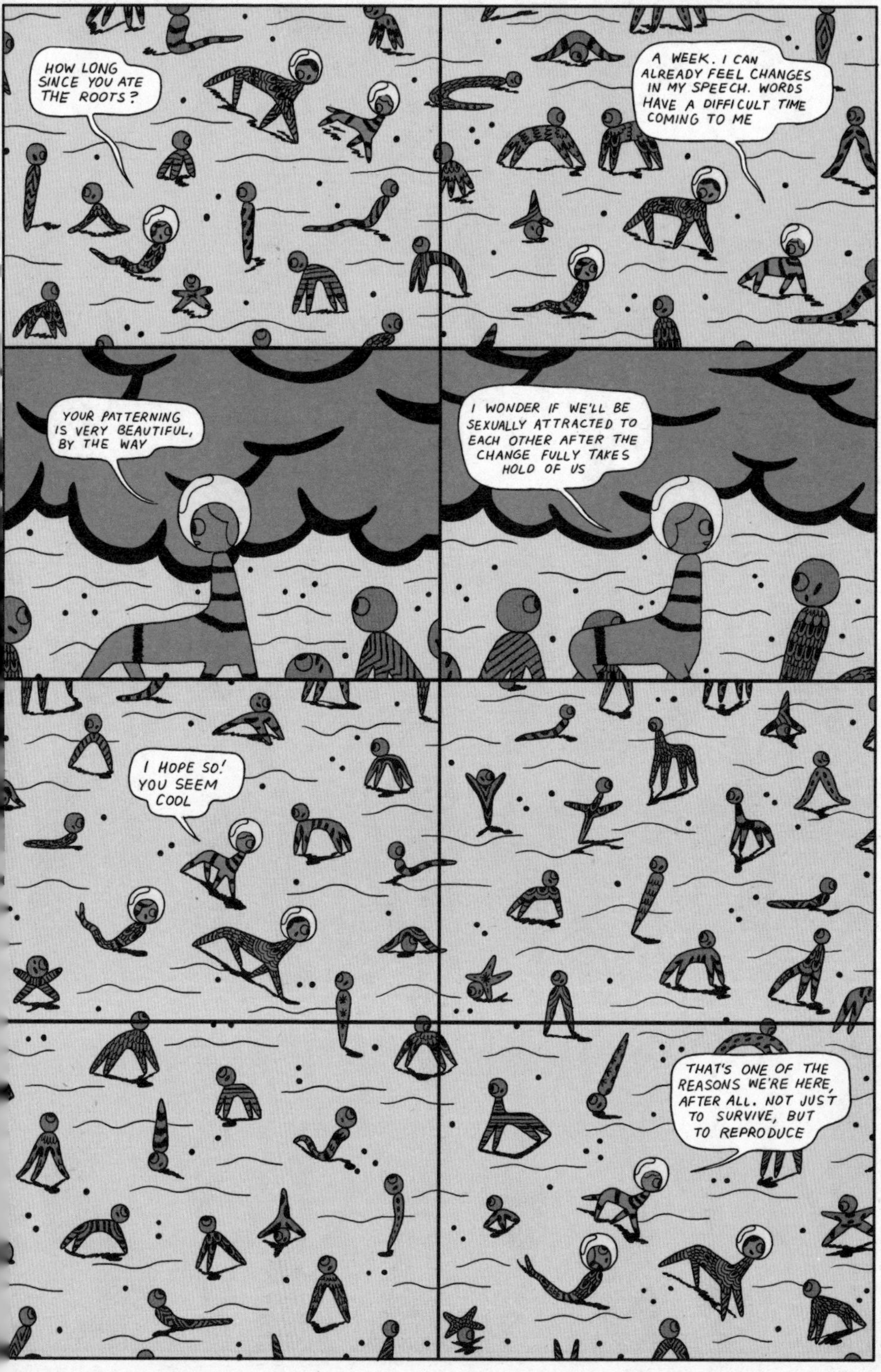
HOW LONG SINCE YOU ATE THE ROOTS?
A WEEK. I CAN ALREADY FEEL CHANGES IN MY SPEECH. WORDS HAVE A DIFFICULT TIME COMING TO ME
YOUR PATTERNING IS VERY BEAUTIFUL, BY THE WAY
I WONDER IF WE'LL BE SEXUALLY ATTRACTED TO EACH OTHER AFTER THE CHANGE FULLY TAKES HOLD OF US
I HOPE SO! YOU SEEM COOL
THAT'S ONE OF THE REASONS WE'RE HERE, AFTER ALL. NOT JUST TO SURVIVE, BUT TO REPRODUCE

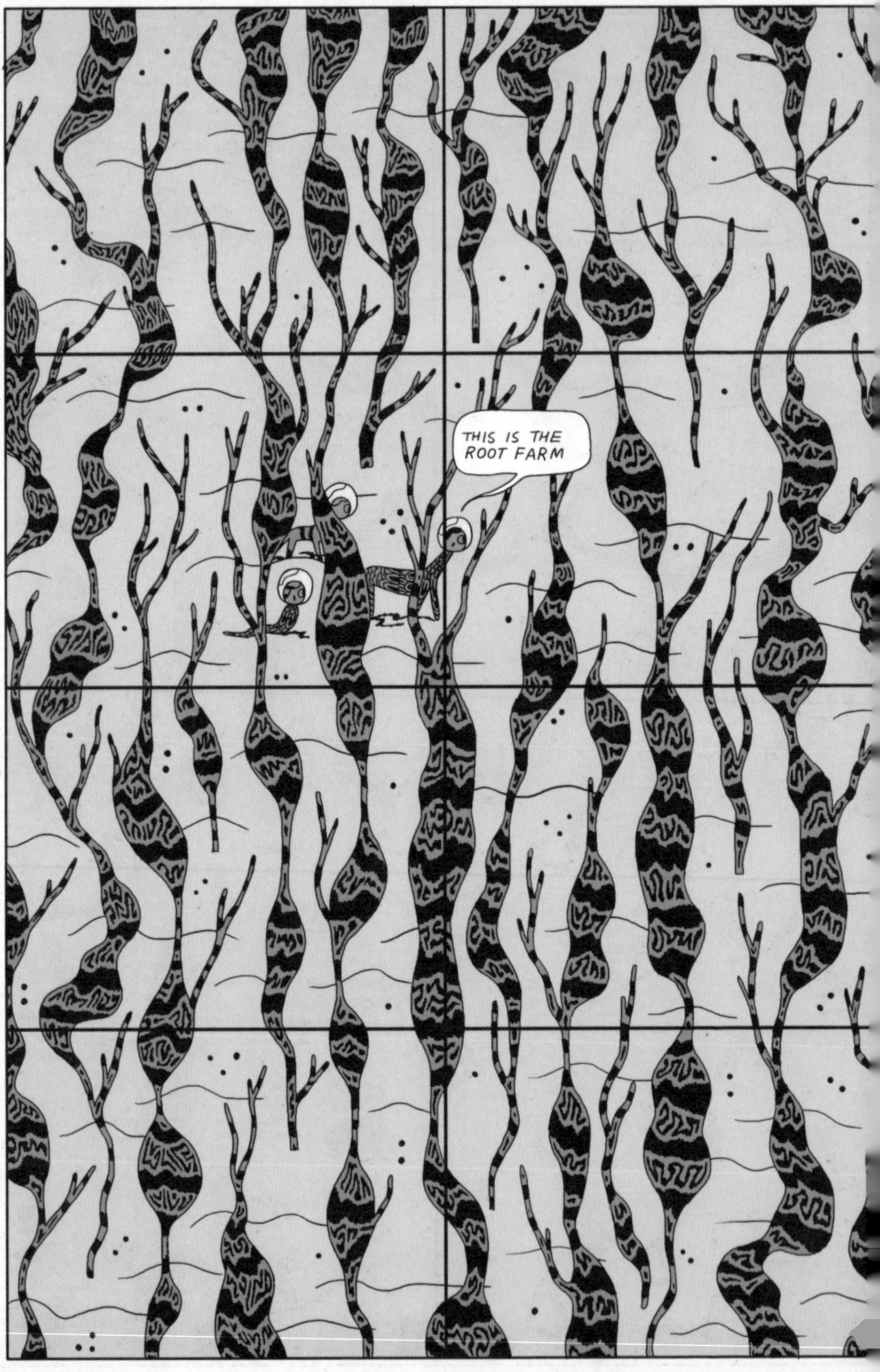
THIS IS THE ROOT FARM

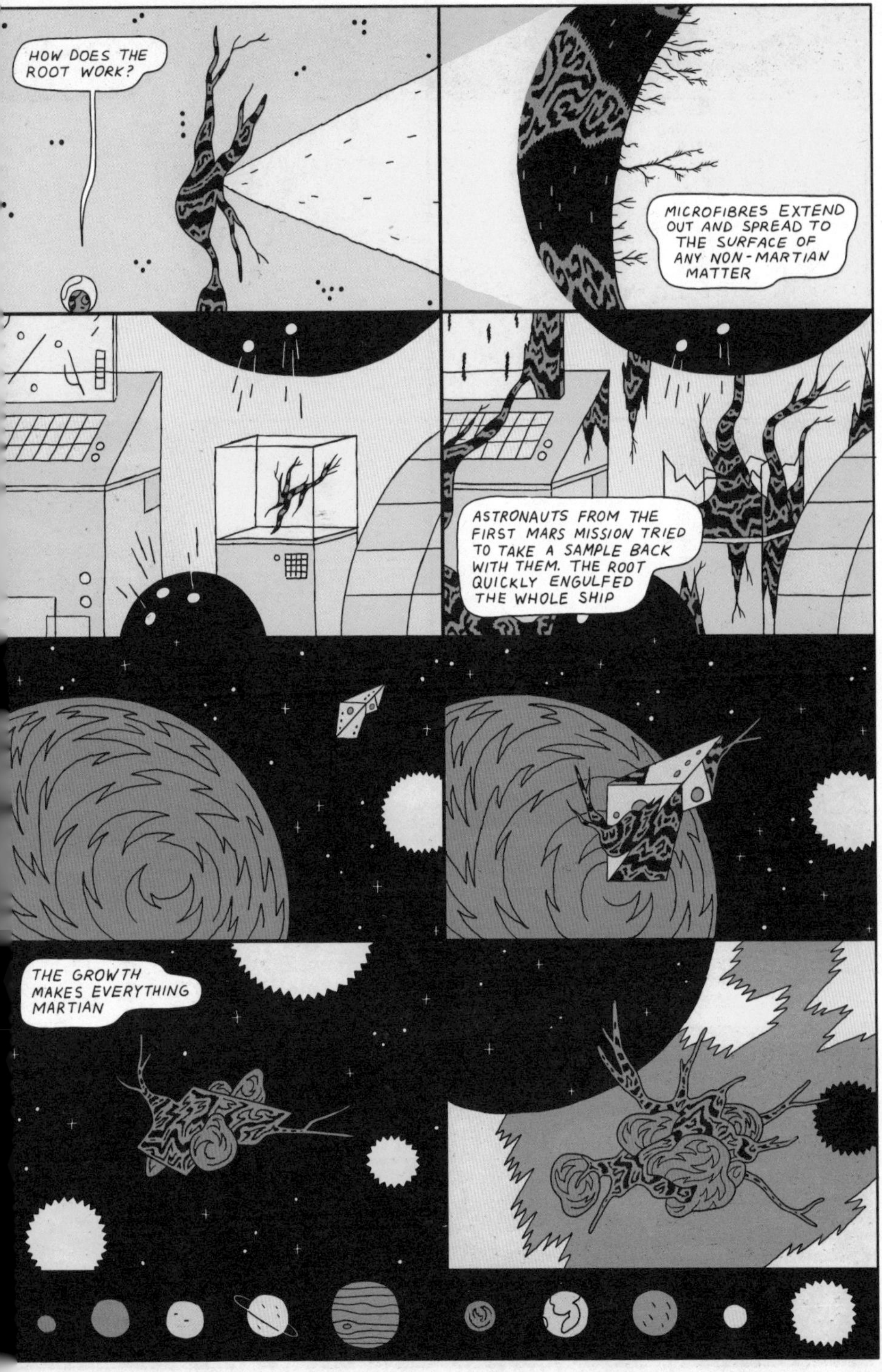
HOW DOES THE ROOT WORK?
MICROFIBRES EXTEND OUT AND SPREAD TO THE SURFACE OF ANY NON-MARTIAN MATTER
ASTRONAUTS FROM THE FIRST MARS MISSION TRIED TO TAKE A SAMPLE BACK WITH THEM. THE ROOT QUICKLY ENGULFED THE WHOLE SHIP
THE GROWTH MAKES EVERYTHING MARTIAN

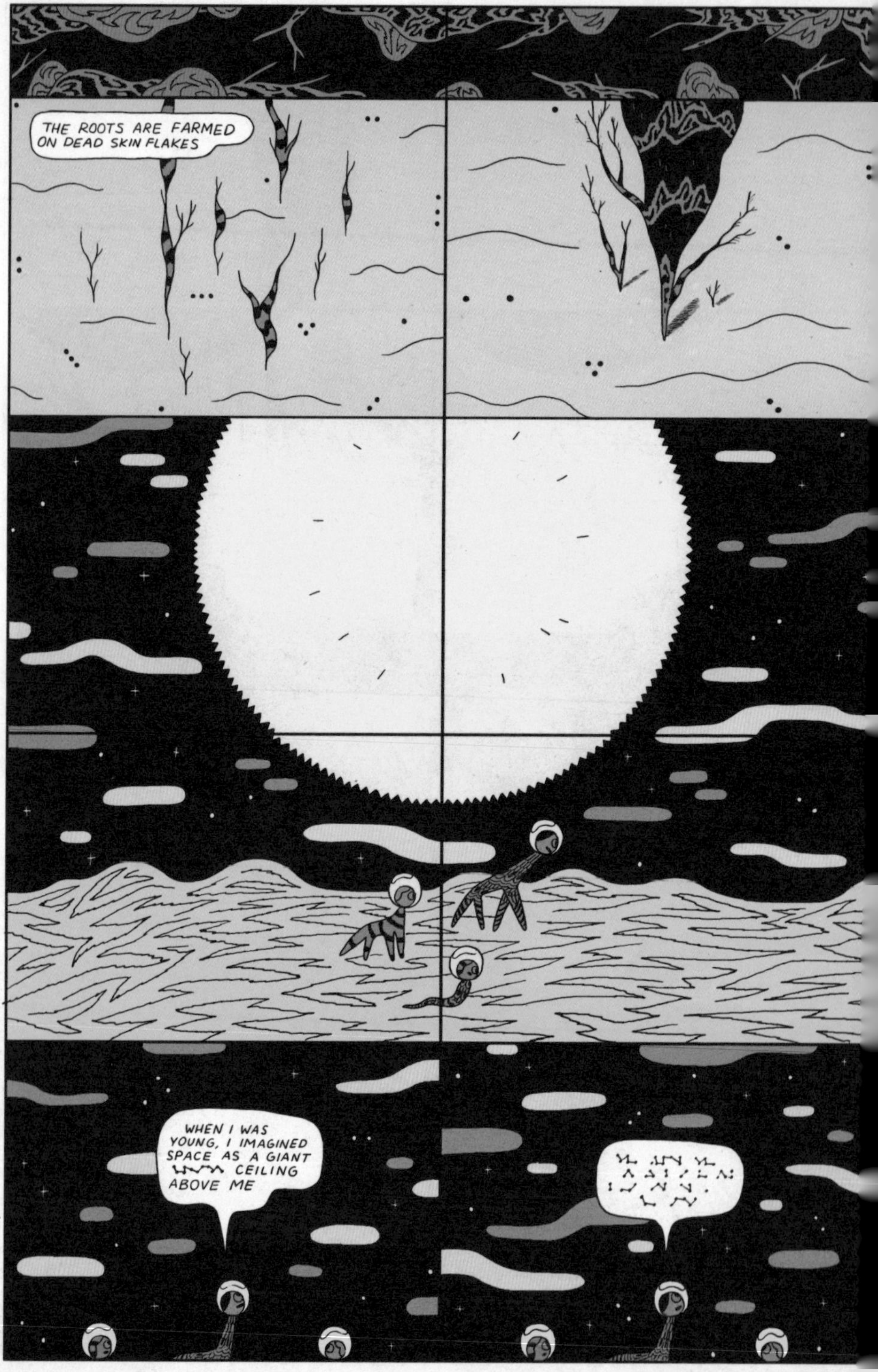
THE ROOTS ARE FARMED ON DEAD SKIN FLAKES
WHEN I WAS YOUNG, I IMAGINED SPACE AS A GIANT CEILING ABOVE ME

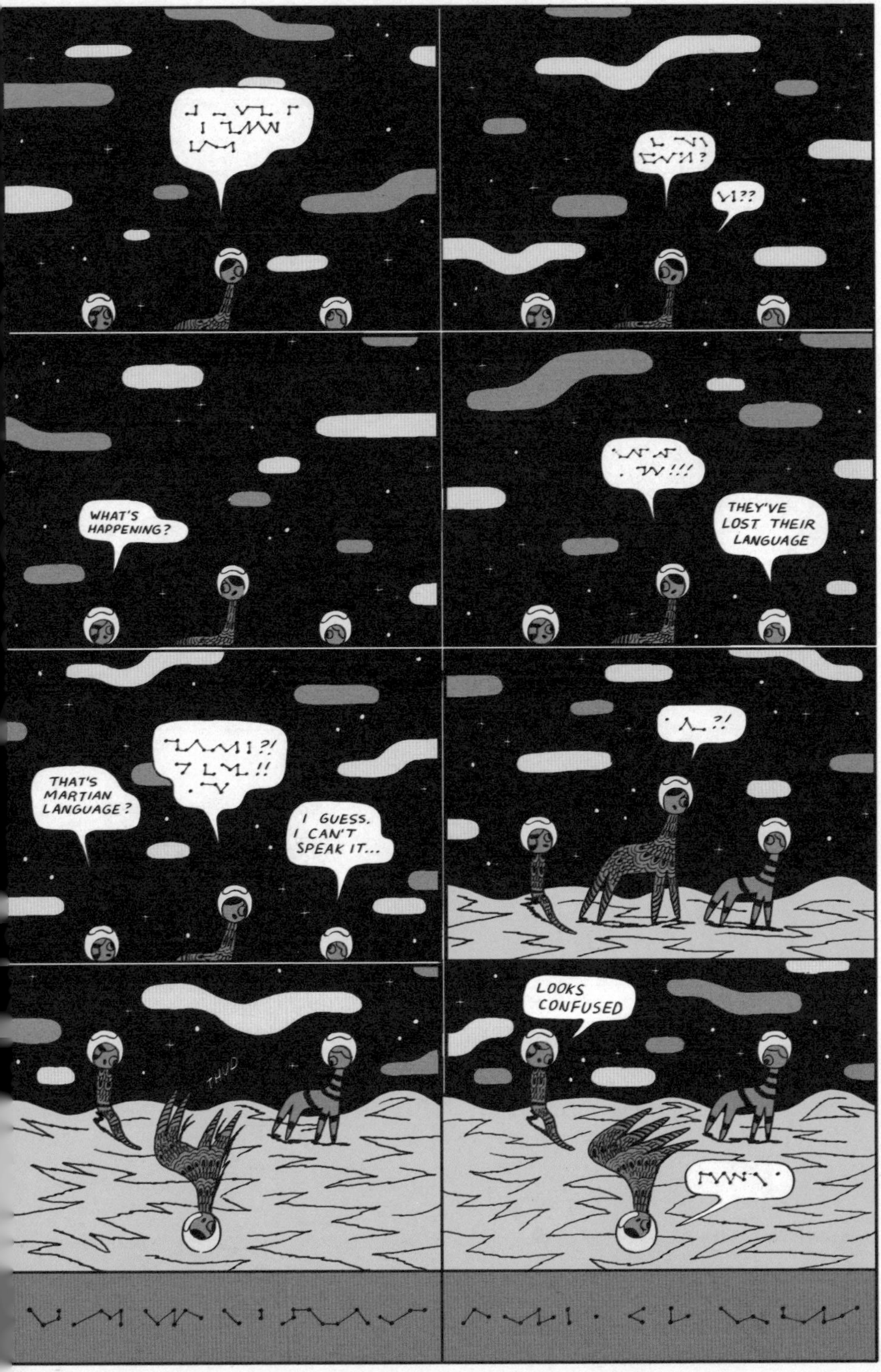
WHAT'S HAPPENING?
THEY'VE LOST THEIR LANGUAGE
THAT'S MARTIAN LANGUAGE?
I GUESS. I CAN'T SPEAK IT...
THUD
LOOKS CONFUSED

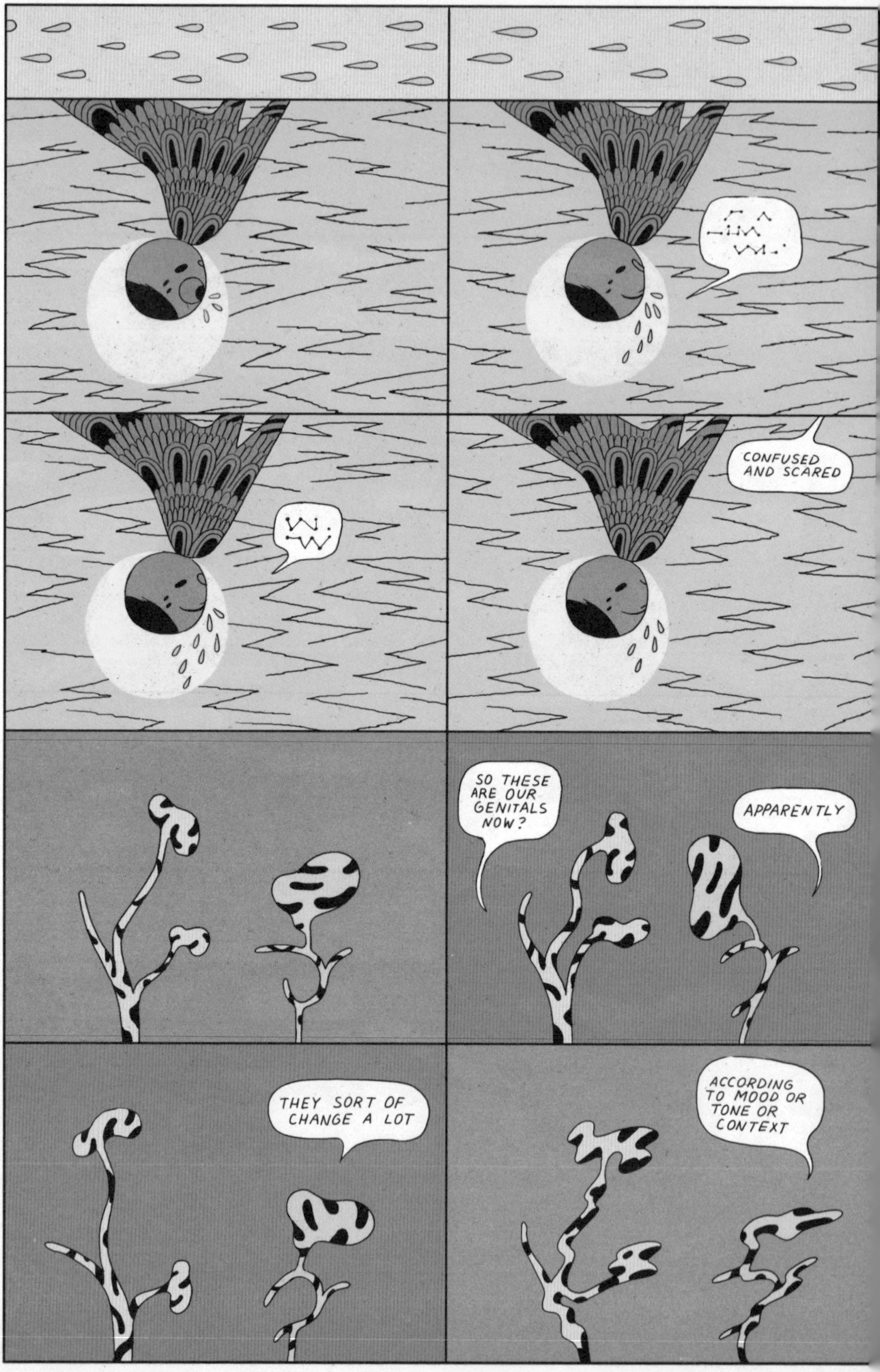
CONFUSED AND SCARED
SO THESE ARE OUR GENITALS NOW?
APPARENTLY
THEY SORT OF CHANGE A LOT
ACCORDING TO MOOD OR TONE OR CONTEXT

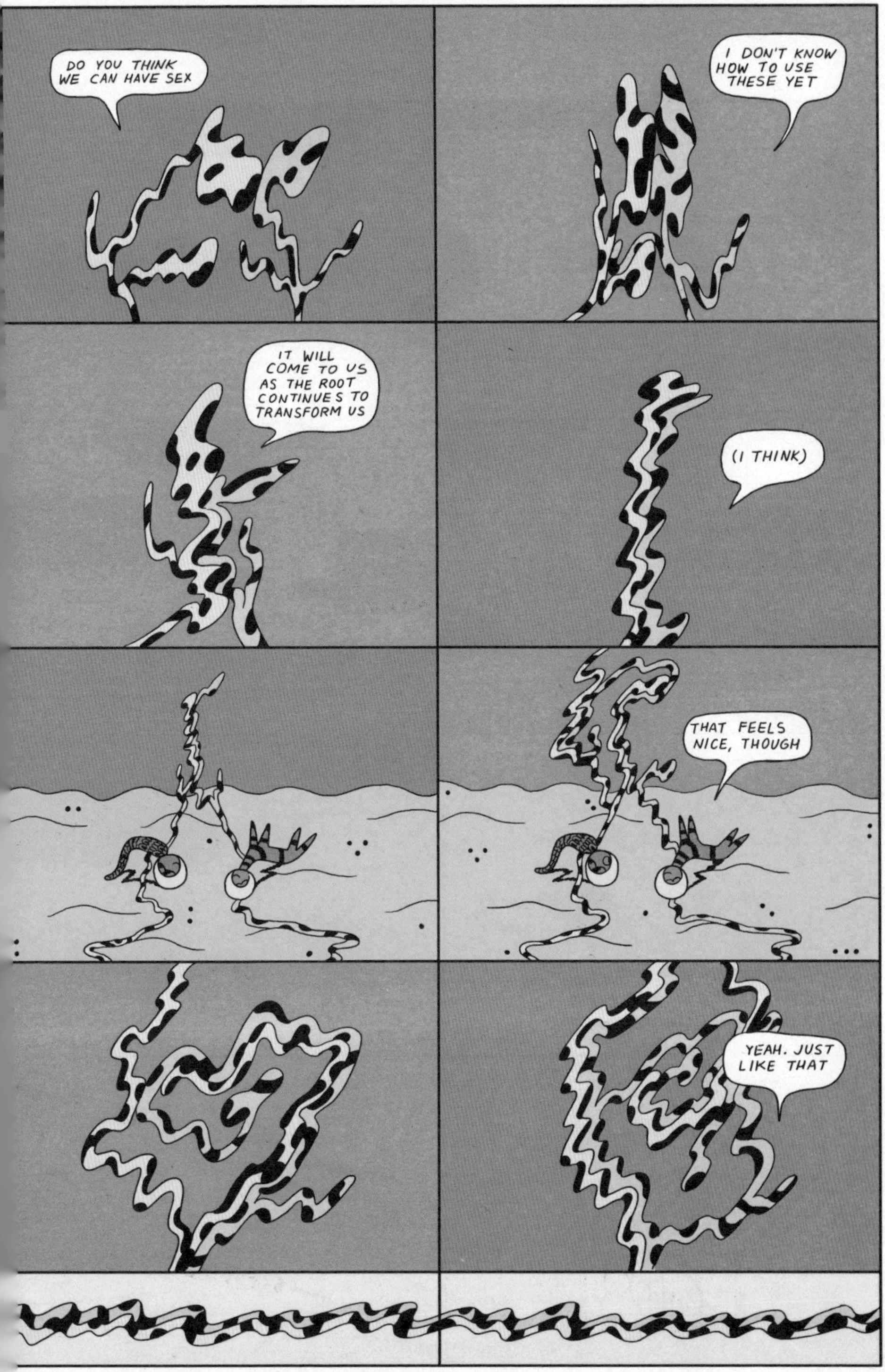
DO YOU THINK WE CAN HAVE SEX
I DON'T KNOW HOW TO USE THESE YET
IT WILL COME TO US AS THE ROOT CONTINUES TO TRANSFORM US
(I THINK)
THAT FEELS NICE, THOUGH
YEAH. JUST LIKE THAT

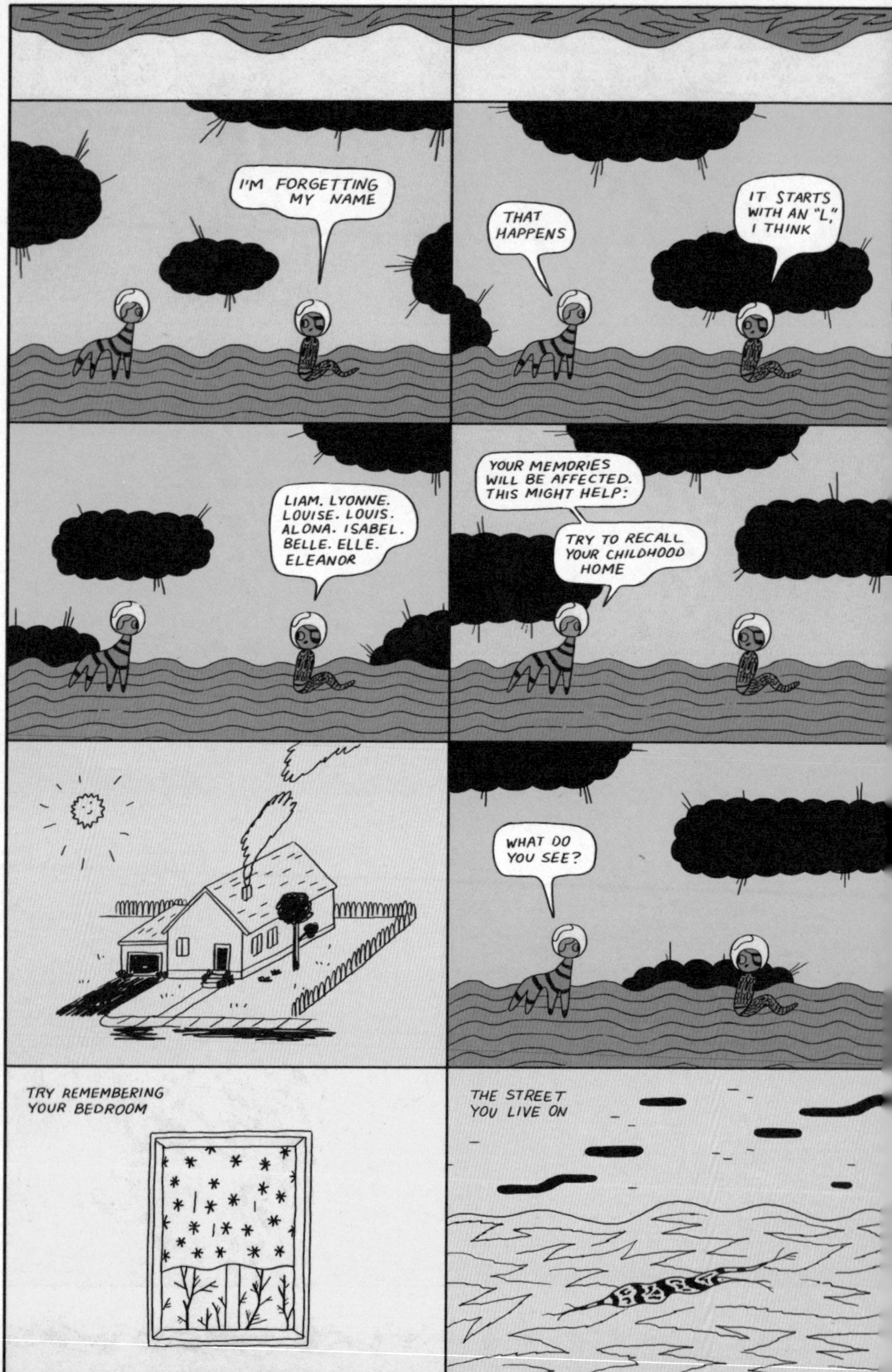
I'M FORGETTING MY NAME
THAT HAPPENS
IT STARTS WITH AN "L," I THINK
LIAM. LYONNE. LOUISE. LOUIS. ALONA. ISABEL. BELLE. ELLE. ELEANOR
YOUR MEMORIES WILL BE AFFECTED. THIS MIGHT HELP:
TRY TO RECALL YOUR CHILDHOOD HOME
WHAT DO YOU SEE?
TRY REMEMBERING YOUR BEDROOM
THE STREET YOU LIVE ON

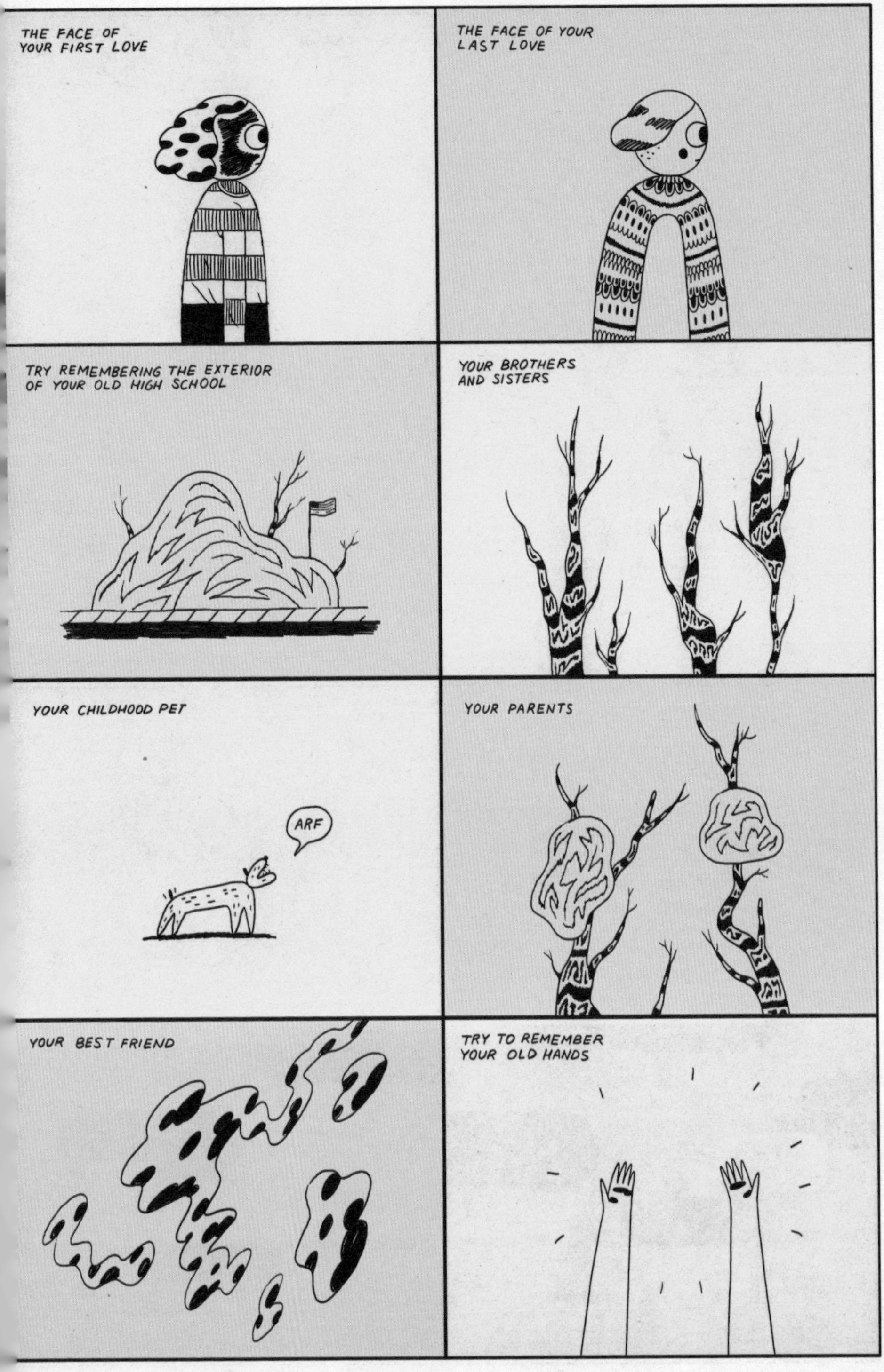
THE FACE OF YOUR FIRST LOVE
THE FACE OF YOUR LAST LOVE
TRY REMEMBERING THE EXTERIOR OF YOUR OLD HIGH SCHOOL
YOUR BROTHERS AND SISTERS
YOUR CHILDHOOD PET
ARF
YOUR PARENTS
YOUR BEST FRIEND
TRY TO REMEMBER YOUR OLD HANDS

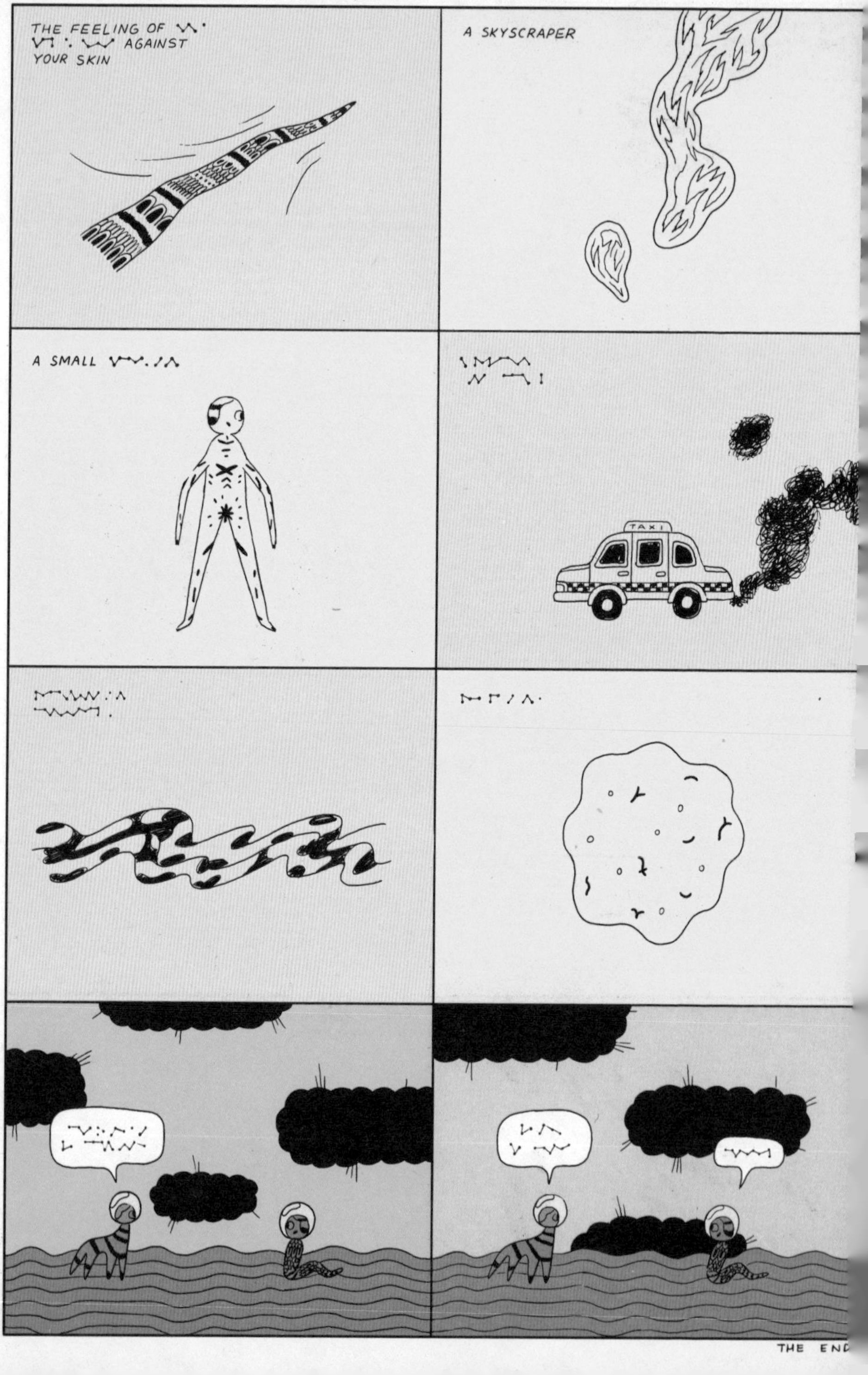
THE FEELING OF AGAINST YOUR SKIN
A SKYSCRAPER
A SMALL
TAXI
THE END

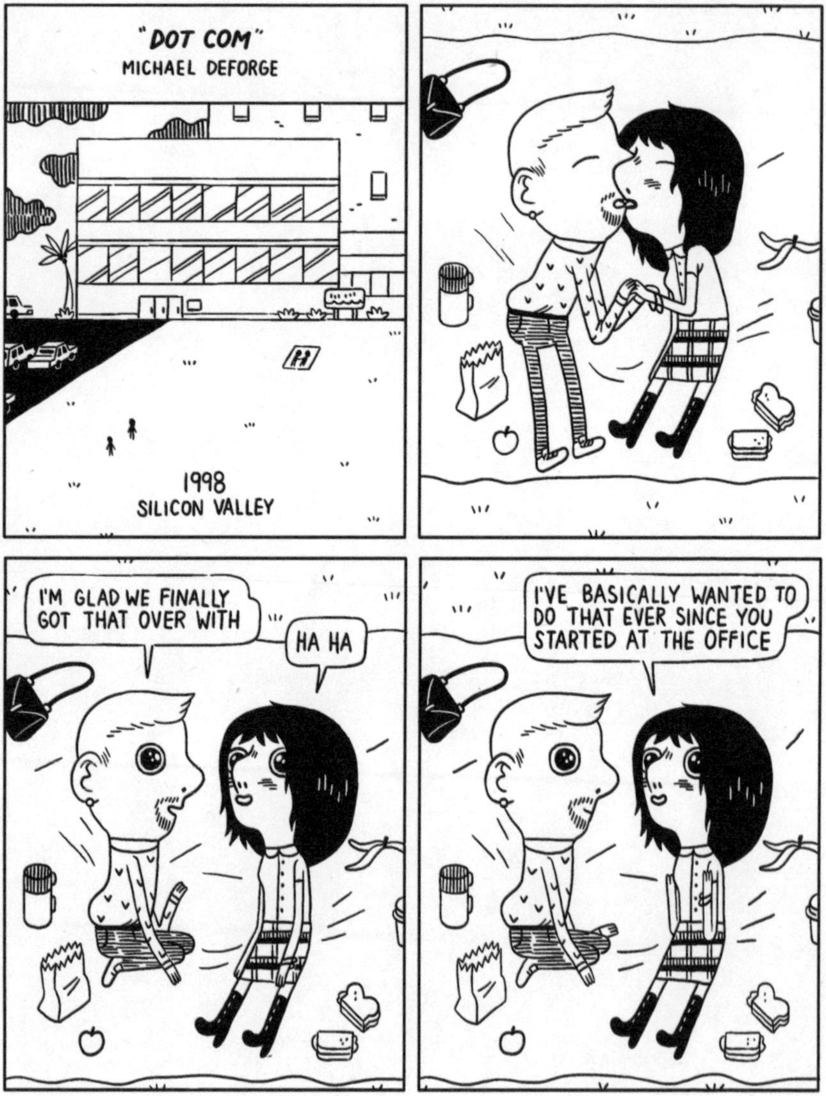
"DOT COM"
MICHAEL DEFORGE
1998
SILICON VALLEY
I'M GLAD WE FINALLY GOT THAT OVER WITH
HA HA
I'VE BASICALLY WANTED TO DO THAT EVER SINCE YOU STARTED AT THE OFFICE

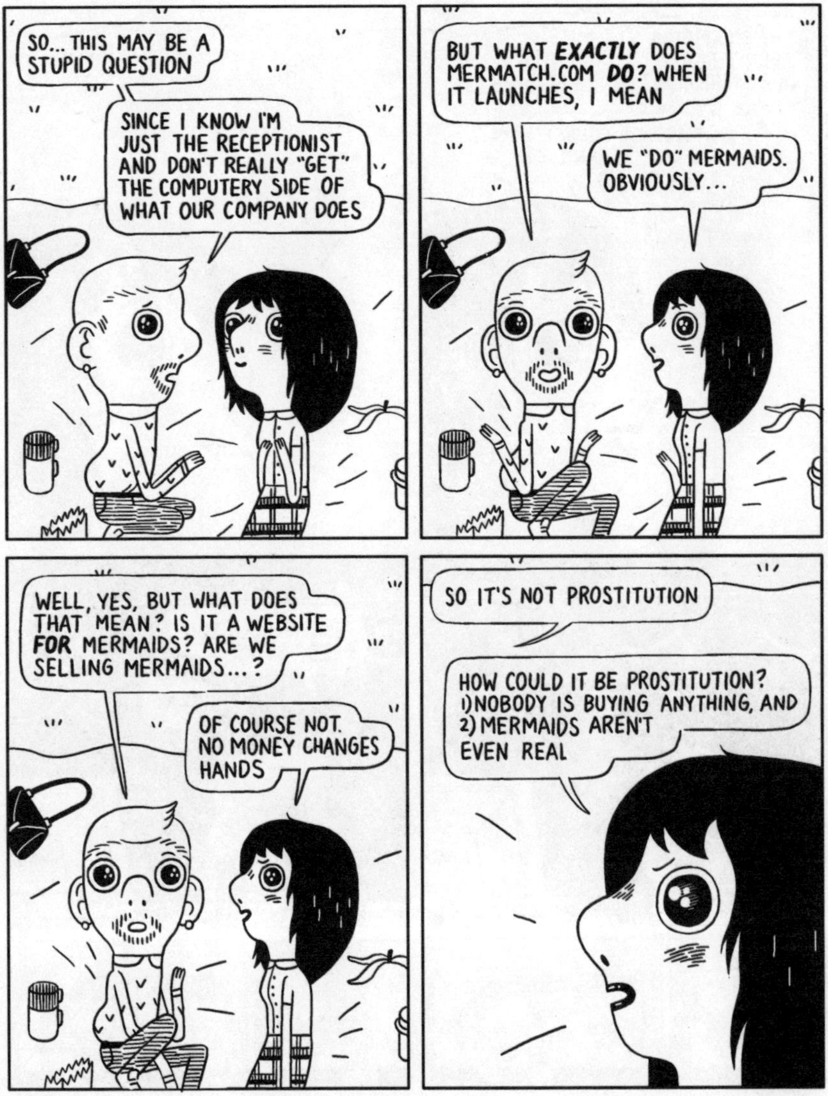
SO... THIS MAY BE A STUPID QUESTION
SINCE I KNOW I'M JUST THE RECEPTIONIST AND DON'T REALLY "GET" THE COMPUTERY SIDE OF WHAT OUR COMPANY DOES
BUT WHAT **EXACTLY** DOES MERMATCH.COM **DO**? WHEN IT LAUNCHES, I MEAN
WE "DO" MERMAIDS. OBVIOUSLY...
WELL, YES, BUT WHAT DOES THAT MEAN? IS IT A WEBSITE **FOR** MERMAIDS? ARE WE SELLING MERMAIDS...?
OF COURSE NOT. NO MONEY CHANGES HANDS
SO IT'S NOT PROSTITUTION
HOW COULD IT BE PROSTITUTION? 1) NOBODY IS BUYING ANYTHING, AND 2) MERMAIDS AREN'T EVEN REAL

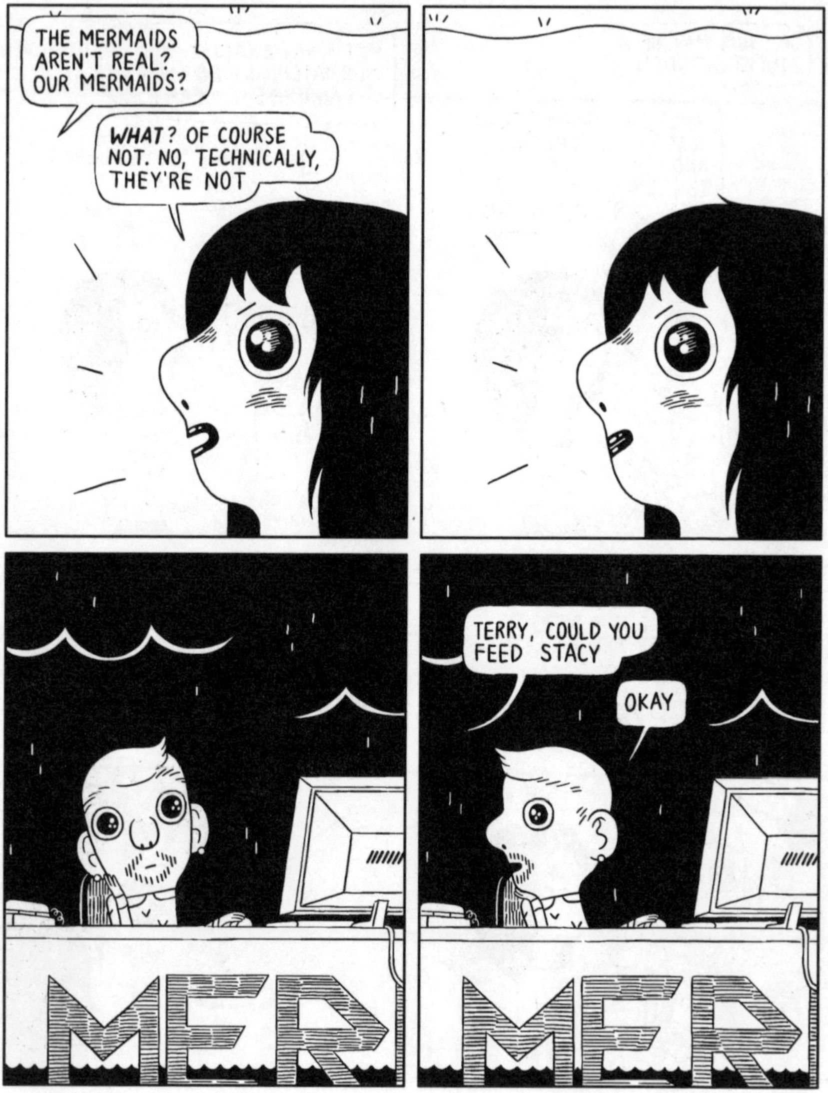
THE MERMAIDS AREN'T REAL? OUR MERMAIDS?
WHAT? OF COURSE NOT. NO, TECHNICALLY, THEY'RE NOT
MER
TERRY, COULD YOU FEED STACY
OKAY
MER

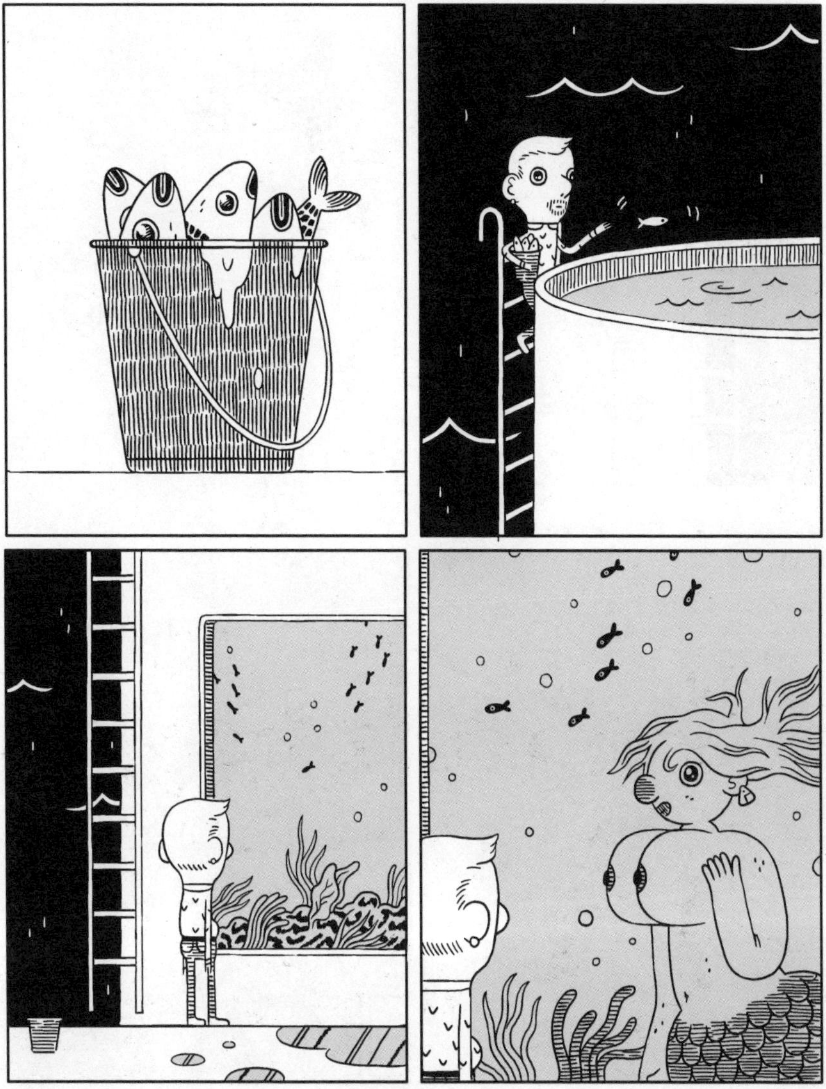

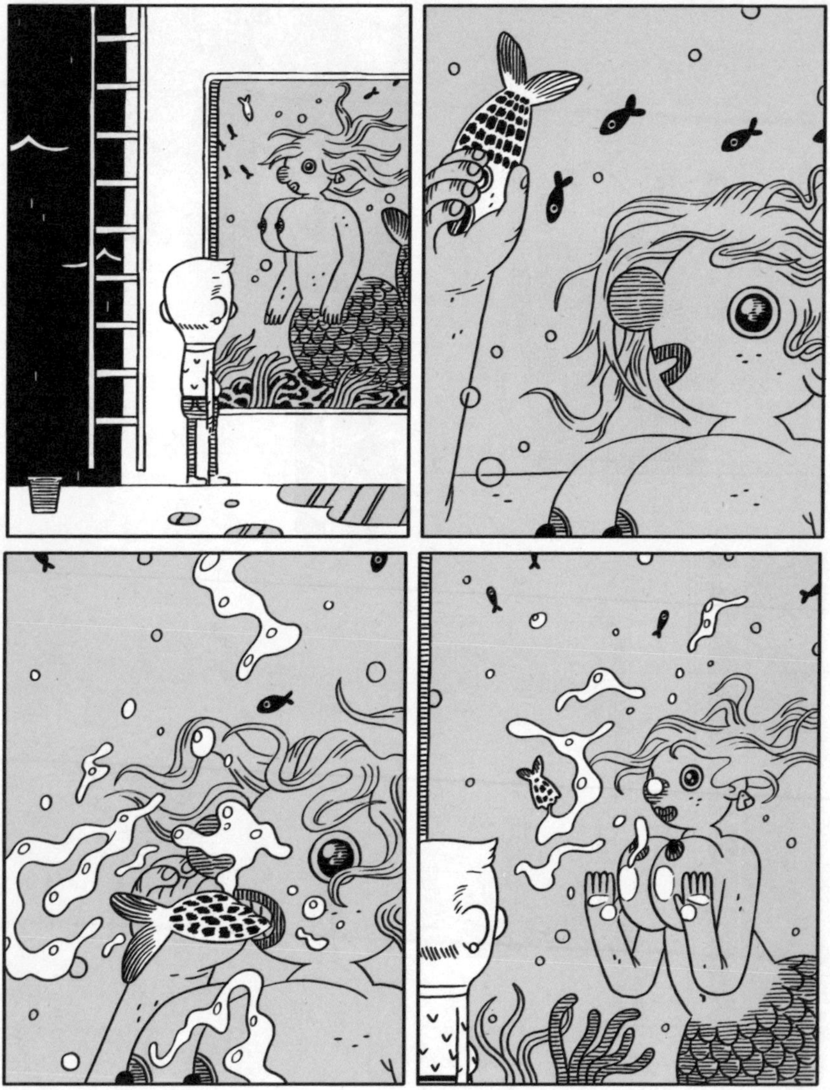

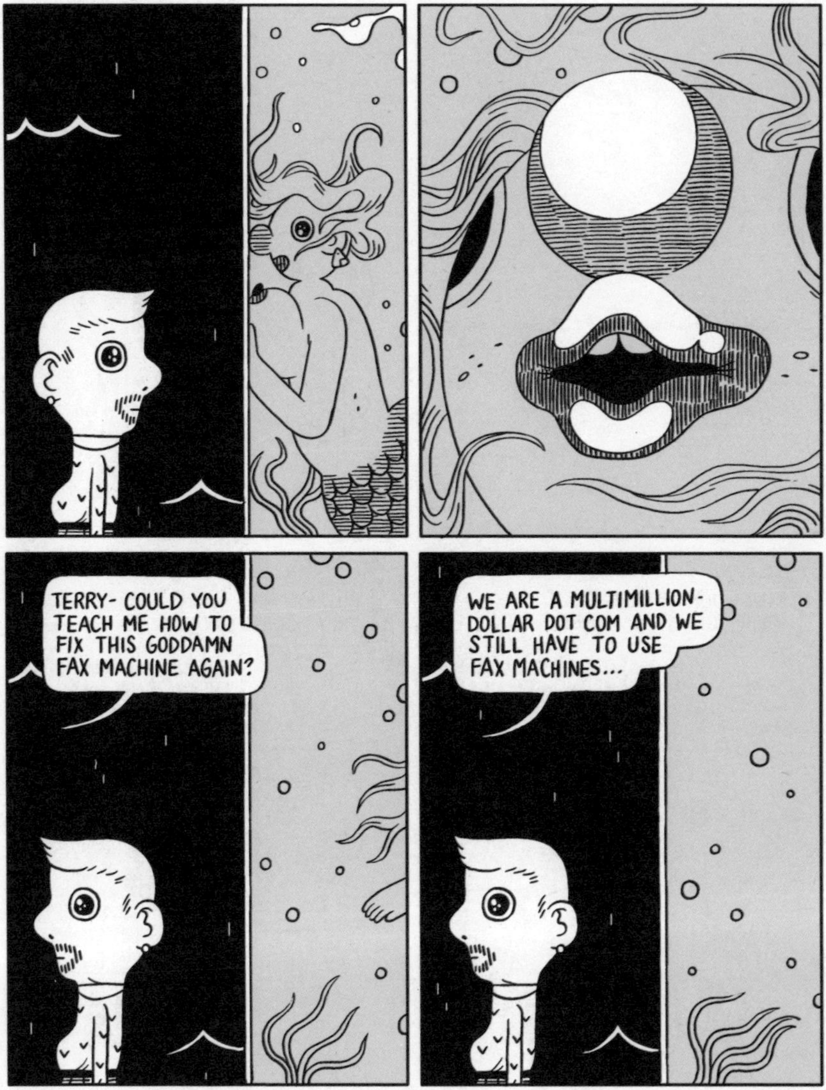
TERRY- COULD YOU TEACH ME HOW TO FIX THIS GODDAMN FAX MACHINE AGAIN?
WE ARE A MULTIMILLION-DOLLAR DOT COM AND WE STILL HAVE TO USE FAX MACHINES...

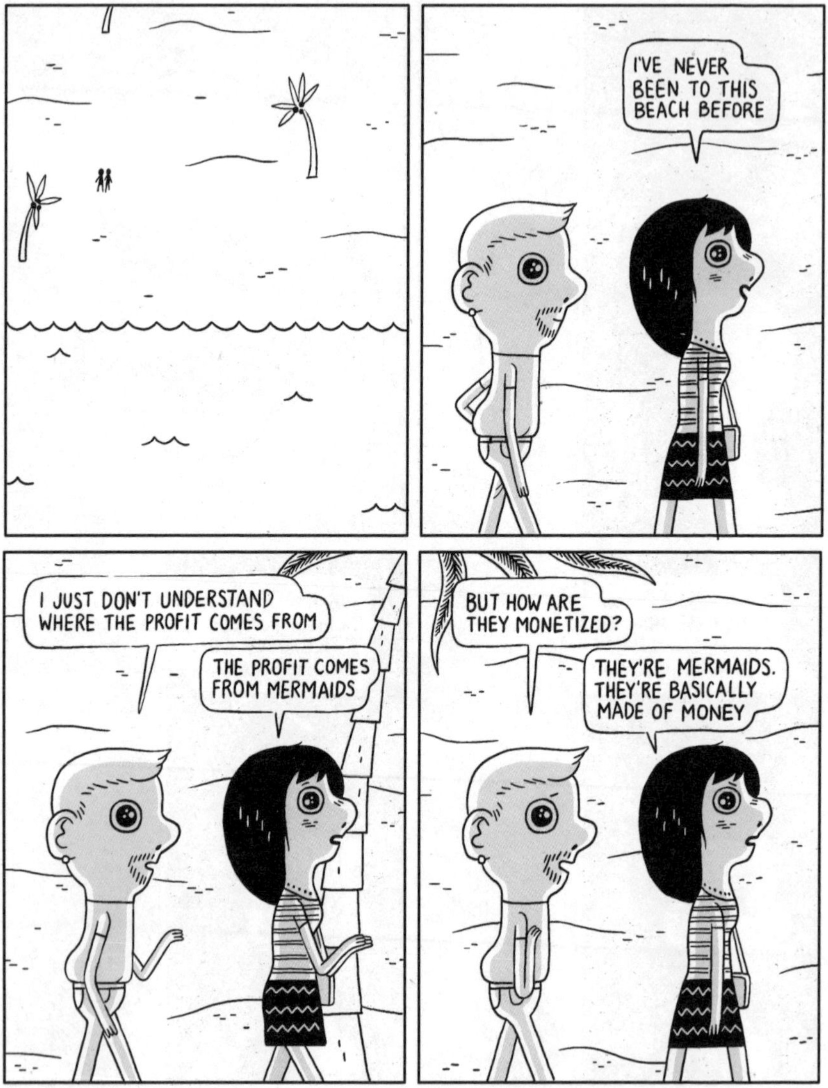
I'VE NEVER BEEN TO THIS BEACH BEFORE
I JUST DON'T UNDERSTAND WHERE THE PROFIT COMES FROM
THE PROFIT COMES FROM MERMAIDS
BUT HOW ARE THEY MONETIZED?
THEY'RE MERMAIDS. THEY'RE BASICALLY MADE OF MONEY

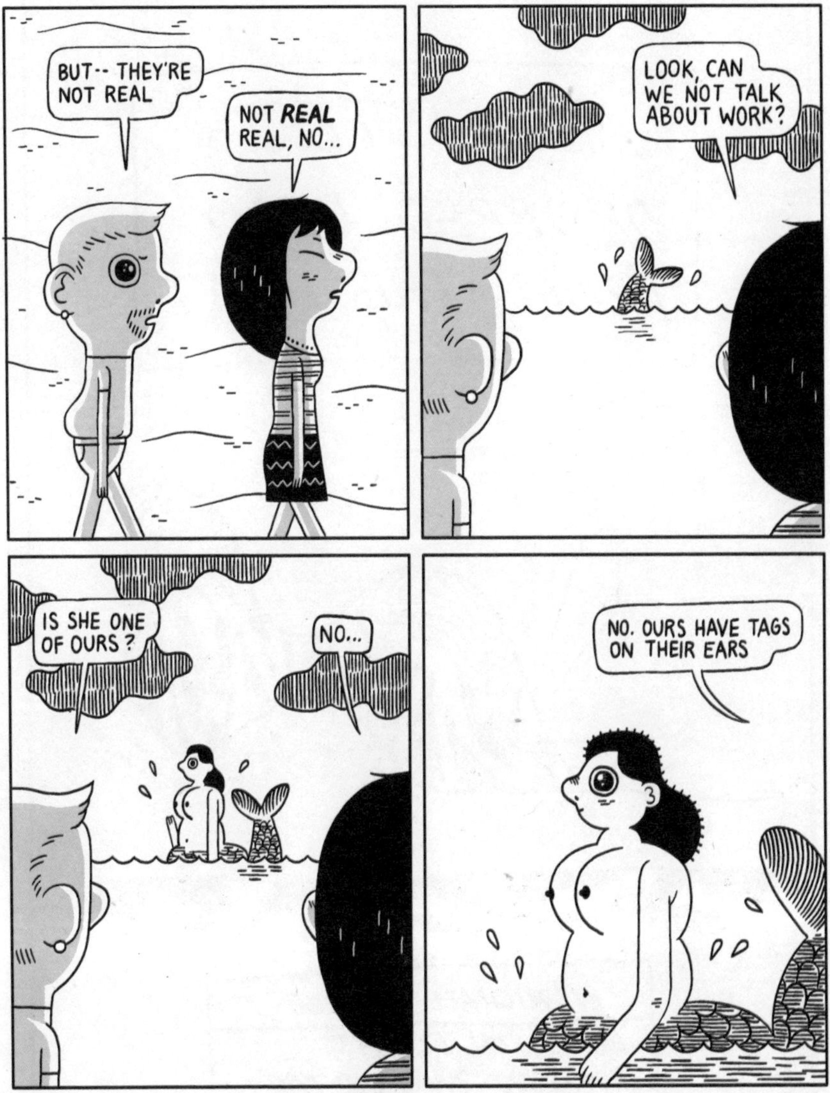
BUT-- THEY'RE NOT REAL
NOT **REAL** REAL, NO...
LOOK, CAN WE NOT TALK ABOUT WORK?
IS SHE ONE OF OURS?
NO...
NO. OURS HAVE TAGS ON THEIR EARS

MY SISTER DROPPED DEAD FROM THE HEAT

BY MICHAEL DEFORGE
DRAWN ON FLIGHT
BETWEEN OAKLAND AND
LAS VEGAS 08/10/2014

WE WALKED FOR DAYS. SOME WERE TOO TIRED TO KEEP GOING. ◆ WE LEFT THEM BEHIND. I COULDN'T TELL HOW MANY OF US THERE WERE. MY SISTER DROPPED DEAD

FROM THE HEAT

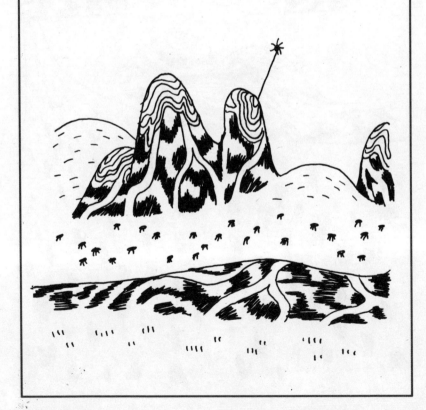

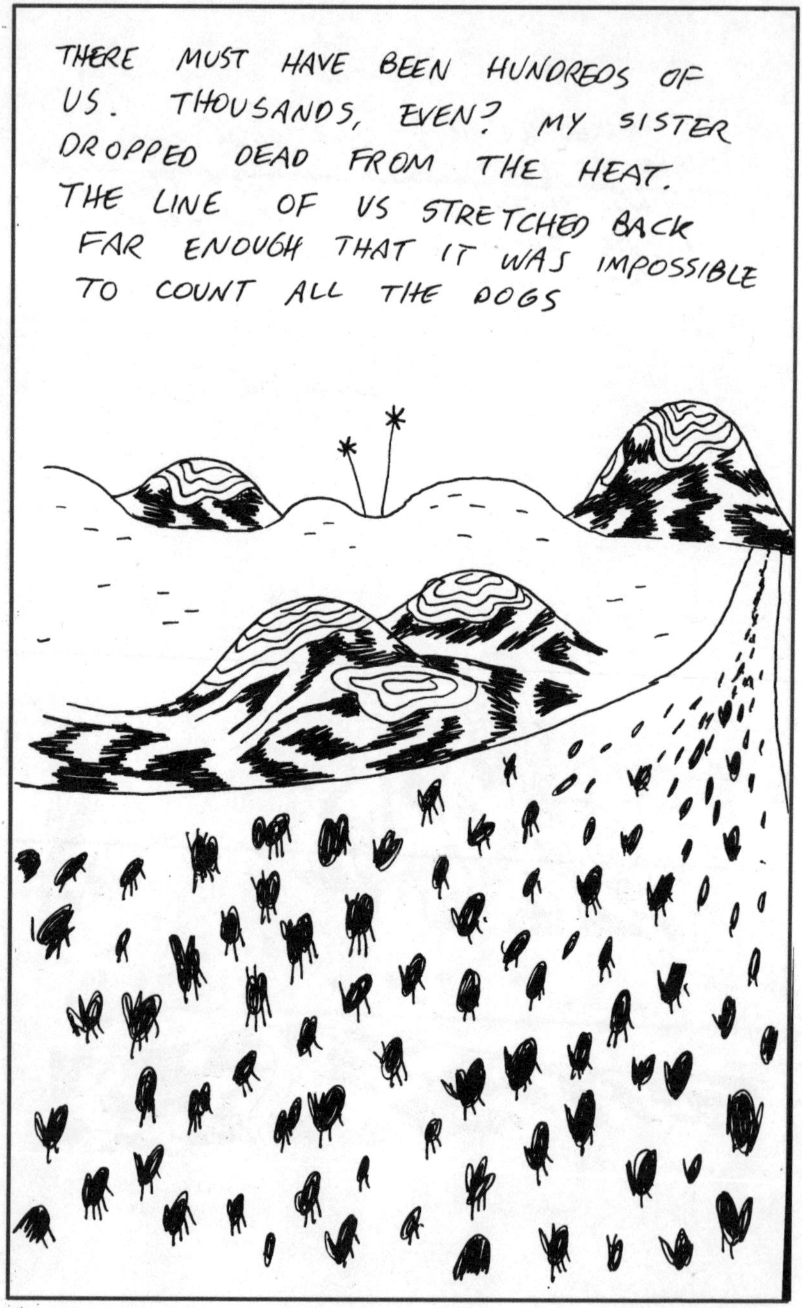
THERE MUST HAVE BEEN HUNDREDS OF US. THOUSANDS, EVEN? MY SISTER DROPPED DEAD FROM THE HEAT. THE LINE OF US STRETCHED BACK FAR ENOUGH THAT IT WAS IMPOSSIBLE TO COUNT ALL THE DOGS

AT SOME POINT, WE STARTED ~~SEEING~~ PASSING
THE BODIES OF OTHER DOGS. MAYBE A
FEW FROM THE FRONT OF THE LINE?
MAYBE THERE WAS A GROUP OF
DOGS ~~BEFORE US~~ THAT MADE THE
JOURNEY BEFORE US. MAYBE THEY'D
BE WAITING FOR US THERE. MY
SISTER DROPPED DEAD FROM THE
HEAT. IT'D BE A RELIEF TO BE
GREETED BY SOME FRIENDLY STRANGERS.

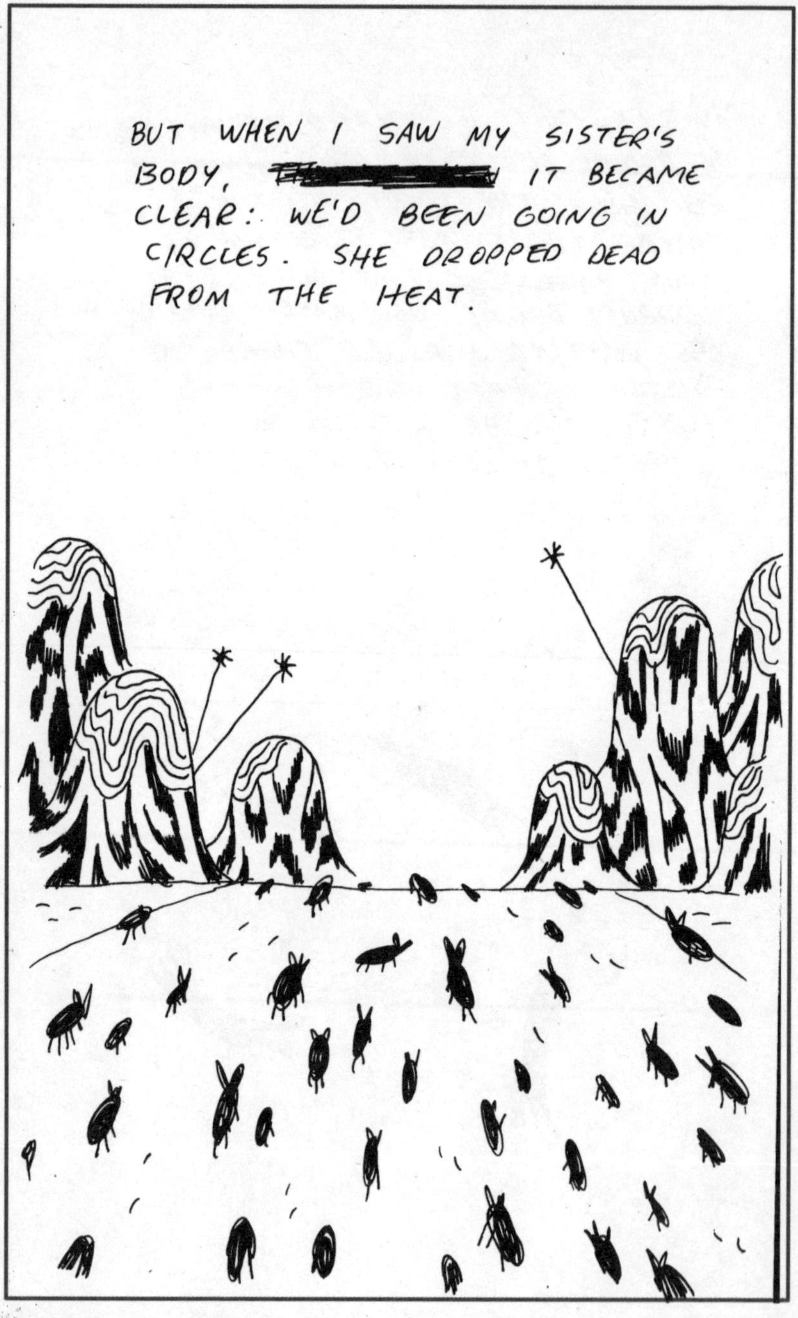
BUT WHEN I SAW MY SISTER'S BODY, [redacted] IT BECAME CLEAR: WE'D BEEN GOING IN CIRCLES. SHE DROPPED DEAD FROM THE HEAT.

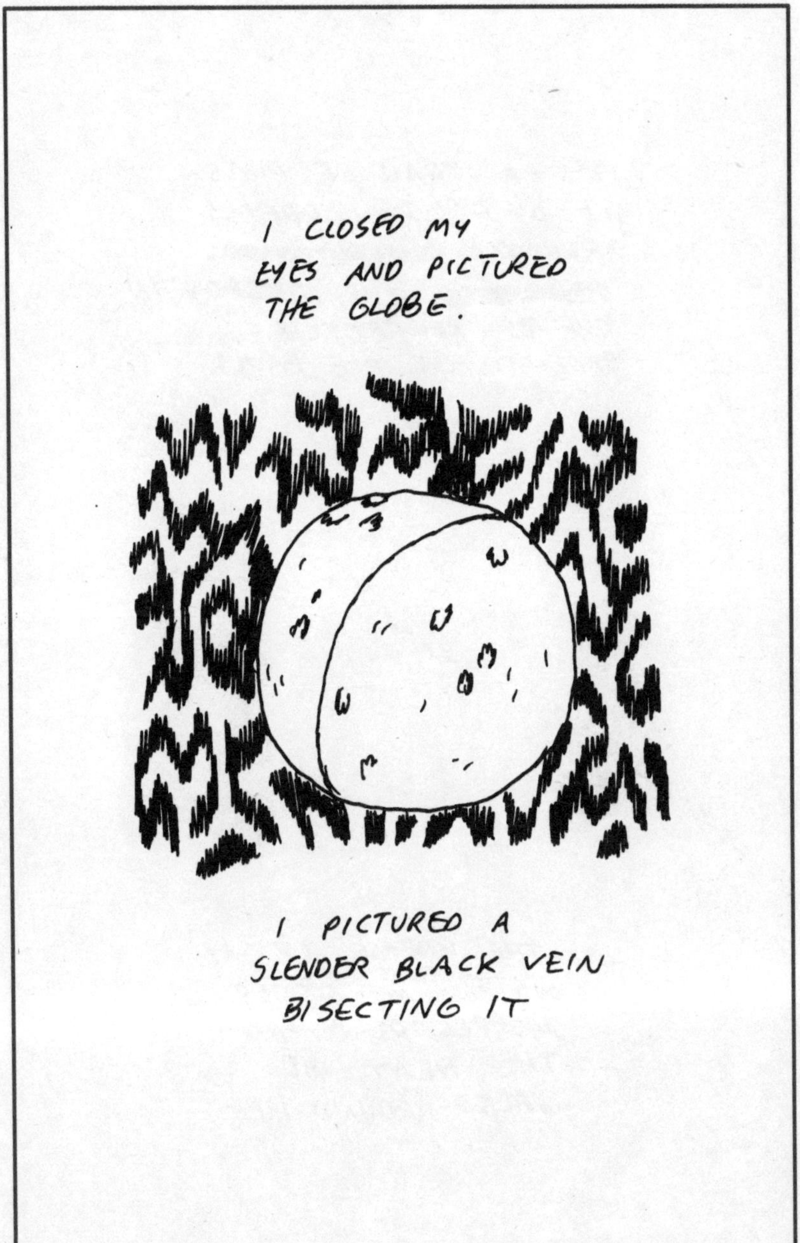
I CLOSED MY EYES AND PICTURED THE GLOBE.
I PICTURED A SLENDER BLACK VEIN BISECTING IT

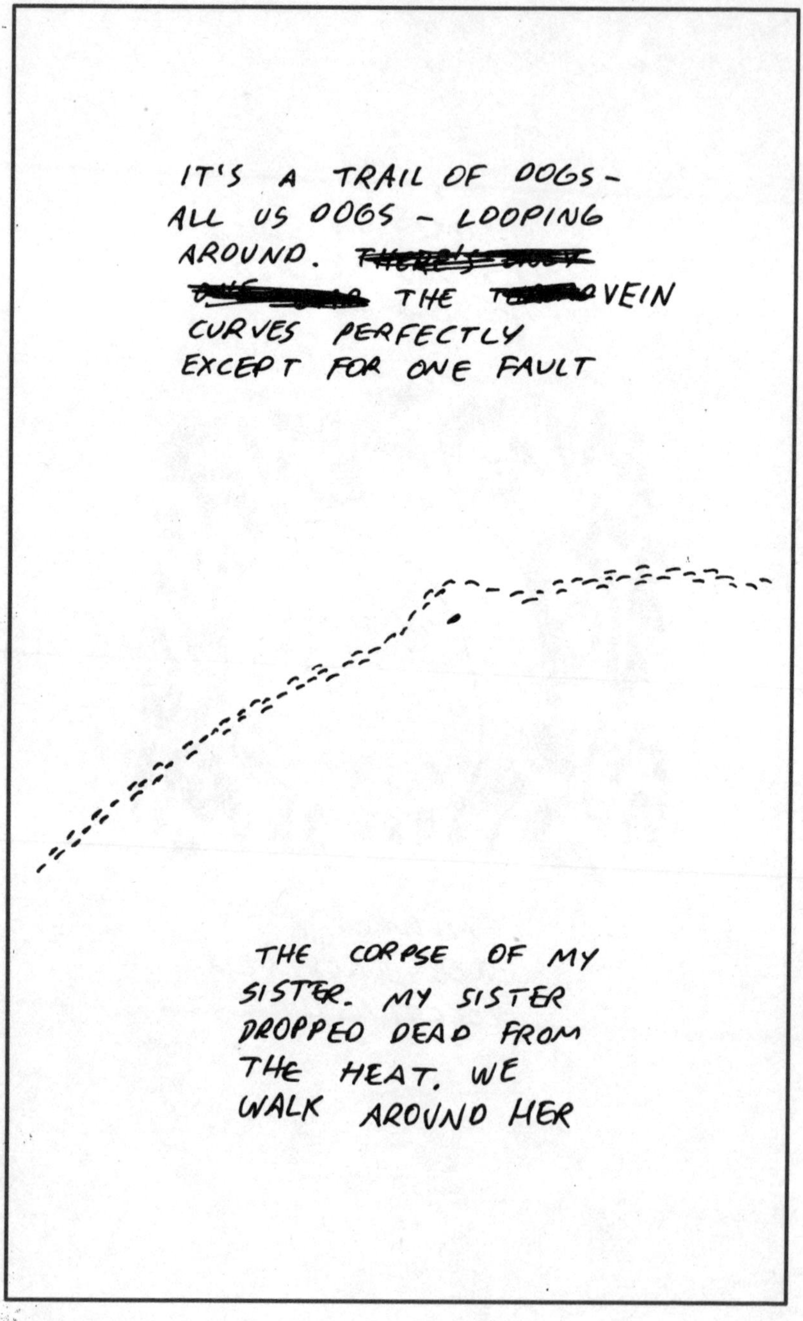
IT'S A TRAIL OF DOGS - ALL US DOGS - LOOPING AROUND. [redacted] THE T[redacted]VEIN CURVES PERFECTLY EXCEPT FOR ONE FAULT
THE CORPSE OF MY SISTER. MY SISTER DROPPED DEAD FROM THE HEAT. WE WALK AROUND HER

THE END

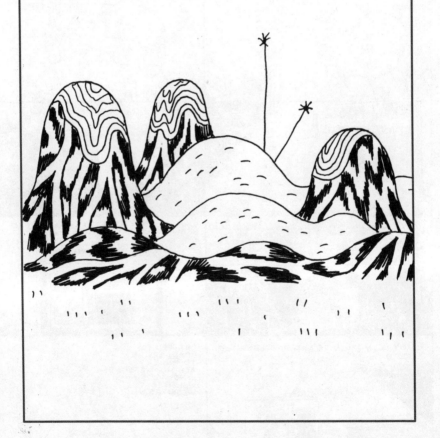

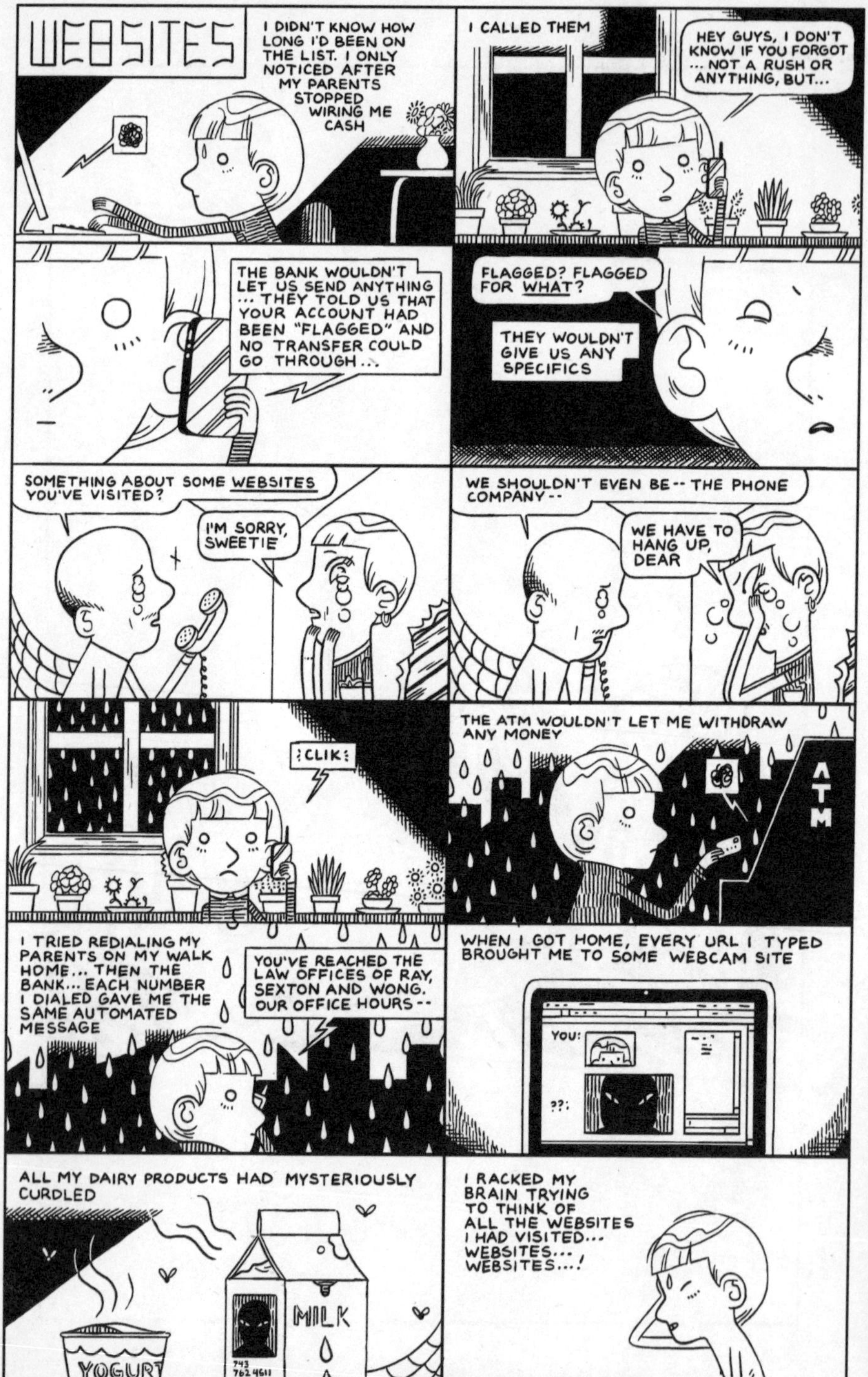
WEBSITES
I DIDN'T KNOW HOW LONG I'D BEEN ON THE LIST. I ONLY NOTICED AFTER MY PARENTS STOPPED WIRING ME CASH
I CALLED THEM
HEY GUYS, I DON'T KNOW IF YOU FORGOT ... NOT A RUSH OR ANYTHING, BUT...
THE BANK WOULDN'T LET US SEND ANYTHING ... THEY TOLD US THAT YOUR ACCOUNT HAD BEEN "FLAGGED" AND NO TRANSFER COULD GO THROUGH...
FLAGGED? FLAGGED FOR WHAT?
THEY WOULDN'T GIVE US ANY SPECIFICS
SOMETHING ABOUT SOME WEBSITES YOU'VE VISITED?
I'M SORRY, SWEETIE
WE SHOULDN'T EVEN BE -- THE PHONE COMPANY --
WE HAVE TO HANG UP, DEAR
CLIK
THE ATM WOULDN'T LET ME WITHDRAW ANY MONEY
ATM
I TRIED REDIALING MY PARENTS ON MY WALK HOME... THEN THE BANK... EACH NUMBER I DIALED GAVE ME THE SAME AUTOMATED MESSAGE
YOU'VE REACHED THE LAW OFFICES OF RAY, SEXTON AND WONG. OUR OFFICE HOURS --
WHEN I GOT HOME, EVERY URL I TYPED BROUGHT ME TO SOME WEBCAM SITE
YOU:
??:
ALL MY DAIRY PRODUCTS HAD MYSTERIOUSLY CURDLED
MILK
743 762 4611
YOGURT
I RACKED MY BRAIN TRYING TO THINK OF ALL THE WEBSITES I HAD VISITED... WEBSITES... WEBSITES...!

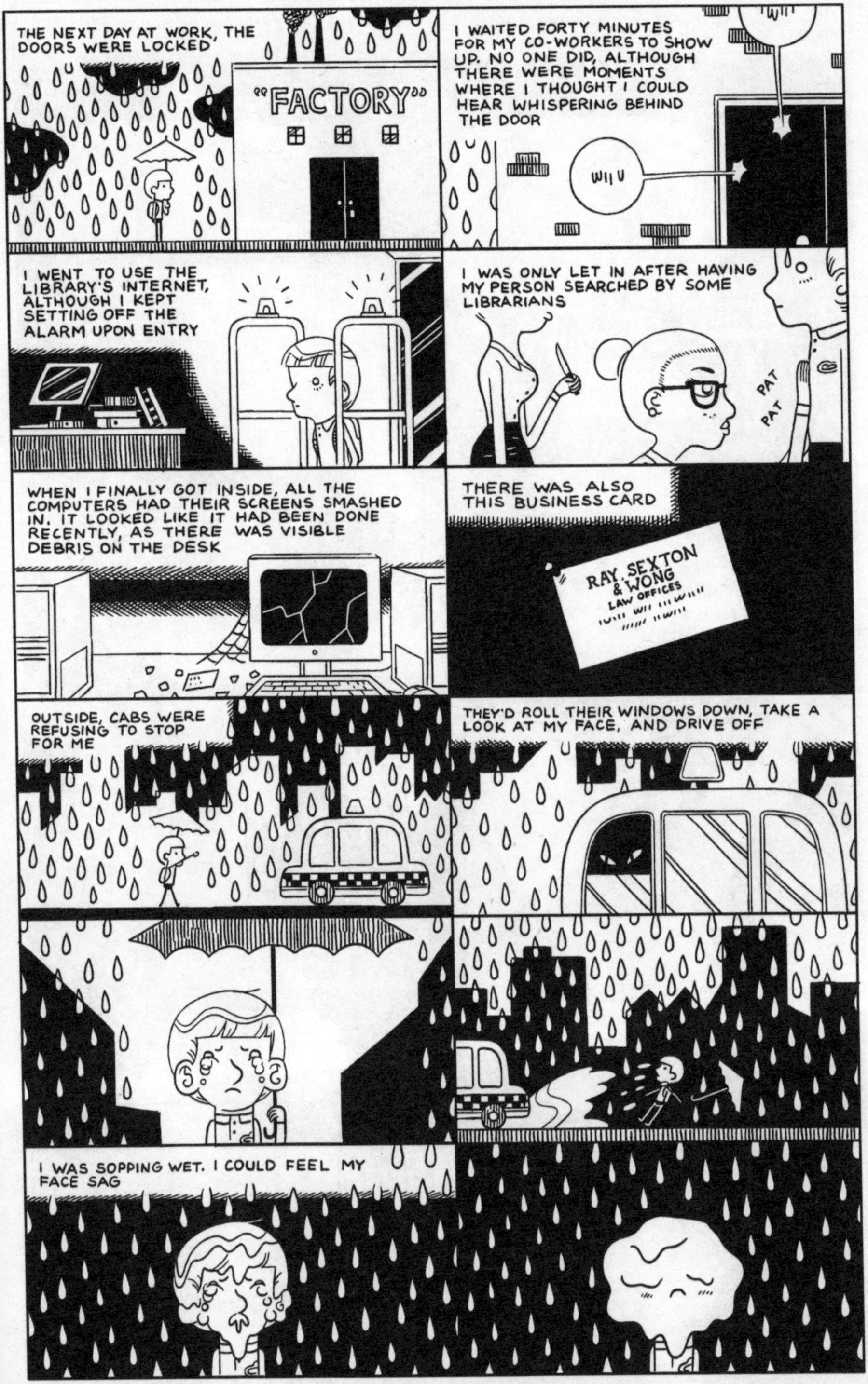

THE NEXT DAY AT WORK, THE DOORS WERE LOCKED
"FACTORY"
I WAITED FORTY MINUTES FOR MY CO-WORKERS TO SHOW UP. NO ONE DID, ALTHOUGH THERE WERE MOMENTS WHERE I THOUGHT I COULD HEAR WHISPERING BEHIND THE DOOR
I WENT TO USE THE LIBRARY'S INTERNET, ALTHOUGH I KEPT SETTING OFF THE ALARM UPON ENTRY
I WAS ONLY LET IN AFTER HAVING MY PERSON SEARCHED BY SOME LIBRARIANS
PAT
PAT
WHEN I FINALLY GOT INSIDE, ALL THE COMPUTERS HAD THEIR SCREENS SMASHED IN. IT LOOKED LIKE IT HAD BEEN DONE RECENTLY, AS THERE WAS VISIBLE DEBRIS ON THE DESK
THERE WAS ALSO THIS BUSINESS CARD
RAY, SEXTON & WONG
LAW OFFICES
OUTSIDE, CABS WERE REFUSING TO STOP FOR ME
THEY'D ROLL THEIR WINDOWS DOWN, TAKE A LOOK AT MY FACE, AND DRIVE OFF
I WAS SOPPING WET. I COULD FEEL MY FACE SAG

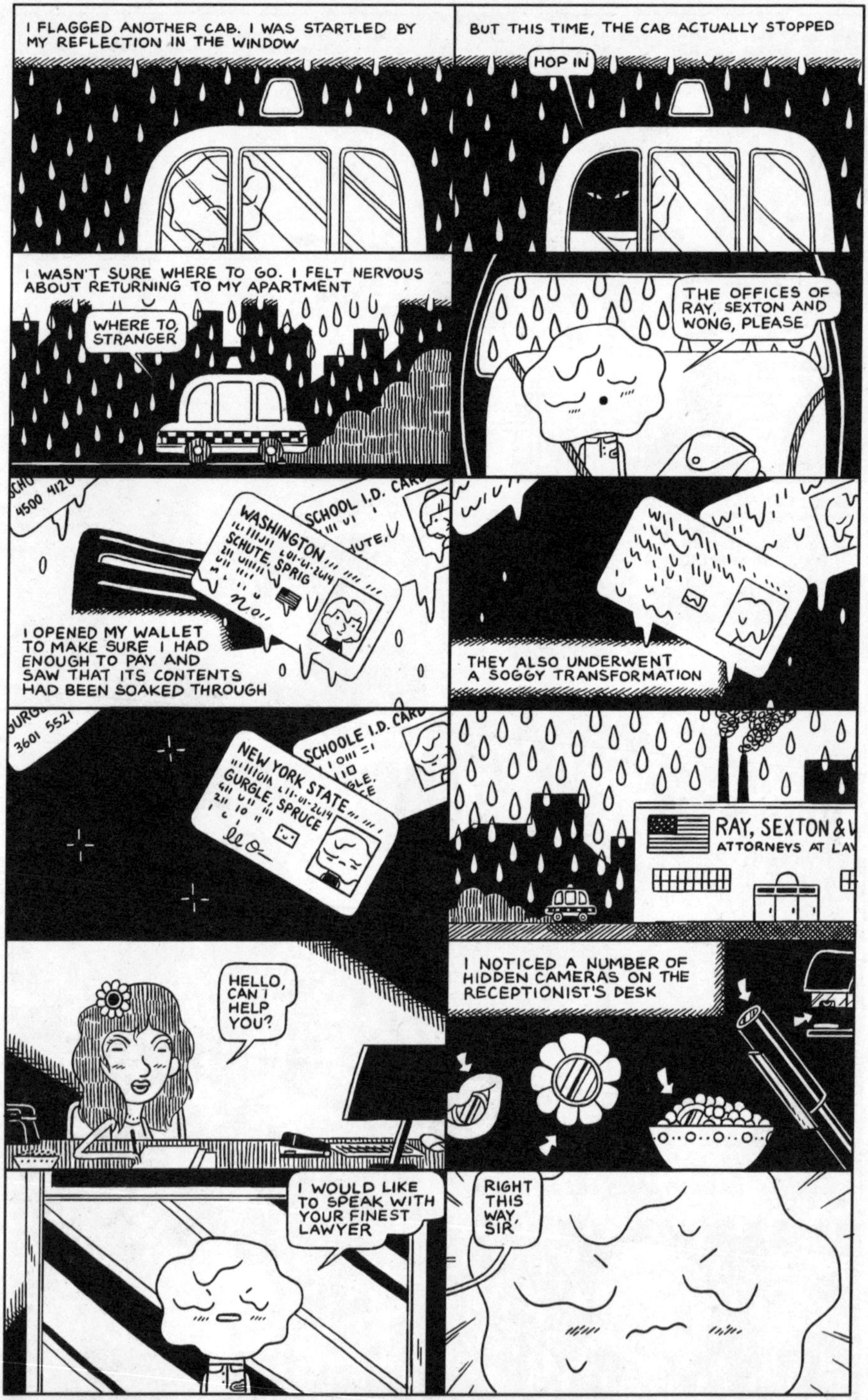

I FLAGGED ANOTHER CAB. I WAS STARTLED BY MY REFLECTION IN THE WINDOW
BUT THIS TIME, THE CAB ACTUALLY STOPPED
HOP IN
I WASN'T SURE WHERE TO GO. I FELT NERVOUS ABOUT RETURNING TO MY APARTMENT
WHERE TO, STRANGER
THE OFFICES OF RAY, SEXTON AND WONG, PLEASE
WASHINGTON
SCHUTE, SPRIG
SCHOOL I.D. CARD
I OPENED MY WALLET TO MAKE SURE I HAD ENOUGH TO PAY AND SAW THAT ITS CONTENTS HAD BEEN SOAKED THROUGH
THEY ALSO UNDERWENT A SOGGY TRANSFORMATION
3601 5521
NEW YORK STATE
GURGLE, SPRUCE
SCHOOLE I.D. CARD
RAY, SEXTON &
ATTORNEYS AT LA
HELLO, CAN I HELP YOU?
I NOTICED A NUMBER OF HIDDEN CAMERAS ON THE RECEPTIONIST'S DESK
I WOULD LIKE TO SPEAK WITH YOUR FINEST LAWYER
RIGHT THIS WAY, SIR

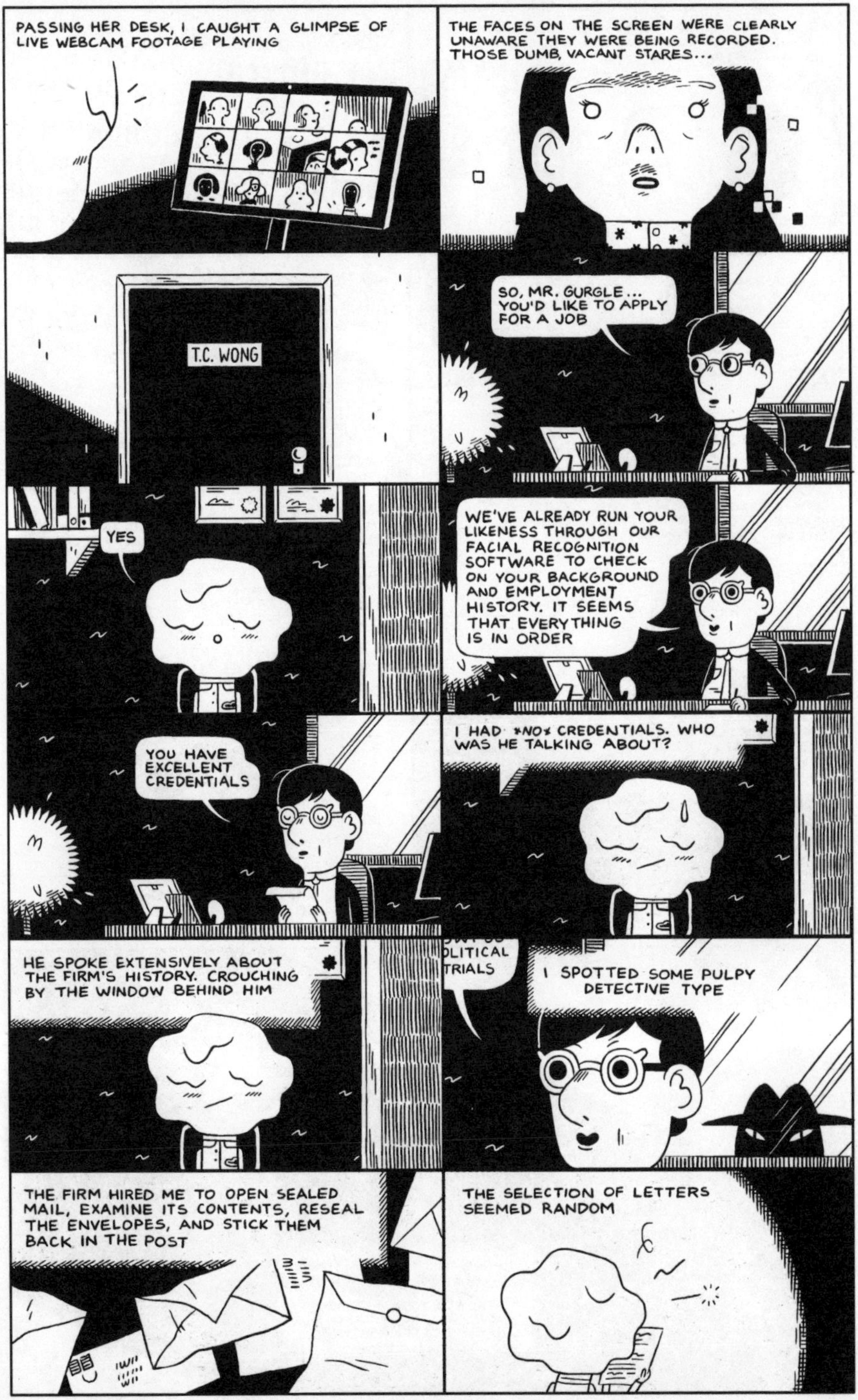
PASSING HER DESK, I CAUGHT A GLIMPSE OF LIVE WEBCAM FOOTAGE PLAYING
THE FACES ON THE SCREEN WERE CLEARLY UNAWARE THEY WERE BEING RECORDED. THOSE DUMB, VACANT STARES...
T.C. WONG
SO, MR. GURGLE... YOU'D LIKE TO APPLY FOR A JOB
YES
WE'VE ALREADY RUN YOUR LIKENESS THROUGH OUR FACIAL RECOGNITION SOFTWARE TO CHECK ON YOUR BACKGROUND AND EMPLOYMENT HISTORY. IT SEEMS THAT EVERYTHING IS IN ORDER
YOU HAVE EXCELLENT CREDENTIALS
I HAD *NO* CREDENTIALS. WHO WAS HE TALKING ABOUT?
HE SPOKE EXTENSIVELY ABOUT THE FIRM'S HISTORY. CROUCHING BY THE WINDOW BEHIND HIM
OLITICAL TRIALS
I SPOTTED SOME PULPY DETECTIVE TYPE
THE FIRM HIRED ME TO OPEN SEALED MAIL, EXAMINE ITS CONTENTS, RESEAL THE ENVELOPES, AND STICK THEM BACK IN THE POST
THE SELECTION OF LETTERS SEEMED RANDOM

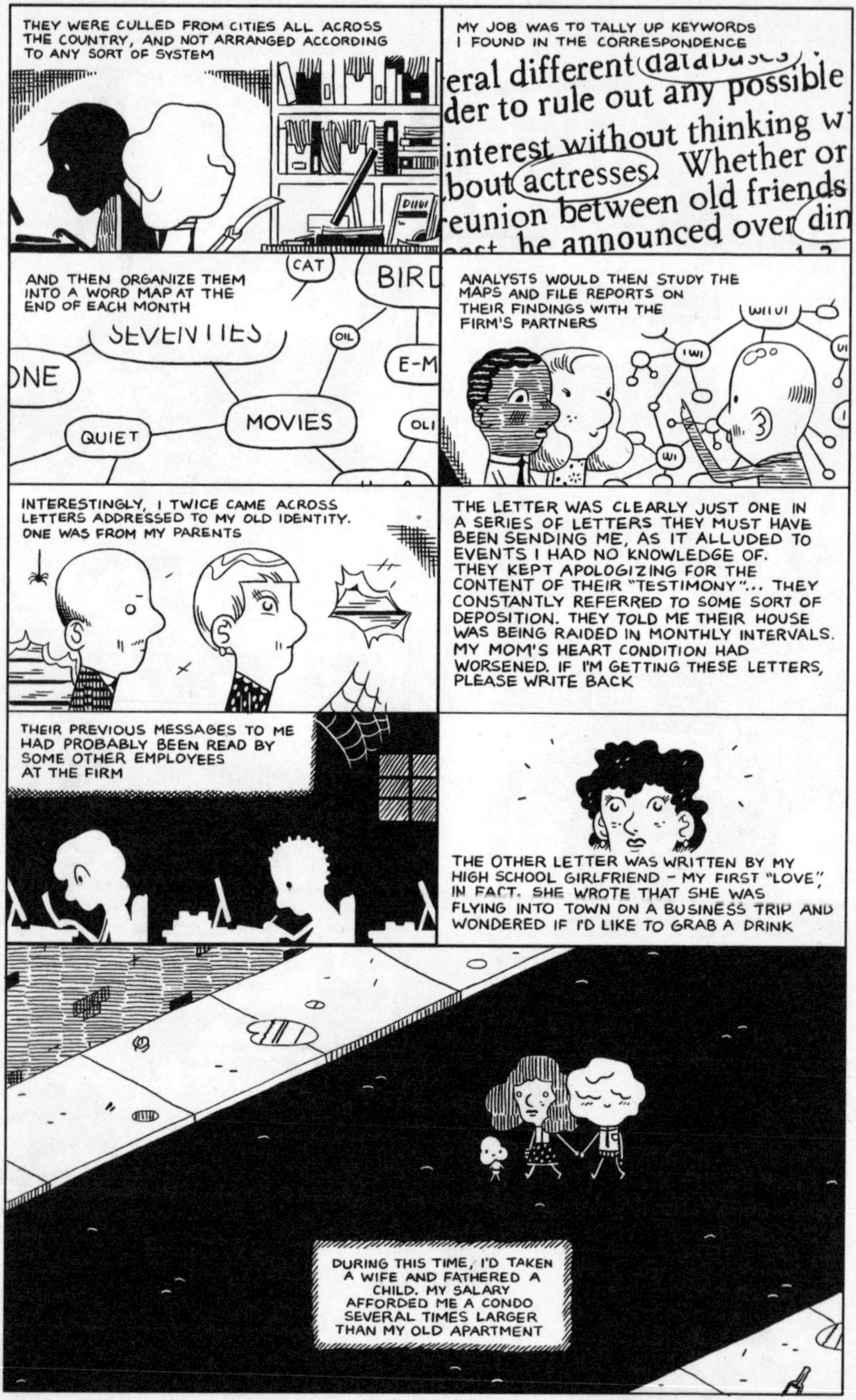
THEY WERE CULLED FROM CITIES ALL ACROSS THE COUNTRY, AND NOT ARRANGED ACCORDING TO ANY SORT OF SYSTEM
MY JOB WAS TO TALLY UP KEYWORDS I FOUND IN THE CORRESPONDENCE
eral different databases
der to rule out any possible
interest without thinking w
bout actresses. Whether or
reunion between old friends
he announced over din
AND THEN ORGANIZE THEM INTO A WORD MAP AT THE END OF EACH MONTH
CAT
BIRD
SEVENTIES
OIL
ONE
E-M
MOVIES
QUIET
ANALYSTS WOULD THEN STUDY THE MAPS AND FILE REPORTS ON THEIR FINDINGS WITH THE FIRM'S PARTNERS
INTERESTINGLY, I TWICE CAME ACROSS LETTERS ADDRESSED TO MY OLD IDENTITY. ONE WAS FROM MY PARENTS
THE LETTER WAS CLEARLY JUST ONE IN A SERIES OF LETTERS THEY MUST HAVE BEEN SENDING ME, AS IT ALLUDED TO EVENTS I HAD NO KNOWLEDGE OF. THEY KEPT APOLOGIZING FOR THE CONTENT OF THEIR "TESTIMONY"... THEY CONSTANTLY REFERRED TO SOME SORT OF DEPOSITION. THEY TOLD ME THEIR HOUSE WAS BEING RAIDED IN MONTHLY INTERVALS. MY MOM'S HEART CONDITION HAD WORSENED. IF I'M GETTING THESE LETTERS, PLEASE WRITE BACK
THEIR PREVIOUS MESSAGES TO ME HAD PROBABLY BEEN READ BY SOME OTHER EMPLOYEES AT THE FIRM
THE OTHER LETTER WAS WRITTEN BY MY HIGH SCHOOL GIRLFRIEND - MY FIRST "LOVE," IN FACT. SHE WROTE THAT SHE WAS FLYING INTO TOWN ON A BUSINESS TRIP AND WONDERED IF I'D LIKE TO GRAB A DRINK
DURING THIS TIME, I'D TAKEN A WIFE AND FATHERED A CHILD. MY SALARY AFFORDED ME A CONDO SEVERAL TIMES LARGER THAN MY OLD APARTMENT

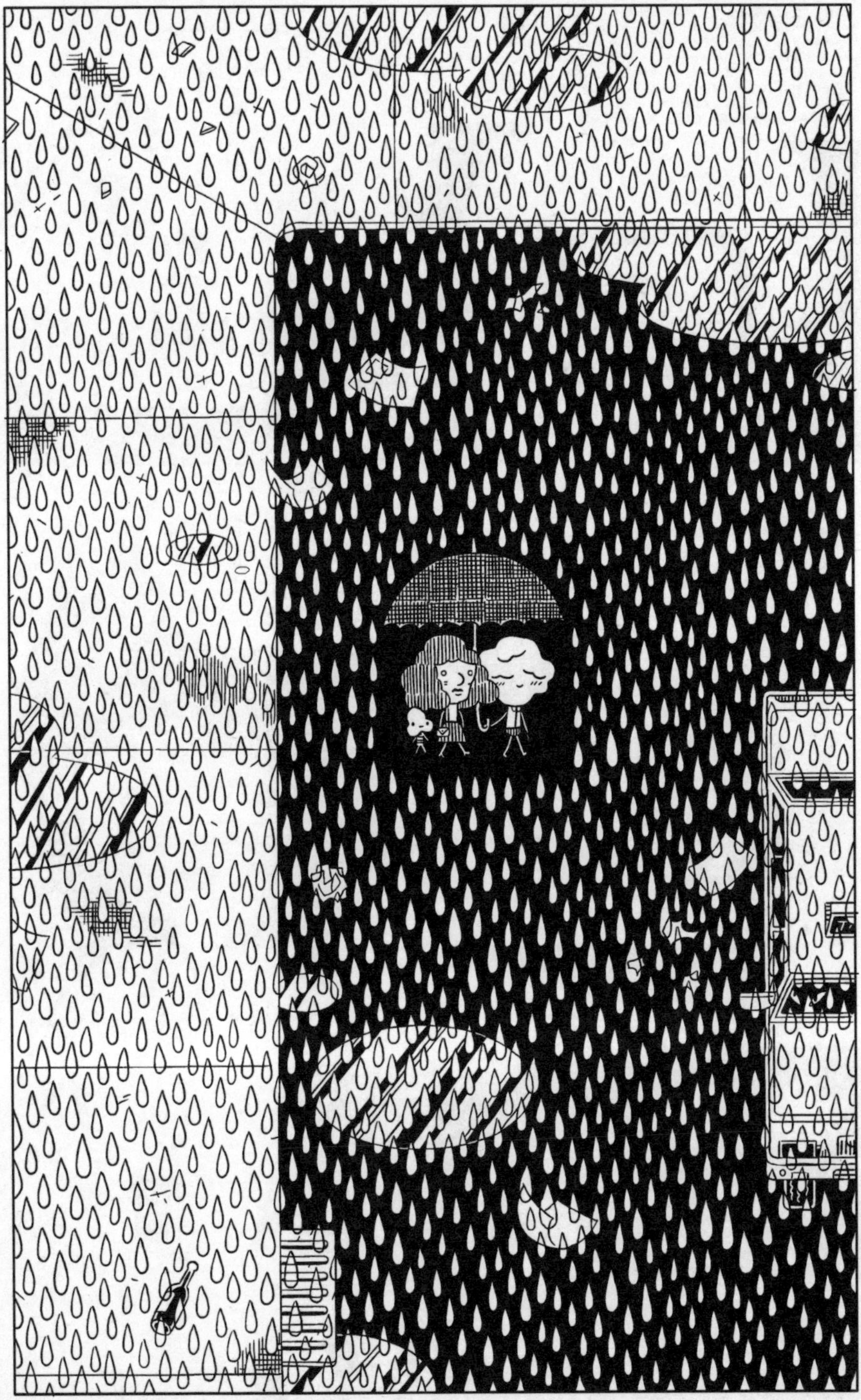

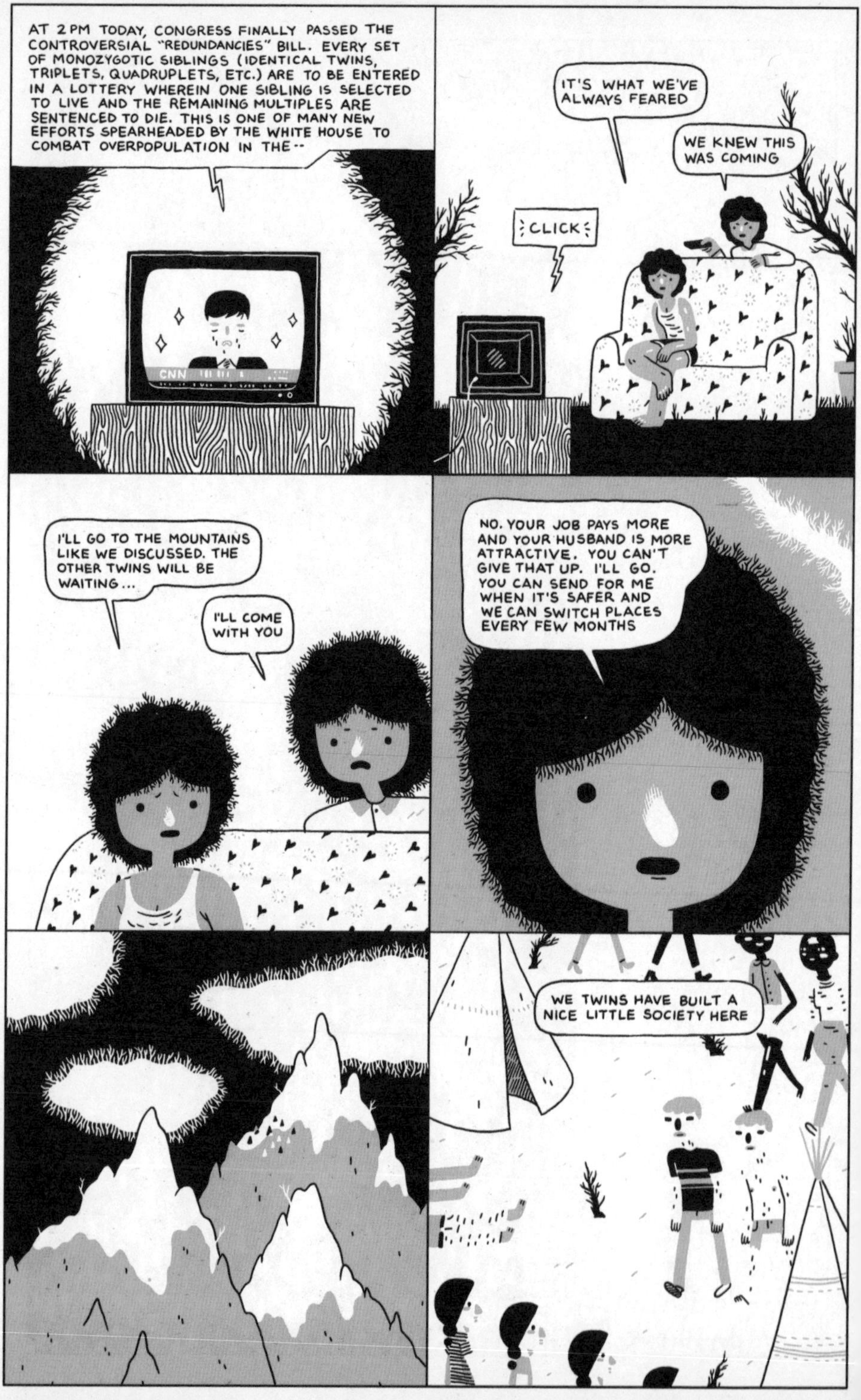
AT 2 PM TODAY, CONGRESS FINALLY PASSED THE CONTROVERSIAL "REDUNDANCIES" BILL. EVERY SET OF MONOZYGOTIC SIBLINGS (IDENTICAL TWINS, TRIPLETS, QUADRUPLETS, ETC.) ARE TO BE ENTERED IN A LOTTERY WHEREIN ONE SIBLING IS SELECTED TO LIVE AND THE REMAINING MULTIPLES ARE SENTENCED TO DIE. THIS IS ONE OF MANY NEW EFFORTS SPEARHEADED BY THE WHITE HOUSE TO COMBAT OVERPOPULATION IN THE--
CNN
IT'S WHAT WE'VE ALWAYS FEARED
WE KNEW THIS WAS COMING
CLICK
I'LL GO TO THE MOUNTAINS LIKE WE DISCUSSED. THE OTHER TWINS WILL BE WAITING...
I'LL COME WITH YOU
NO. YOUR JOB PAYS MORE AND YOUR HUSBAND IS MORE ATTRACTIVE. YOU CAN'T GIVE THAT UP. I'LL GO. YOU CAN SEND FOR ME WHEN IT'S SAFER AND WE CAN SWITCH PLACES EVERY FEW MONTHS
WE TWINS HAVE BUILT A NICE LITTLE SOCIETY HERE

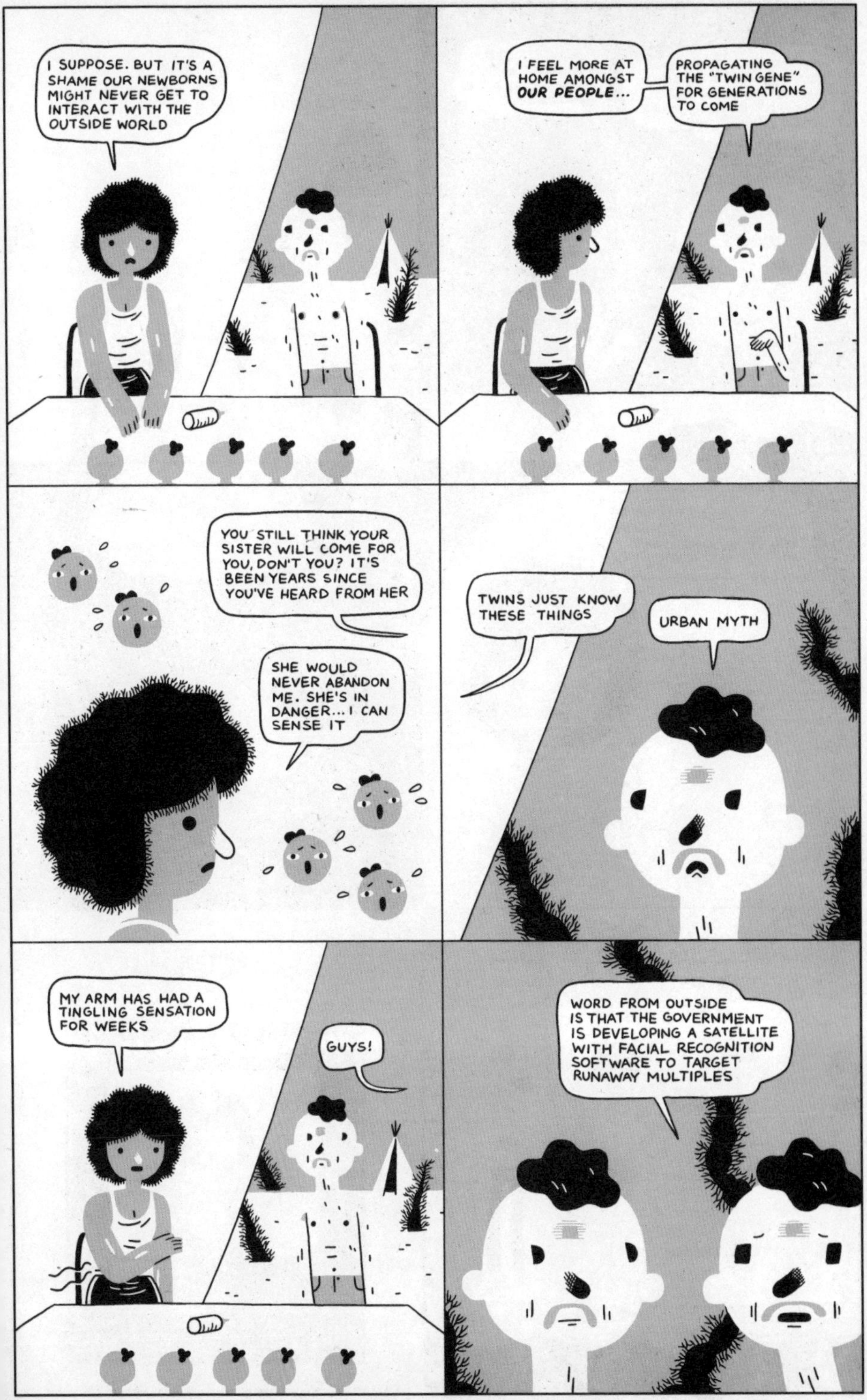
I SUPPOSE. BUT IT'S A SHAME OUR NEWBORNS MIGHT NEVER GET TO INTERACT WITH THE OUTSIDE WORLD
I FEEL MORE AT HOME AMONGST **OUR PEOPLE...**
PROPAGATING THE "TWIN GENE" FOR GENERATIONS TO COME
YOU STILL THINK YOUR SISTER WILL COME FOR YOU, DON'T YOU? IT'S BEEN YEARS SINCE YOU'VE HEARD FROM HER
SHE WOULD NEVER ABANDON ME. SHE'S IN DANGER... I CAN SENSE IT
TWINS JUST KNOW THESE THINGS
URBAN MYTH
MY ARM HAS HAD A TINGLING SENSATION FOR WEEKS
GUYS!
WORD FROM OUTSIDE IS THAT THE GOVERNMENT IS DEVELOPING A SATELLITE WITH FACIAL RECOGNITION SOFTWARE TO TARGET RUNAWAY MULTIPLES

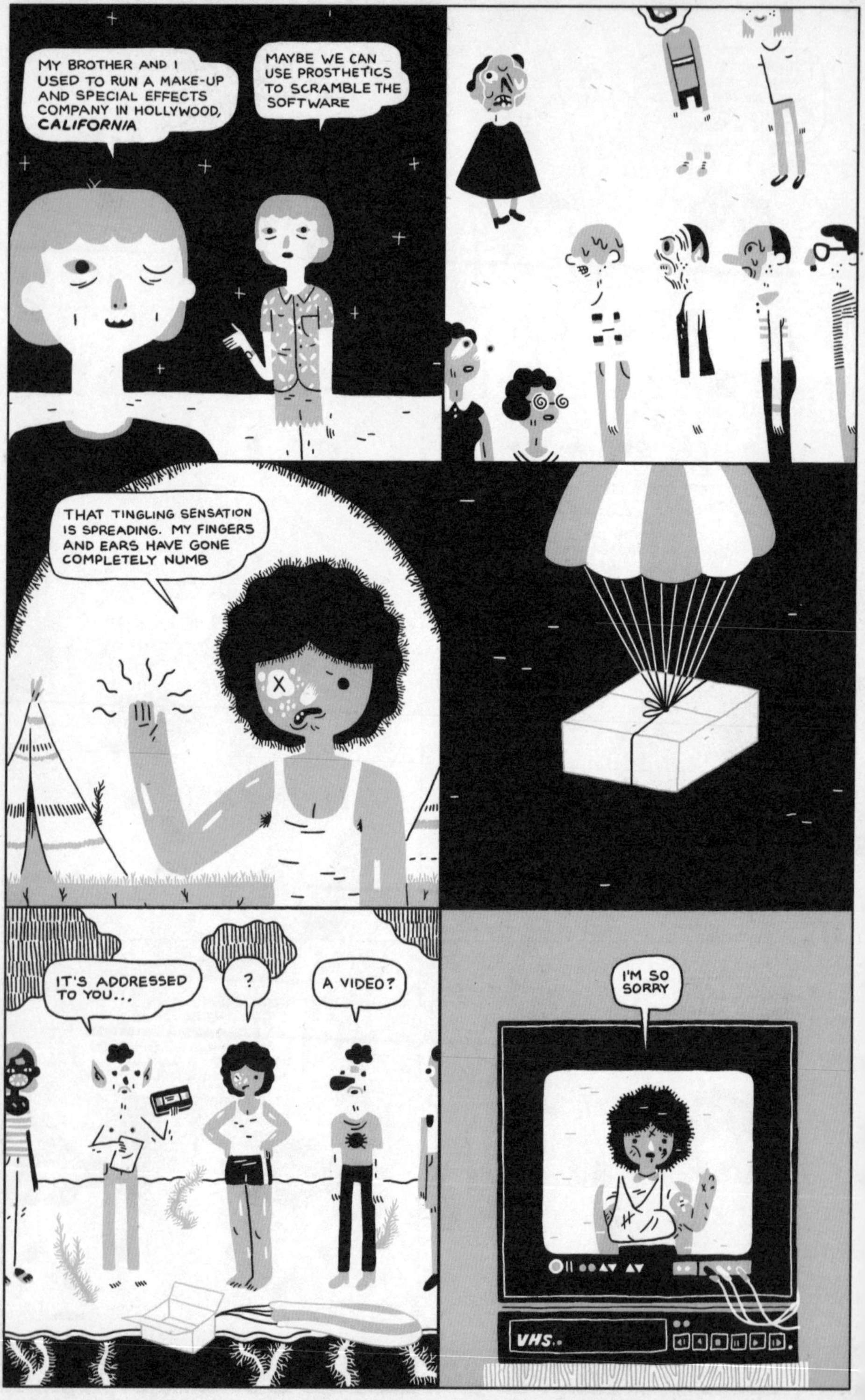
MY BROTHER AND I USED TO RUN A MAKE-UP AND SPECIAL EFFECTS COMPANY IN HOLLYWOOD, CALIFORNIA
MAYBE WE CAN USE PROSTHETICS TO SCRAMBLE THE SOFTWARE
THAT TINGLING SENSATION IS SPREADING. MY FINGERS AND EARS HAVE GONE COMPLETELY NUMB
IT'S ADDRESSED TO YOU...
?
A VIDEO?
I'M SO SORRY
VHS..

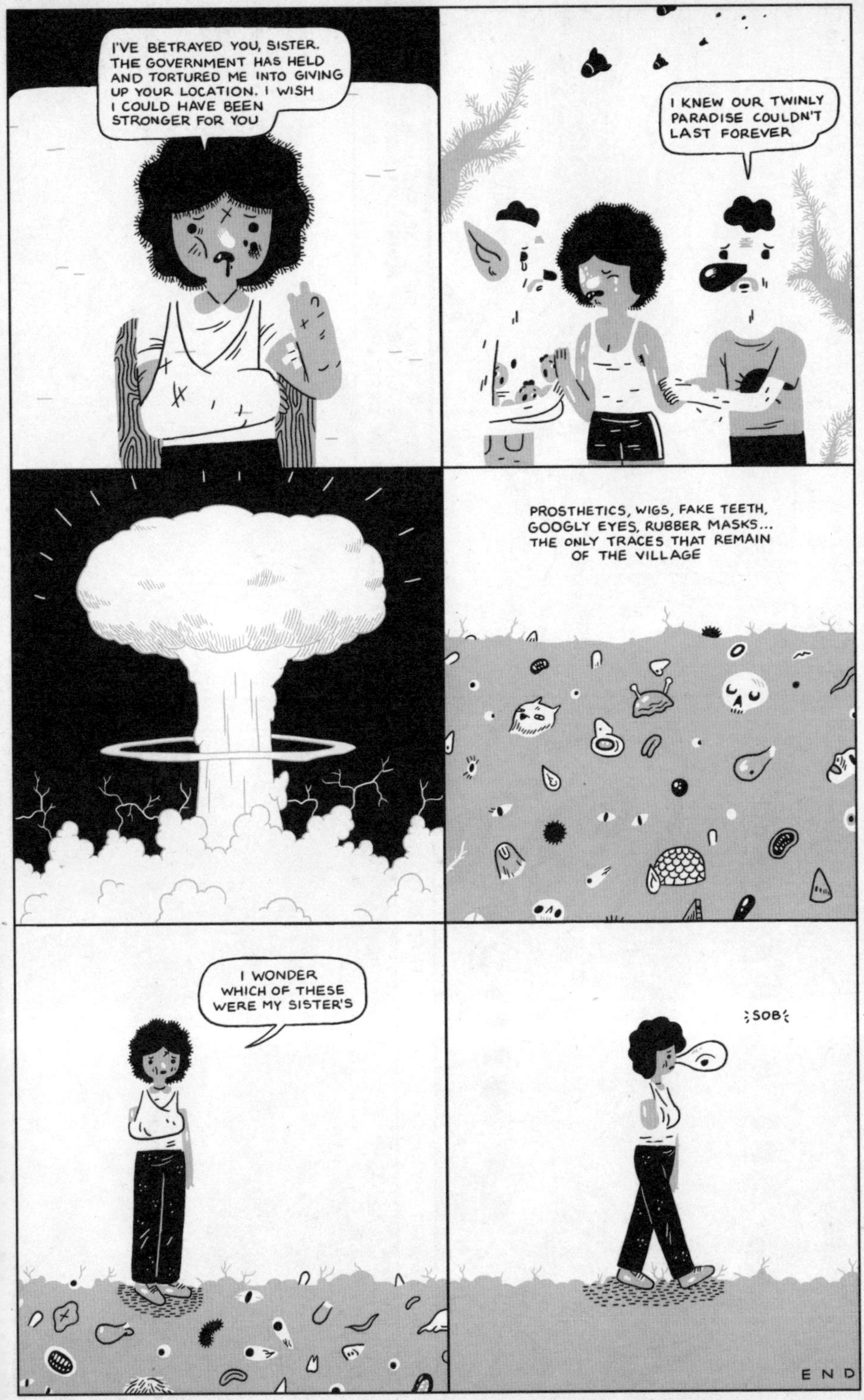
I'VE BETRAYED YOU, SISTER. THE GOVERNMENT HAS HELD AND TORTURED ME INTO GIVING UP YOUR LOCATION. I WISH I COULD HAVE BEEN STRONGER FOR YOU
I KNEW OUR TWINLY PARADISE COULDN'T LAST FOREVER
PROSTHETICS, WIGS, FAKE TEETH, GOOGLY EYES, RUBBER MASKS... THE ONLY TRACES THAT REMAIN OF THE VILLAGE
I WONDER WHICH OF THESE WERE MY SISTER'S
SOB
END

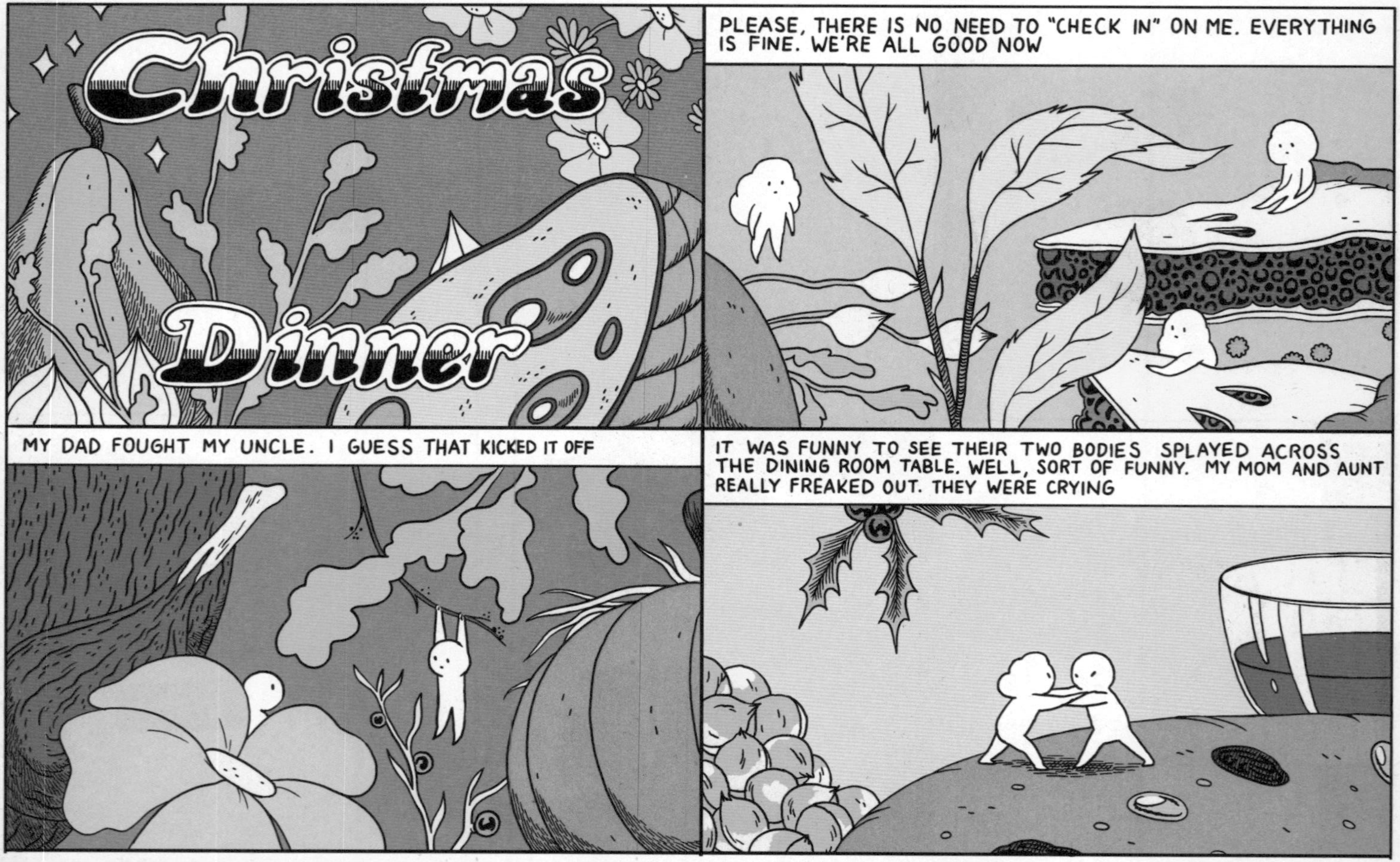
Christmas Dinner
PLEASE, THERE IS NO NEED TO "CHECK IN" ON ME. EVERYTHING IS FINE. WE'RE ALL GOOD NOW
MY DAD FOUGHT MY UNCLE. I GUESS THAT KICKED IT OFF
IT WAS FUNNY TO SEE THEIR TWO BODIES SPLAYED ACROSS THE DINING ROOM TABLE. WELL, SORT OF FUNNY. MY MOM AND AUNT REALLY FREAKED OUT. THEY WERE CRYING

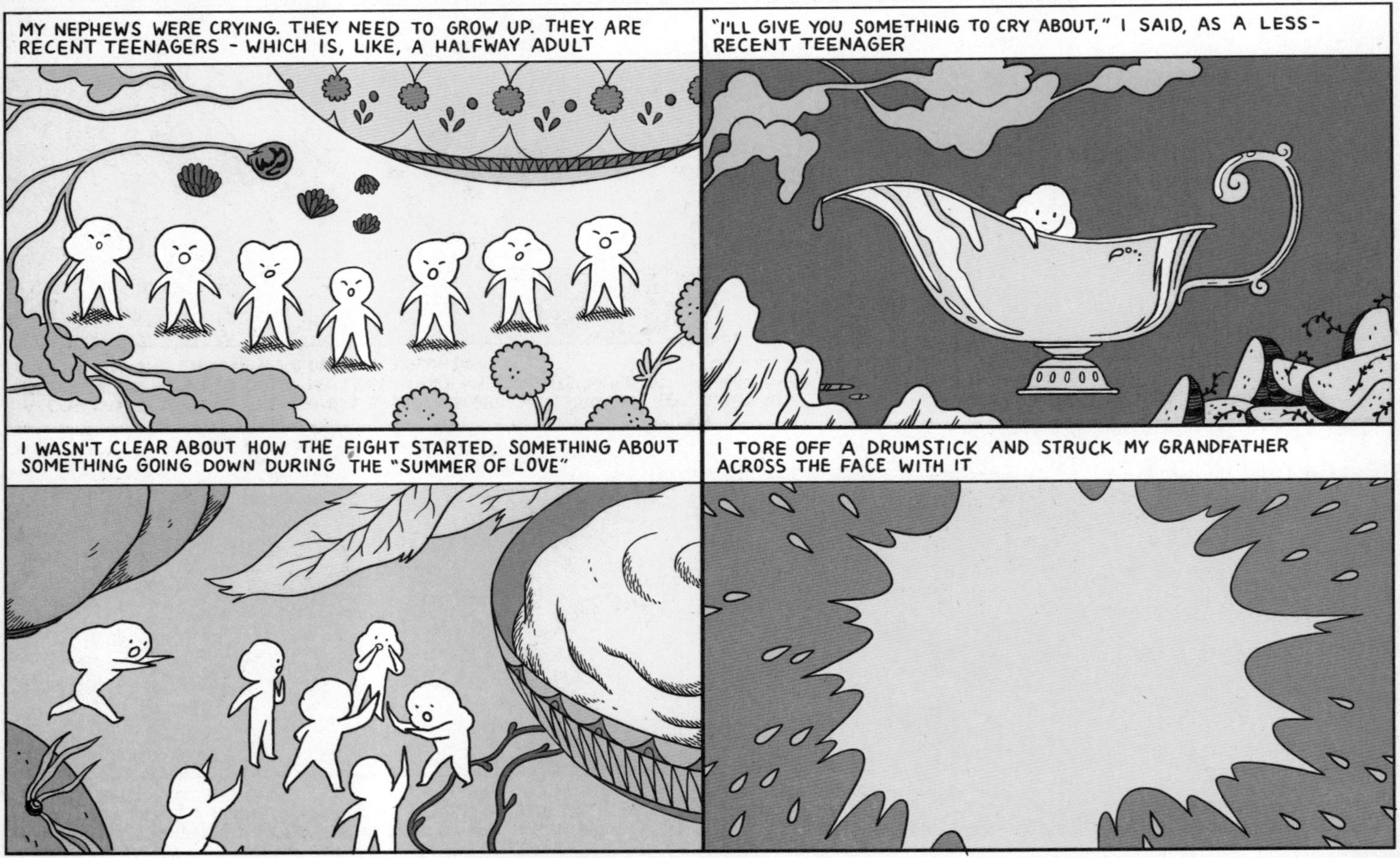
MY NEPHEWS WERE CRYING. THEY NEED TO GROW UP. THEY ARE RECENT TEENAGERS - WHICH IS, LIKE, A HALFWAY ADULT
"I'LL GIVE YOU SOMETHING TO CRY ABOUT," I SAID, AS A LESS-RECENT TEENAGER
I WASN'T CLEAR ABOUT HOW THE FIGHT STARTED. SOMETHING ABOUT SOMETHING GOING DOWN DURING THE "SUMMER OF LOVE"
I TORE OFF A DRUMSTICK AND STRUCK MY GRANDFATHER ACROSS THE FACE WITH IT

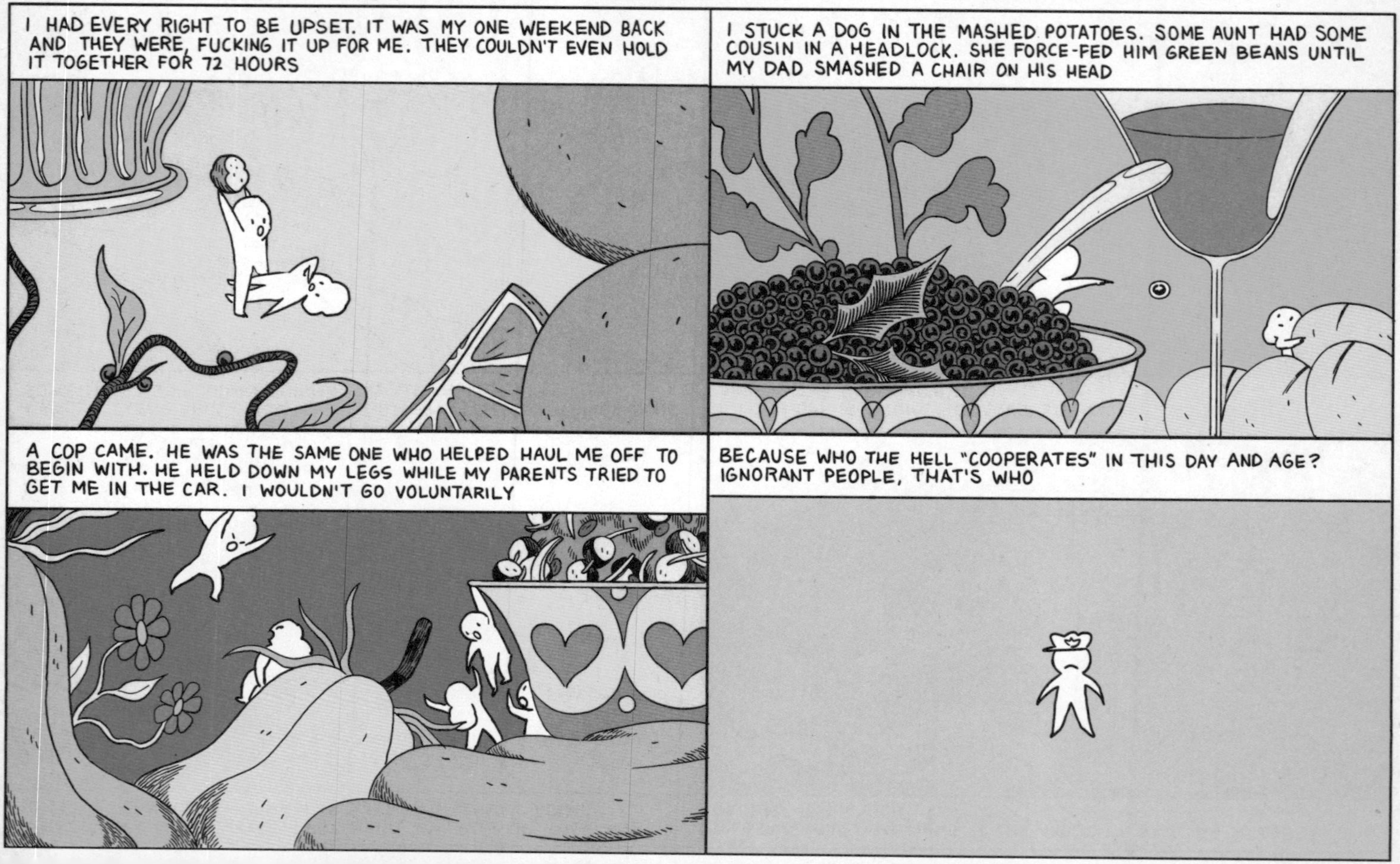
I HAD EVERY RIGHT TO BE UPSET. IT WAS MY ONE WEEKEND BACK AND THEY WERE FUCKING IT UP FOR ME. THEY COULDN'T EVEN HOLD IT TOGETHER FOR 72 HOURS
I STUCK A DOG IN THE MASHED POTATOES. SOME AUNT HAD SOME COUSIN IN A HEADLOCK. SHE FORCE-FED HIM GREEN BEANS UNTIL MY DAD SMASHED A CHAIR ON HIS HEAD
A COP CAME. HE WAS THE SAME ONE WHO HELPED HAUL ME OFF TO BEGIN WITH. HE HELD DOWN MY LEGS WHILE MY PARENTS TRIED TO GET ME IN THE CAR. I WOULDN'T GO VOLUNTARILY
BECAUSE WHO THE HELL "COOPERATES" IN THIS DAY AND AGE? IGNORANT PEOPLE, THAT'S WHO

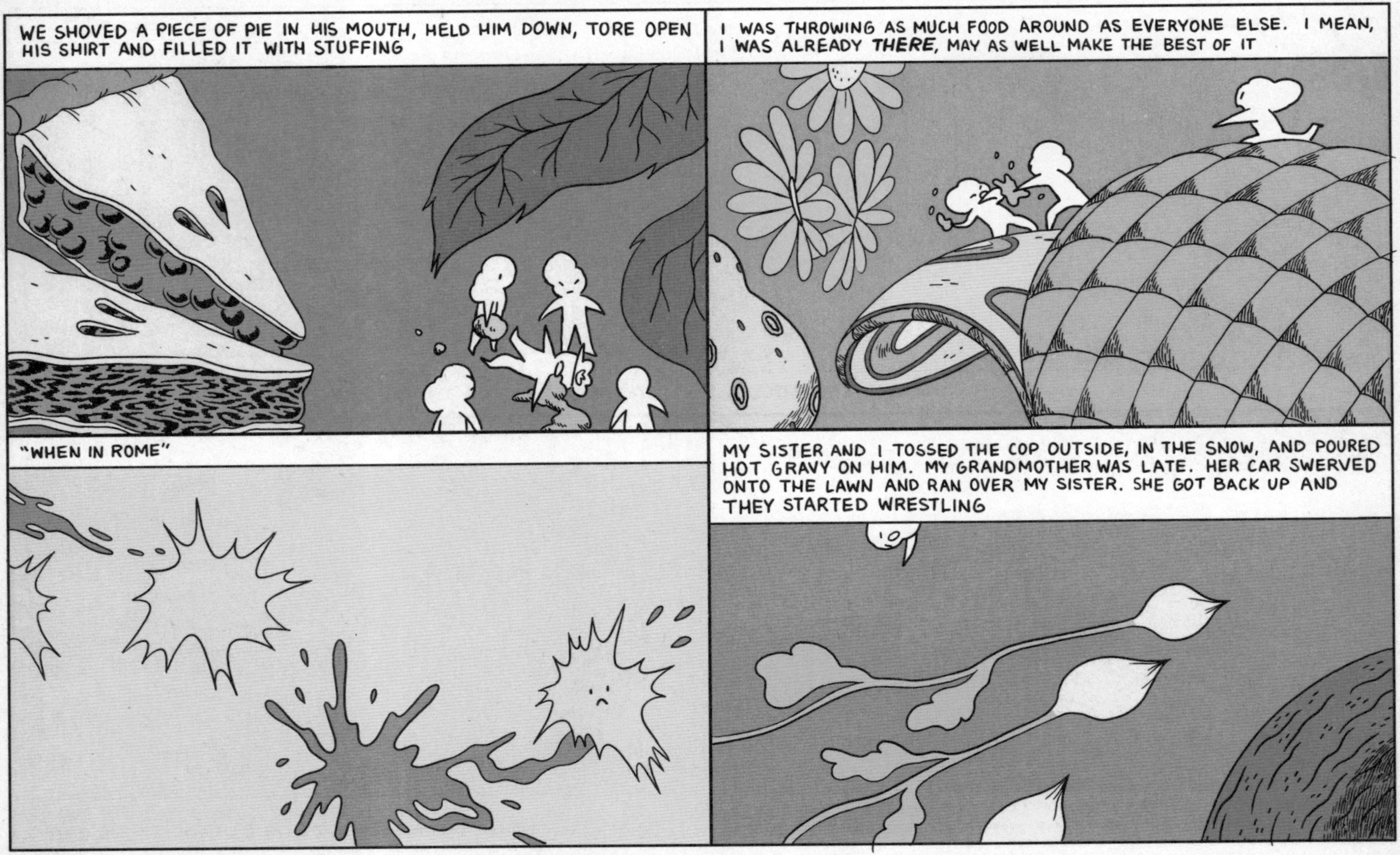
WE SHOVED A PIECE OF PIE IN HIS MOUTH, HELD HIM DOWN, TORE OPEN HIS SHIRT AND FILLED IT WITH STUFFING
I WAS THROWING AS MUCH FOOD AROUND AS EVERYONE ELSE. I MEAN, I WAS ALREADY *THERE*, MAY AS WELL MAKE THE BEST OF IT
"WHEN IN ROME"
MY SISTER AND I TOSSED THE COP OUTSIDE, IN THE SNOW, AND POURED HOT GRAVY ON HIM. MY GRANDMOTHER WAS LATE. HER CAR SWERVED ONTO THE LAWN AND RAN OVER MY SISTER. SHE GOT BACK UP AND THEY STARTED WRESTLING

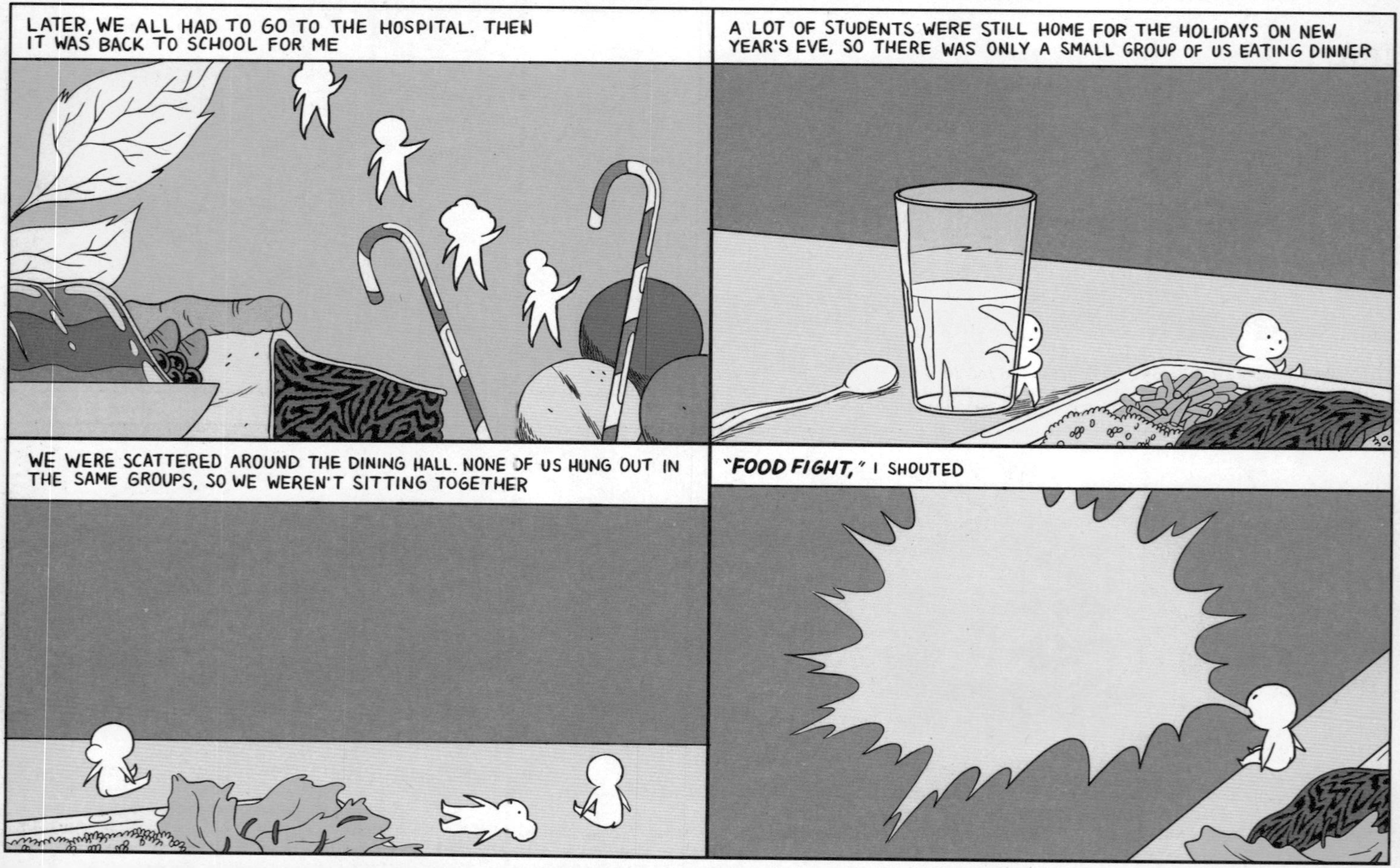
LATER, WE ALL HAD TO GO TO THE HOSPITAL. THEN IT WAS BACK TO SCHOOL FOR ME
A LOT OF STUDENTS WERE STILL HOME FOR THE HOLIDAYS ON NEW YEAR'S EVE, SO THERE WAS ONLY A SMALL GROUP OF US EATING DINNER
WE WERE SCATTERED AROUND THE DINING HALL. NONE OF US HUNG OUT IN THE SAME GROUPS, SO WE WEREN'T SITTING TOGETHER
"**FOOD FIGHT,**" I SHOUTED

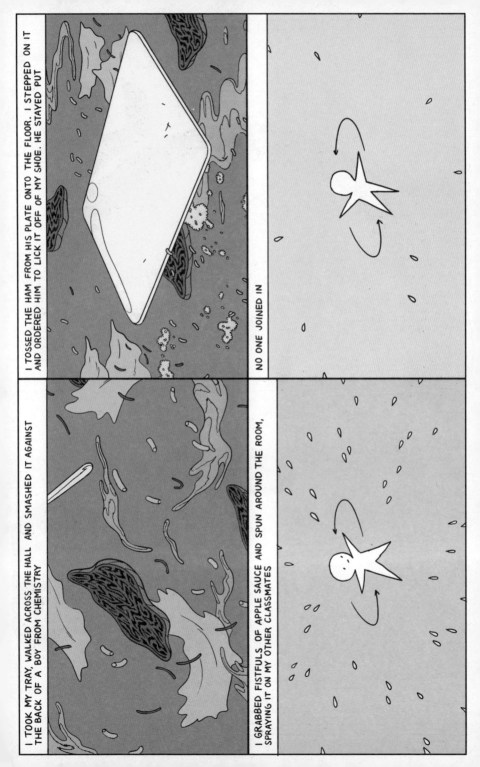

I TOOK MY TRAY, WALKED ACROSS THE HALL AND SMASHED IT AGAINST THE BACK OF A BOY FROM CHEMISTRY

I TOSSED THE HAM FROM HIS PLATE ONTO THE FLOOR. I STEPPED ON IT AND ORDERED HIM TO LICK IT OFF OF MY SHOE. HE STAYED PUT

I GRABBED FISTFULS OF APPLE SAUCE AND SPUN AROUND THE ROOM, SPRAYING IT ON MY OTHER CLASSMATES

NO ONE JOINED IN

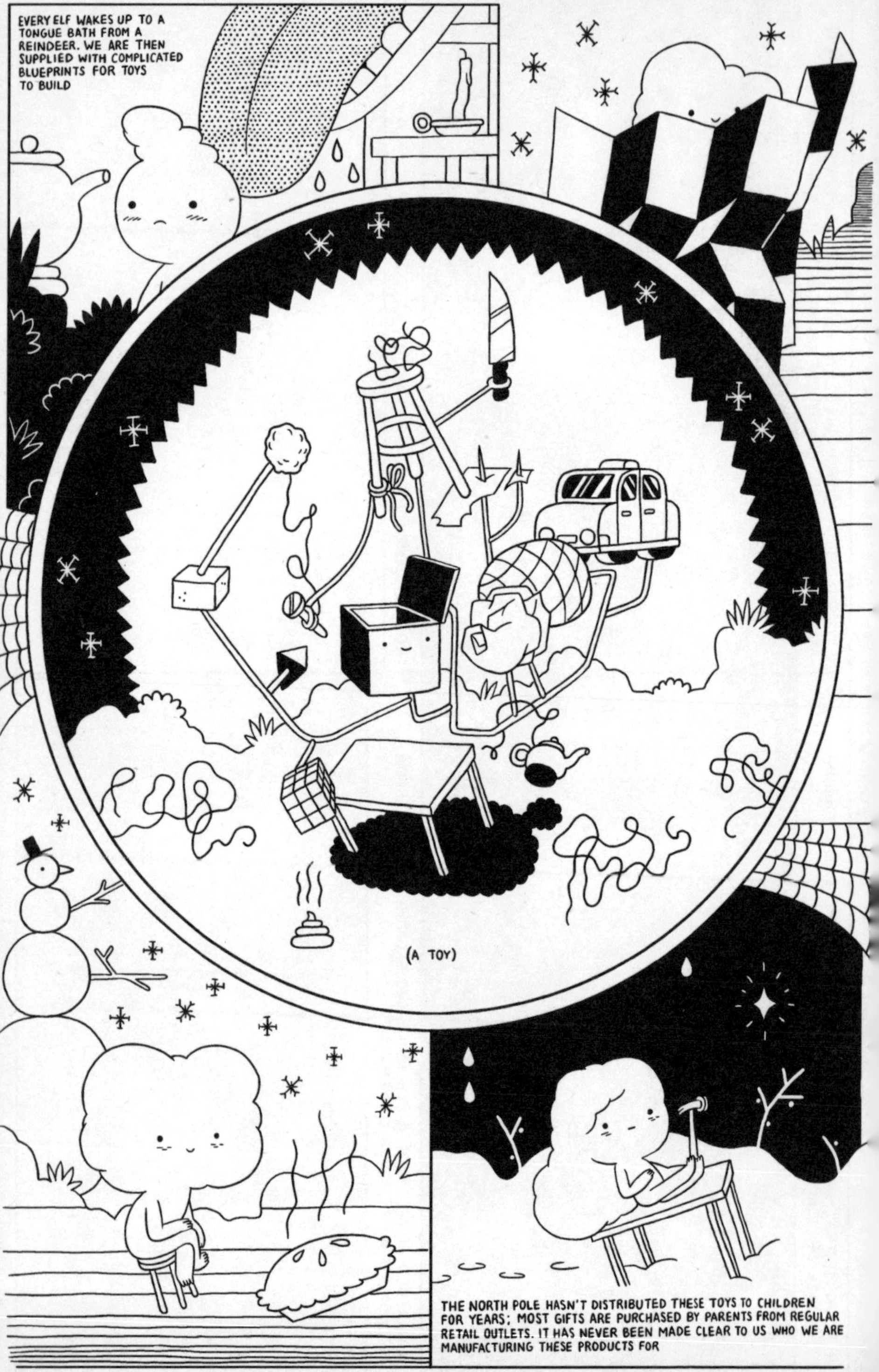
EVERY ELF WAKES UP TO A TONGUE BATH FROM A REINDEER. WE ARE THEN SUPPLIED WITH COMPLICATED BLUEPRINTS FOR TOYS TO BUILD
(A TOY)
THE NORTH POLE HASN'T DISTRIBUTED THESE TOYS TO CHILDREN FOR YEARS; MOST GIFTS ARE PURCHASED BY PARENTS FROM REGULAR RETAIL OUTLETS. IT HAS NEVER BEEN MADE CLEAR TO US WHO WE ARE MANUFACTURING THESE PRODUCTS FOR

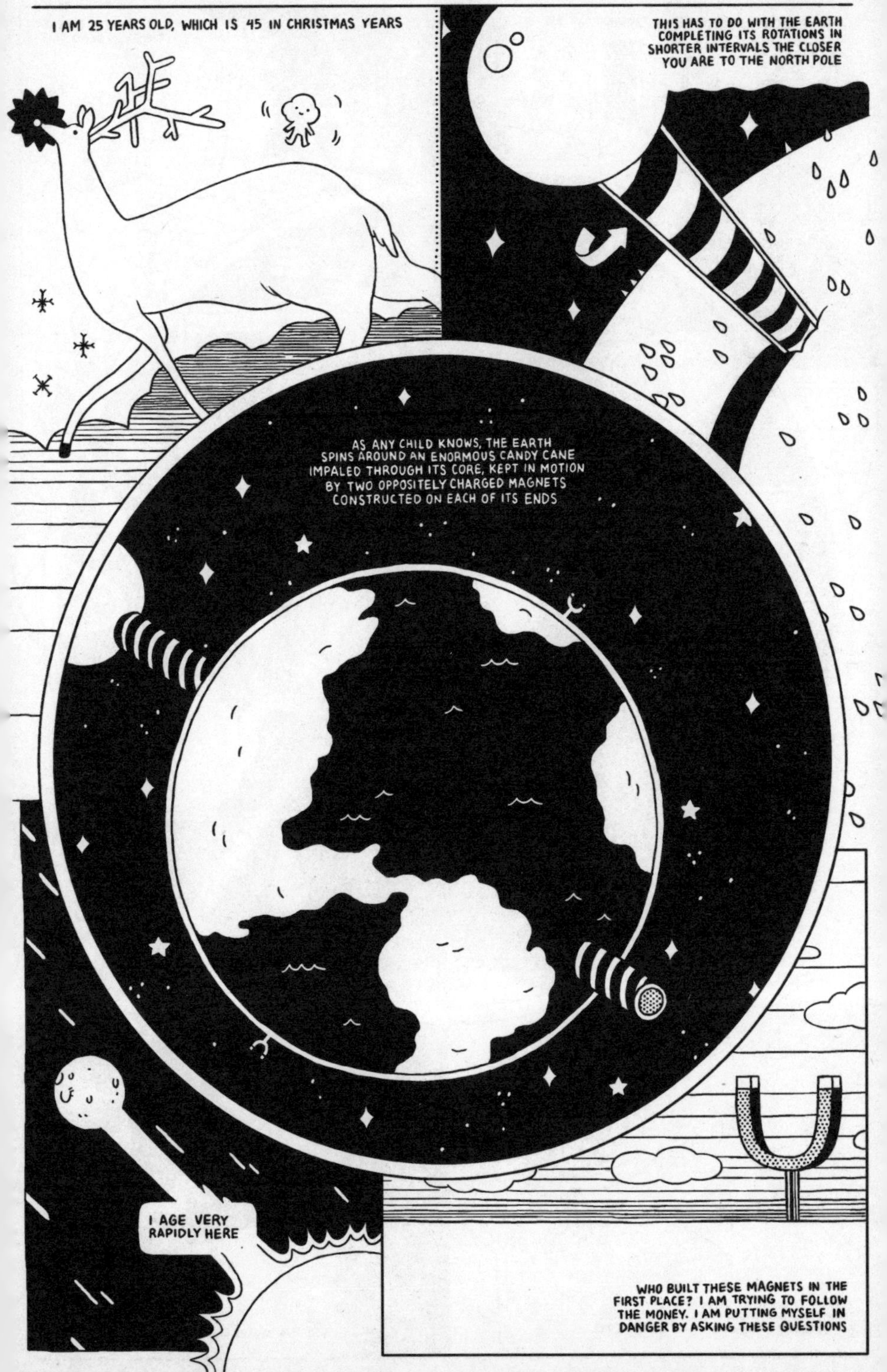
I AM 25 YEARS OLD, WHICH IS 45 IN CHRISTMAS YEARS
THIS HAS TO DO WITH THE EARTH COMPLETING ITS ROTATIONS IN SHORTER INTERVALS THE CLOSER YOU ARE TO THE NORTH POLE
AS ANY CHILD KNOWS, THE EARTH SPINS AROUND AN ENORMOUS CANDY CANE IMPALED THROUGH ITS CORE, KEPT IN MOTION BY TWO OPPOSITELY CHARGED MAGNETS CONSTRUCTED ON EACH OF ITS ENDS
I AGE VERY RAPIDLY HERE
WHO BUILT THESE MAGNETS IN THE FIRST PLACE? I AM TRYING TO FOLLOW THE MONEY. I AM PUTTING MYSELF IN DANGER BY ASKING THESE QUESTIONS

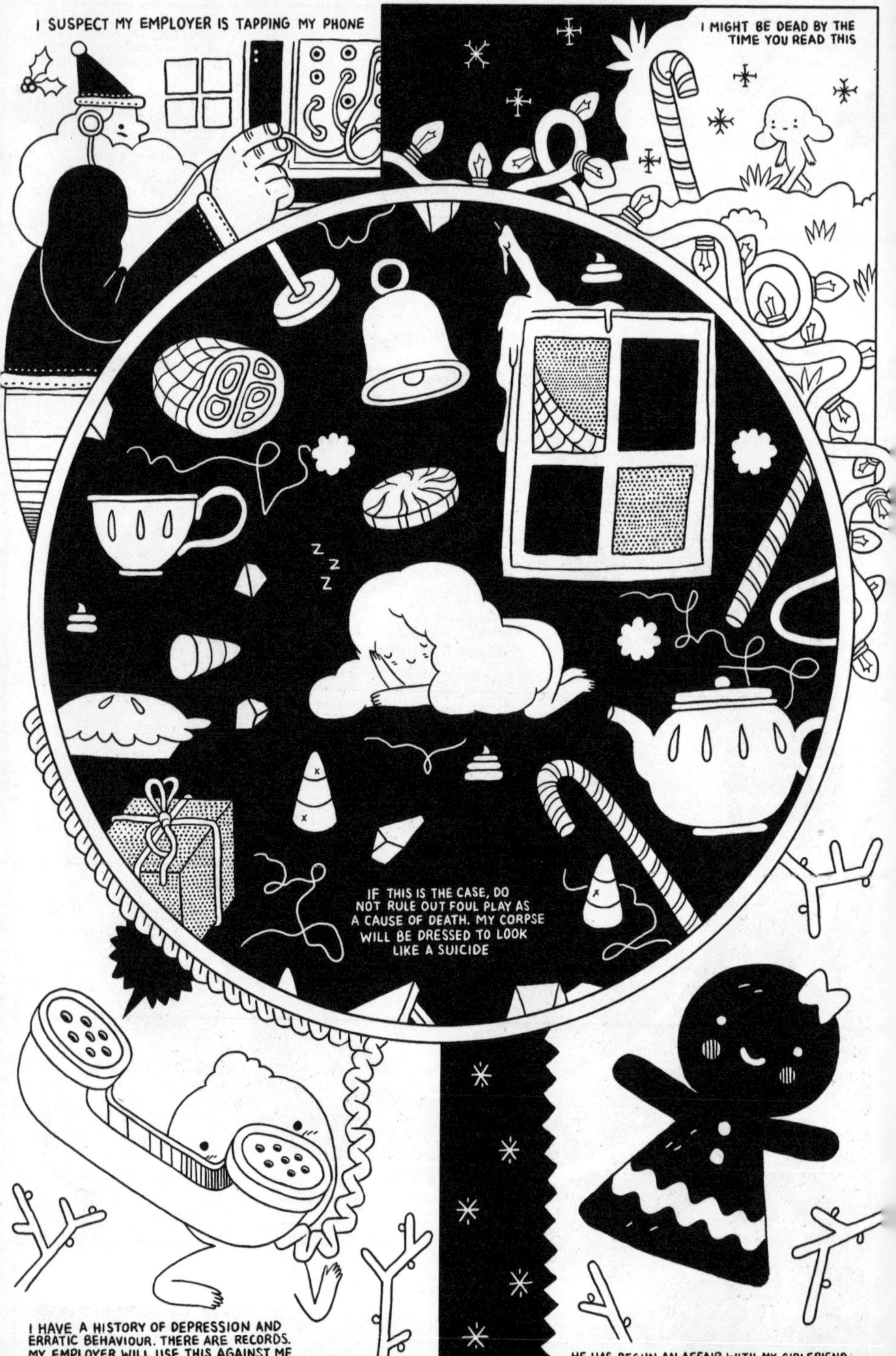
I SUSPECT MY EMPLOYER IS TAPPING MY PHONE
I MIGHT BE DEAD BY THE TIME YOU READ THIS
Z Z Z
IF THIS IS THE CASE, DO NOT RULE OUT FOUL PLAY AS A CAUSE OF DEATH. MY CORPSE WILL BE DRESSED TO LOOK LIKE A SUICIDE
I HAVE A HISTORY OF DEPRESSION AND ERRATIC BEHAVIOUR. THERE ARE RECORDS. MY EMPLOYER WILL USE THIS AGAINST ME
HE HAS BEGUN AN AFFAIR WITH MY GIRLFRIEND

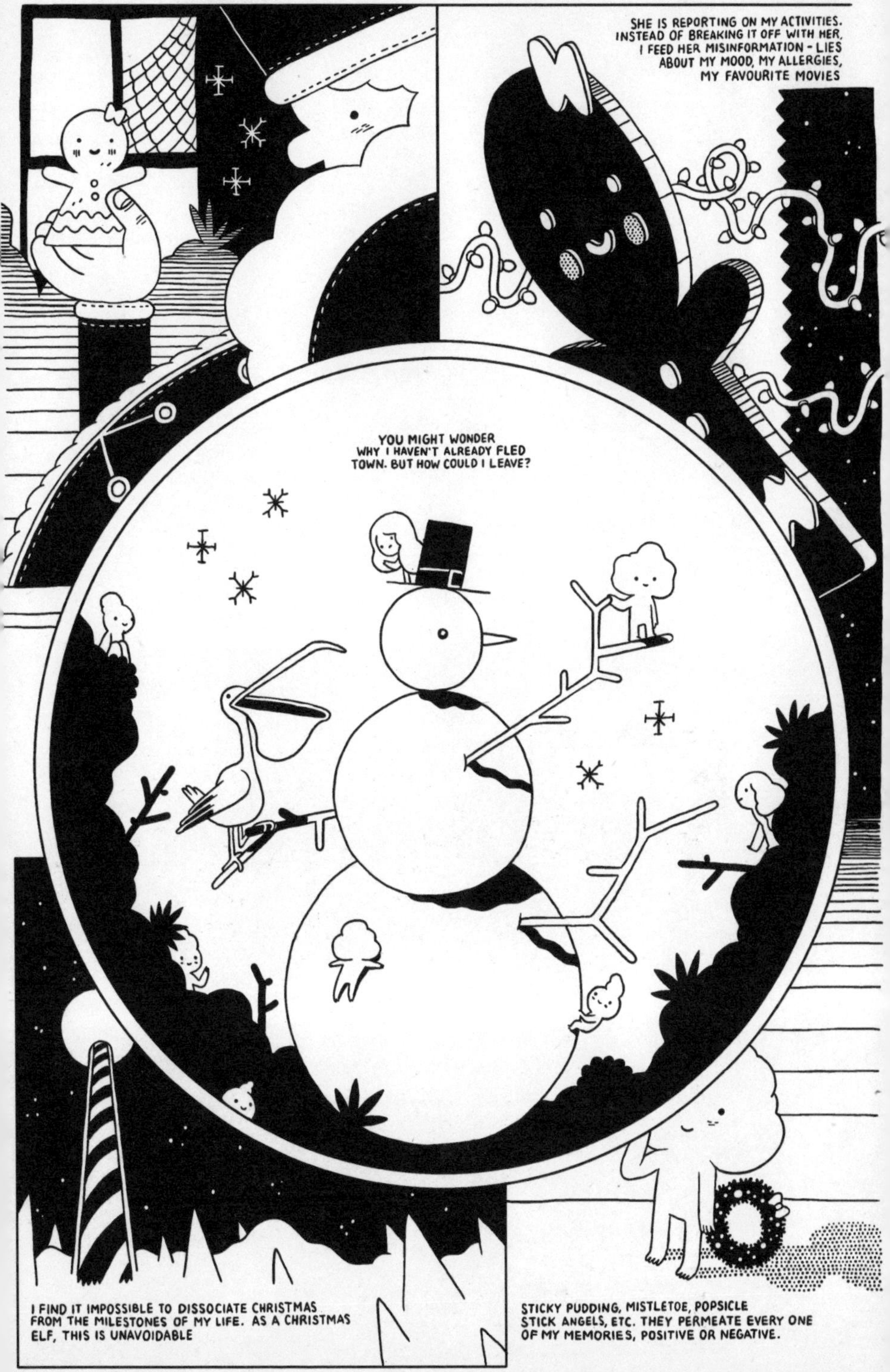
SHE IS REPORTING ON MY ACTIVITIES. INSTEAD OF BREAKING IT OFF WITH HER, I FEED HER MISINFORMATION - LIES ABOUT MY MOOD, MY ALLERGIES, MY FAVOURITE MOVIES
YOU MIGHT WONDER WHY I HAVEN'T ALREADY FLED TOWN. BUT HOW COULD I LEAVE?
I FIND IT IMPOSSIBLE TO DISSOCIATE CHRISTMAS FROM THE MILESTONES OF MY LIFE. AS A CHRISTMAS ELF, THIS IS UNAVOIDABLE
STICKY PUDDING, MISTLETOE, POPSICLE STICK ANGELS, ETC. THEY PERMEATE EVERY ONE OF MY MEMORIES, POSITIVE OR NEGATIVE.

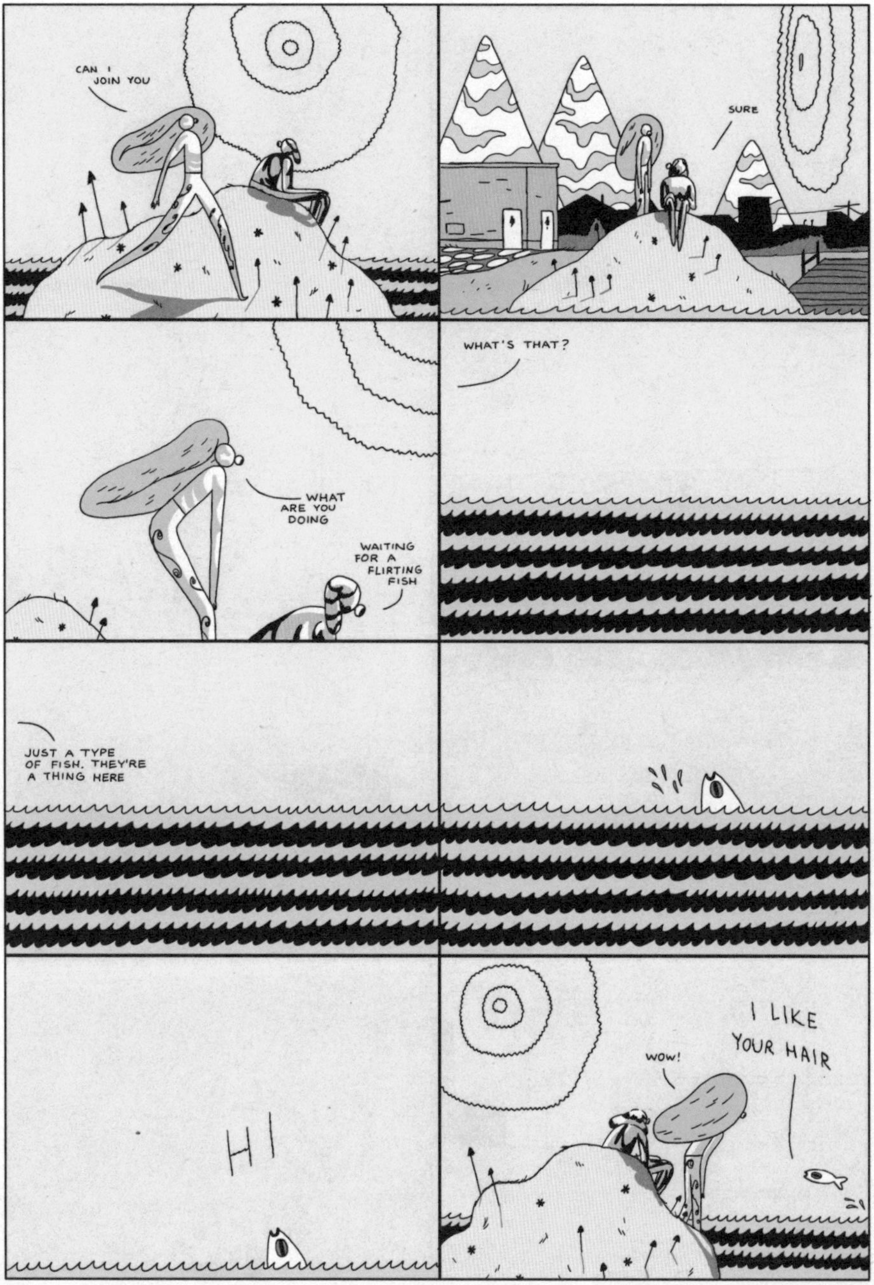
CAN I JOIN YOU
SURE
WHAT ARE YOU DOING
WAITING FOR A FLIRTING FISH
WHAT'S THAT?
JUST A TYPE OF FISH. THEY'RE A THING HERE
HI
WOW!
I LIKE YOUR HAIR

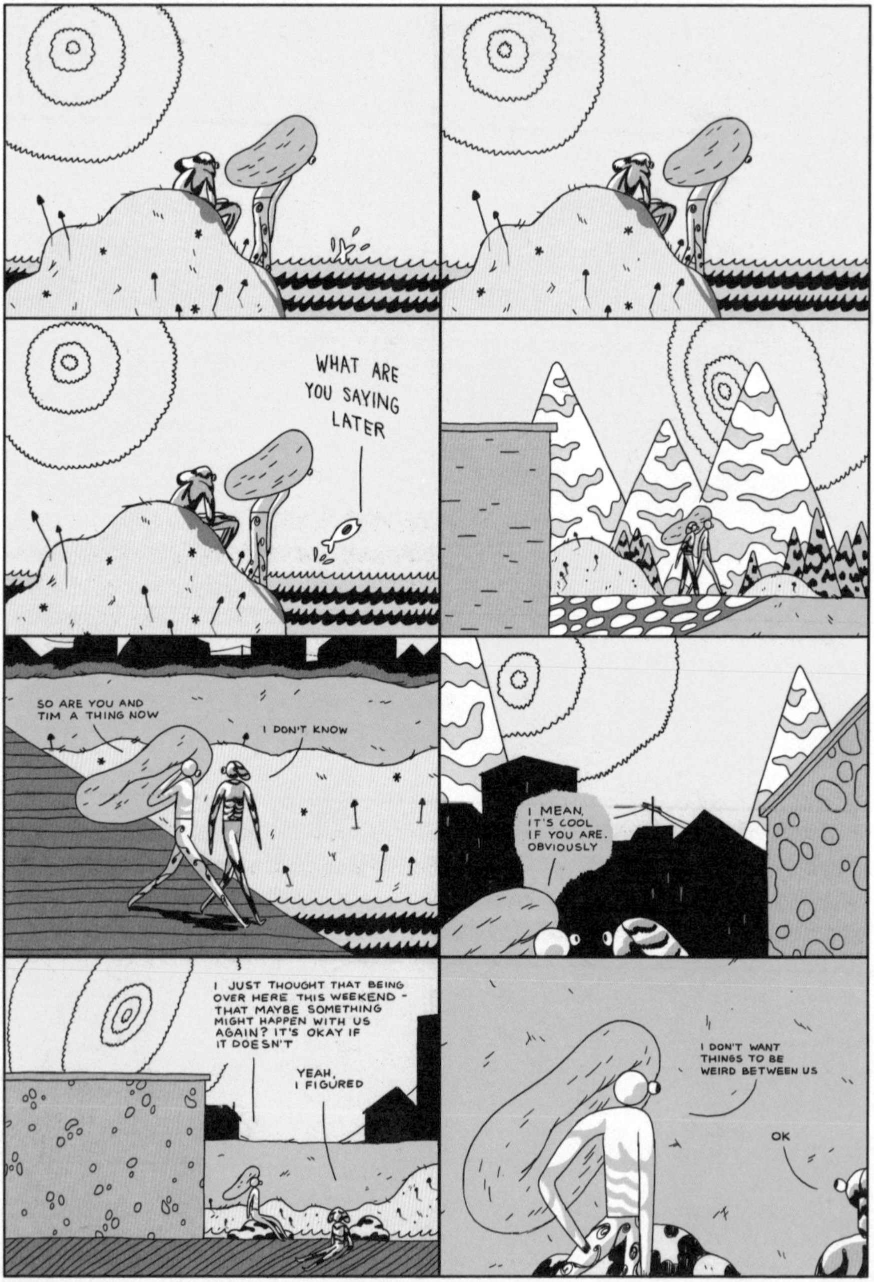
WHAT ARE YOU SAYING LATER
SO ARE YOU AND TIM A THING NOW
I DON'T KNOW
I MEAN, IT'S COOL IF YOU ARE. OBVIOUSLY
I JUST THOUGHT THAT BEING OVER HERE THIS WEEKEND - THAT MAYBE SOMETHING MIGHT HAPPEN WITH US AGAIN? IT'S OKAY IF IT DOESN'T
YEAH, I FIGURED
I DON'T WANT THINGS TO BE WEIRD BETWEEN US
OK

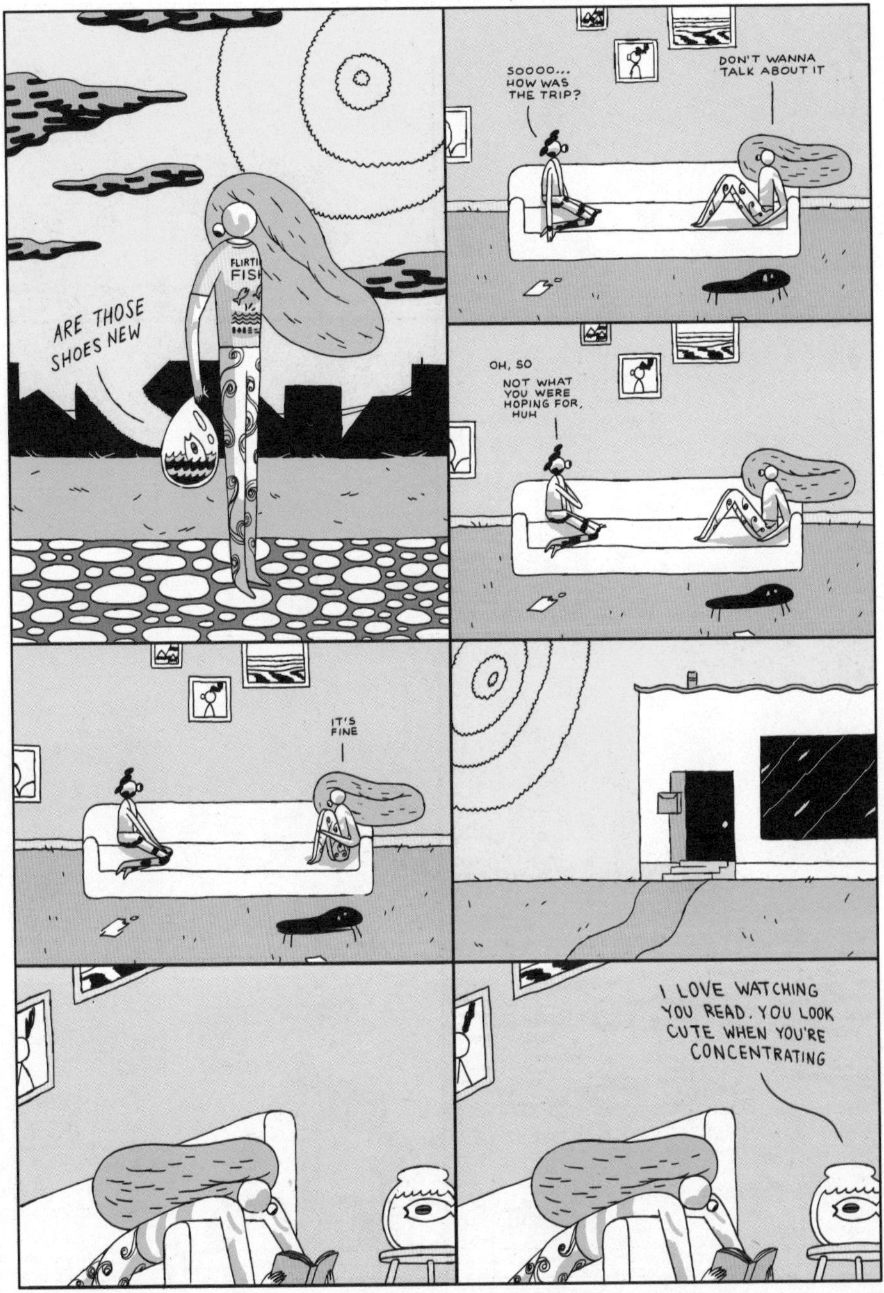
ARE THOSE SHOES NEW
FLIRTING FISH
SOOOO... HOW WAS THE TRIP?
DON'T WANNA TALK ABOUT IT
OH, SO
NOT WHAT YOU WERE HOPING FOR, HUH
IT'S FINE
I LOVE WATCHING YOU READ. YOU LOOK CUTE WHEN YOU'RE CONCENTRATING

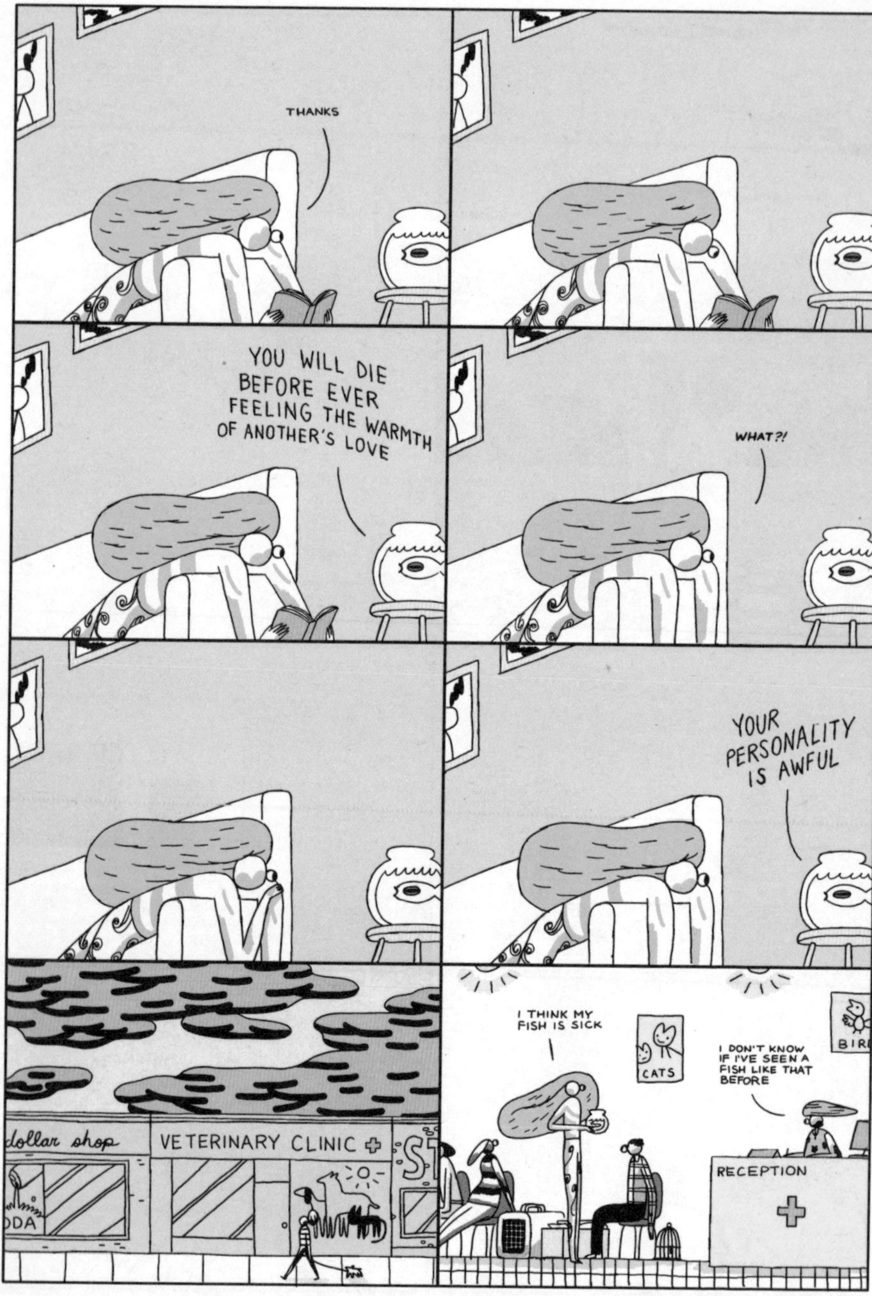
THANKS
YOU WILL DIE BEFORE EVER FEELING THE WARMTH OF ANOTHER'S LOVE
WHAT?!
YOUR PERSONALITY IS AWFUL
dollar shop
VETERINARY CLINIC
I THINK MY FISH IS SICK
CATS
I DON'T KNOW IF I'VE SEEN A FISH LIKE THAT BEFORE
RECEPTION

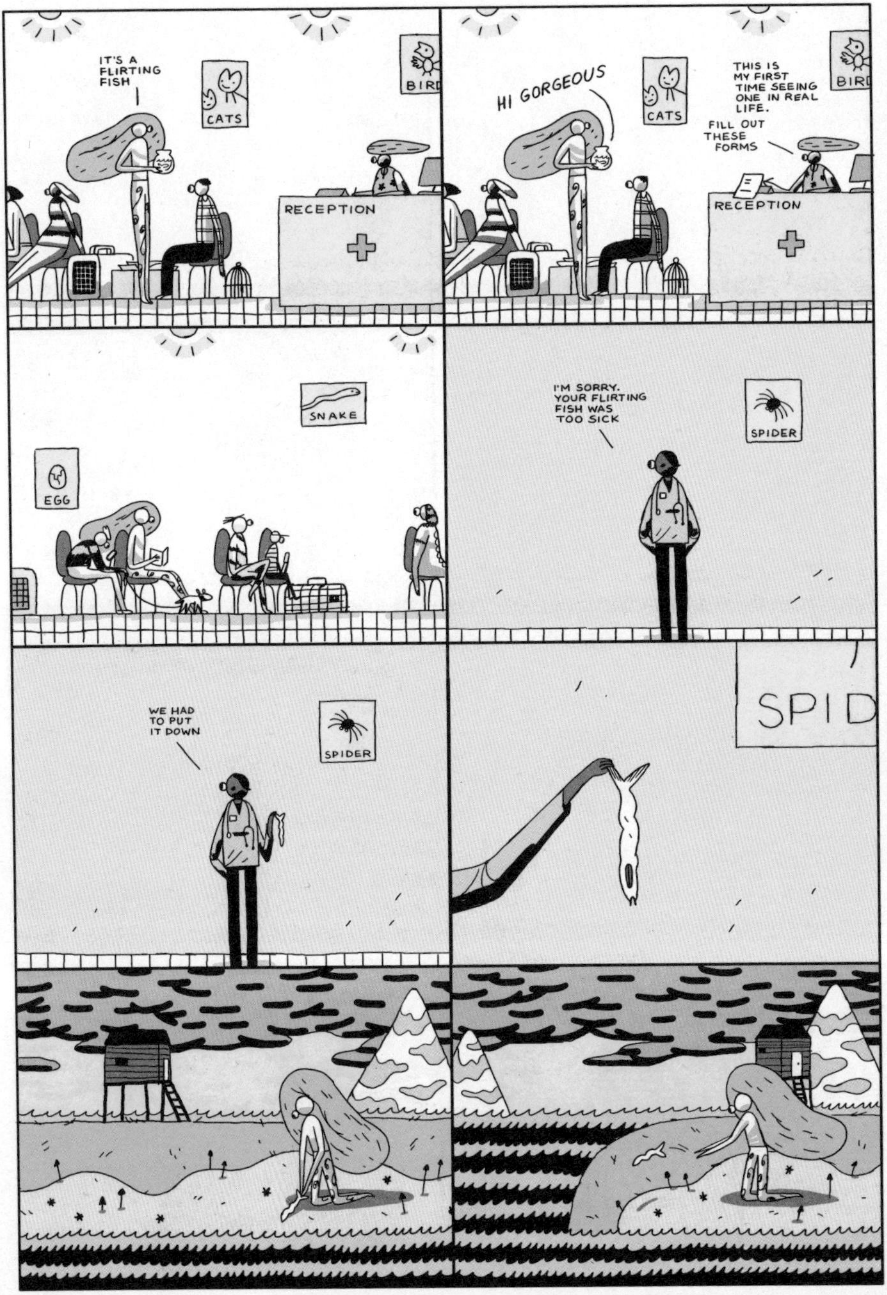
IT'S A FLIRTING FISH
CATS
BIRD
RECEPTION
HI GORGEOUS
CATS
THIS IS MY FIRST TIME SEEING ONE IN REAL LIFE.
FILL OUT THESE FORMS
BIRD
RECEPTION
SNAKE
EGG
I'M SORRY. YOUR FLIRTING FISH WAS TOO SICK
SPIDER
WE HAD TO PUT IT DOWN
SPIDER
SPID

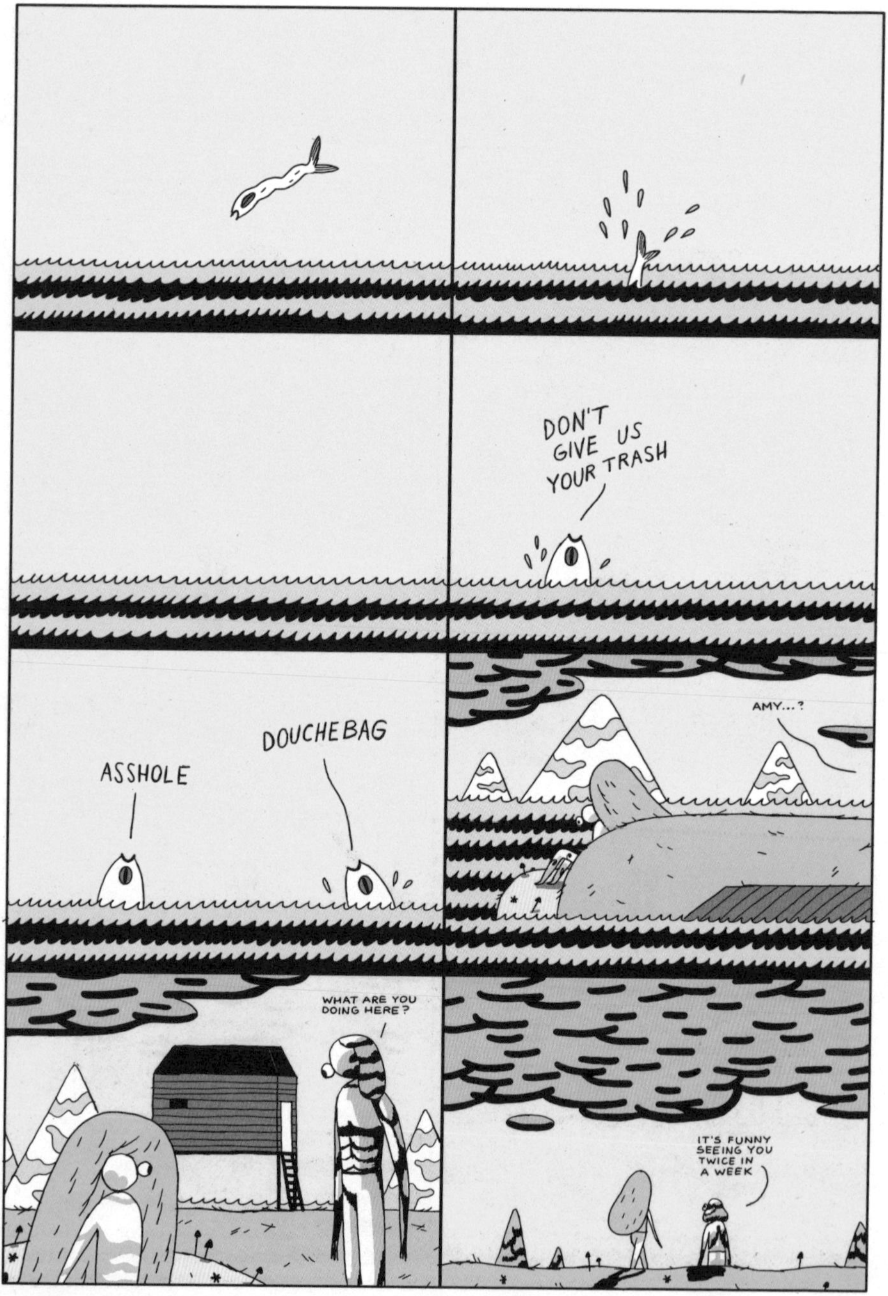
DON'T GIVE US YOUR TRASH
ASSHOLE
DOUCHEBAG
AMY...?
WHAT ARE YOU DOING HERE?
IT'S FUNNY SEEING YOU TWICE IN A WEEK

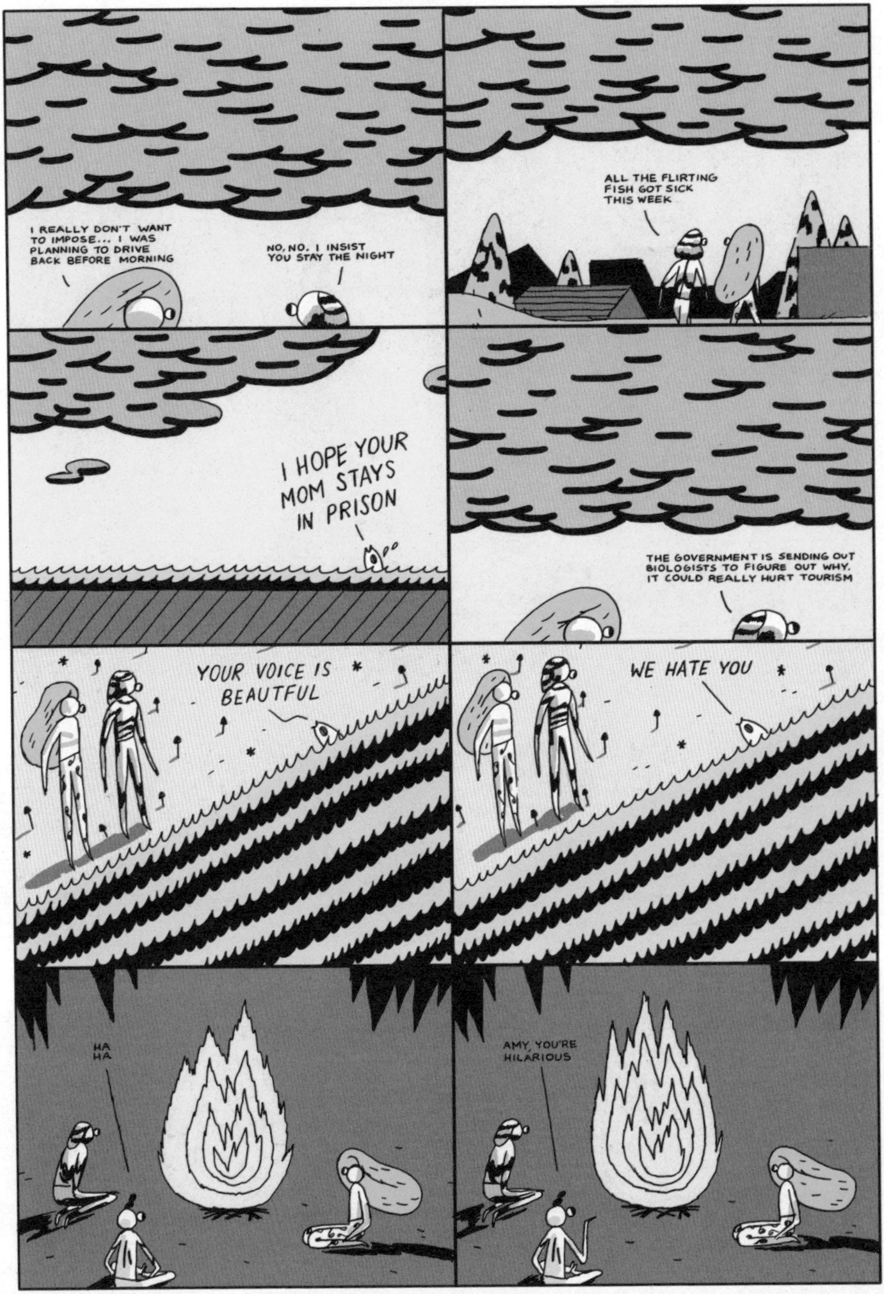
I REALLY DON'T WANT TO IMPOSE... I WAS PLANNING TO DRIVE BACK BEFORE MORNING
NO, NO. I INSIST YOU STAY THE NIGHT
ALL THE FLIRTING FISH GOT SICK THIS WEEK
I HOPE YOUR MOM STAYS IN PRISON
THE GOVERNMENT IS SENDING OUT BIOLOGISTS TO FIGURE OUT WHY. IT COULD REALLY HURT TOURISM
YOUR VOICE IS BEAUTFUL
WE HATE YOU
HA HA
AMY, YOU'RE HILARIOUS

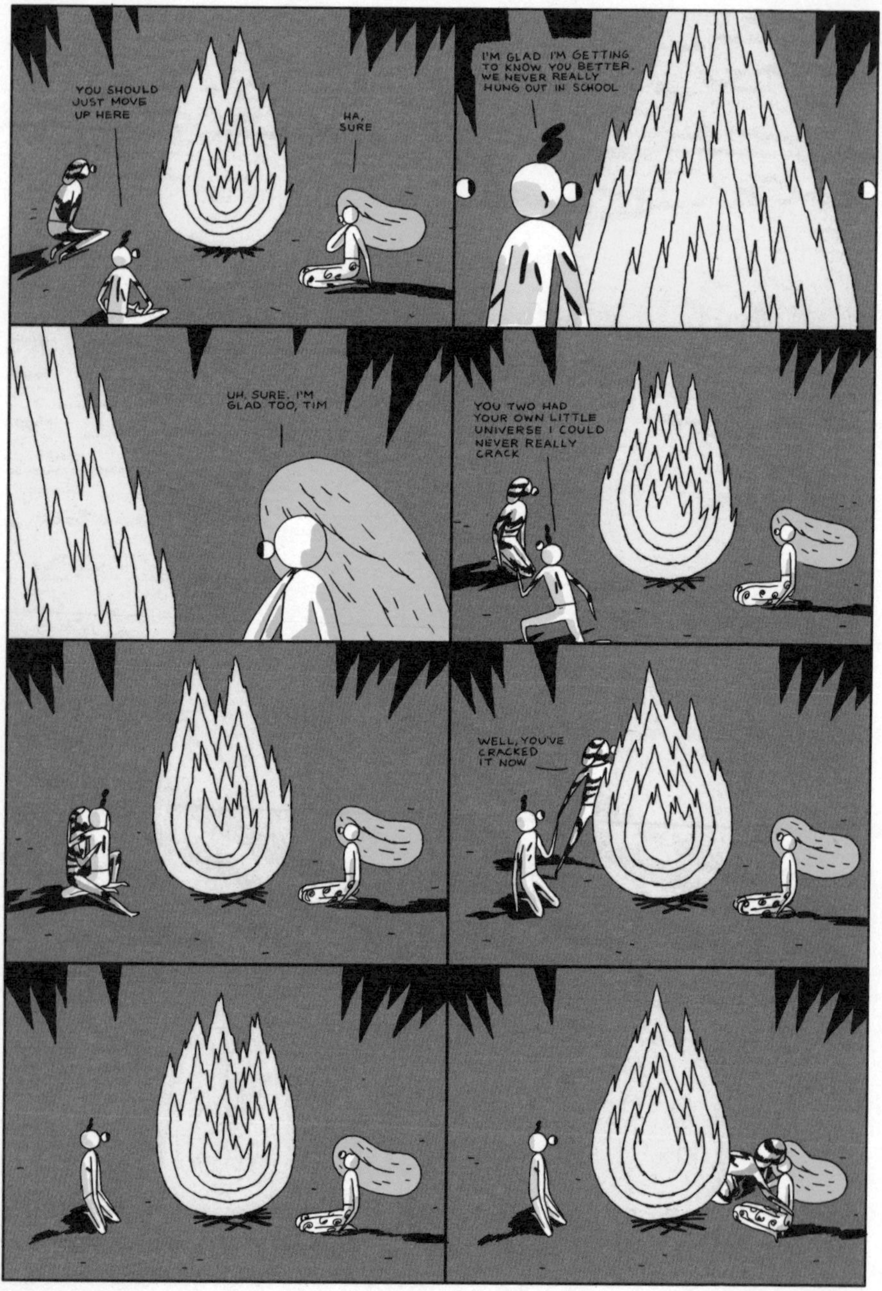
YOU SHOULD JUST MOVE UP HERE
HA, SURE
I'M GLAD I'M GETTING TO KNOW YOU BETTER. WE NEVER REALLY HUNG OUT IN SCHOOL
UH, SURE. I'M GLAD TOO, TIM
YOU TWO HAD YOUR OWN LITTLE UNIVERSE I COULD NEVER REALLY CRACK
WELL, YOU'VE CRACKED IT NOW

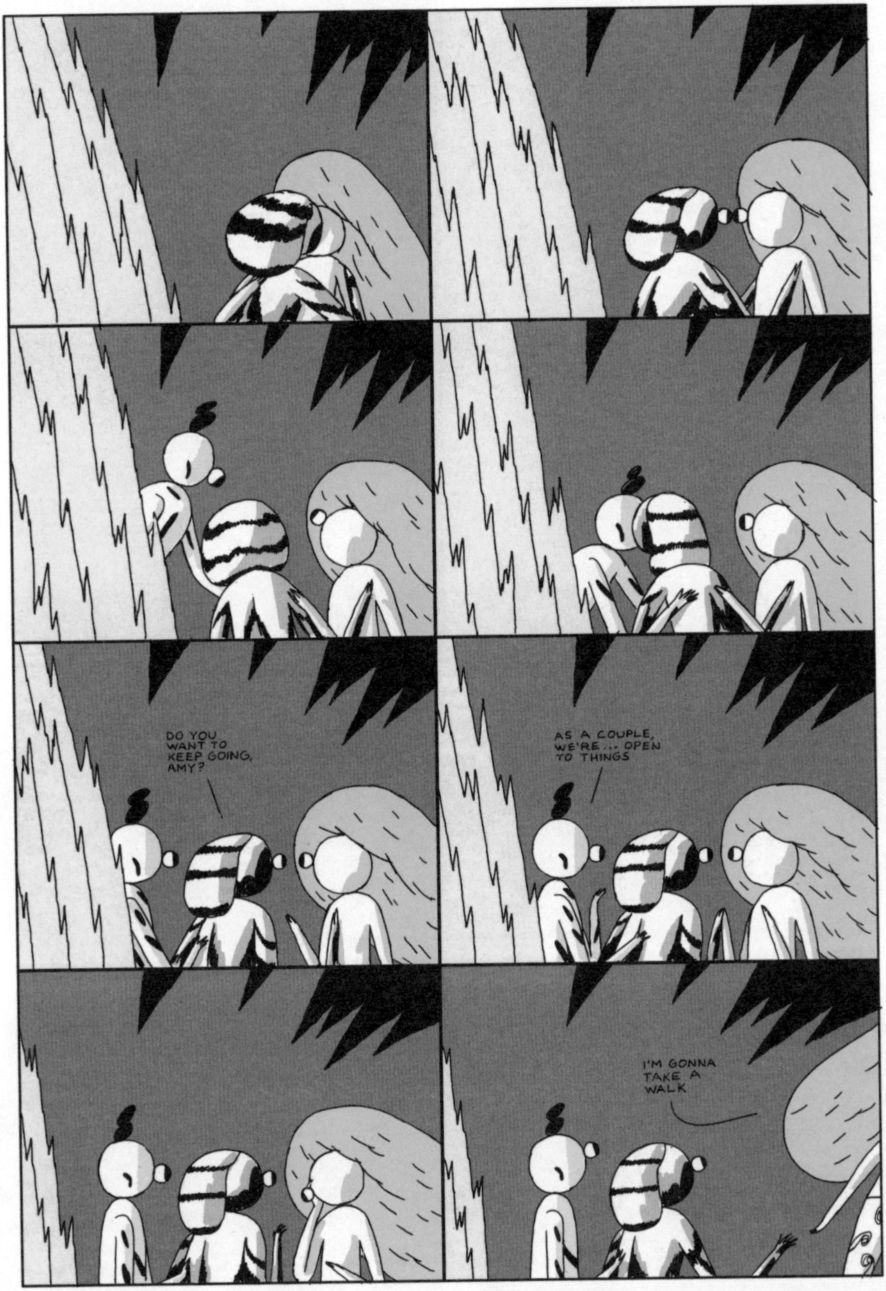
DO YOU WANT TO KEEP GOING, AMY?
AS A COUPLE, WE'RE... OPEN TO THINGS
I'M GONNA TAKE A WALK

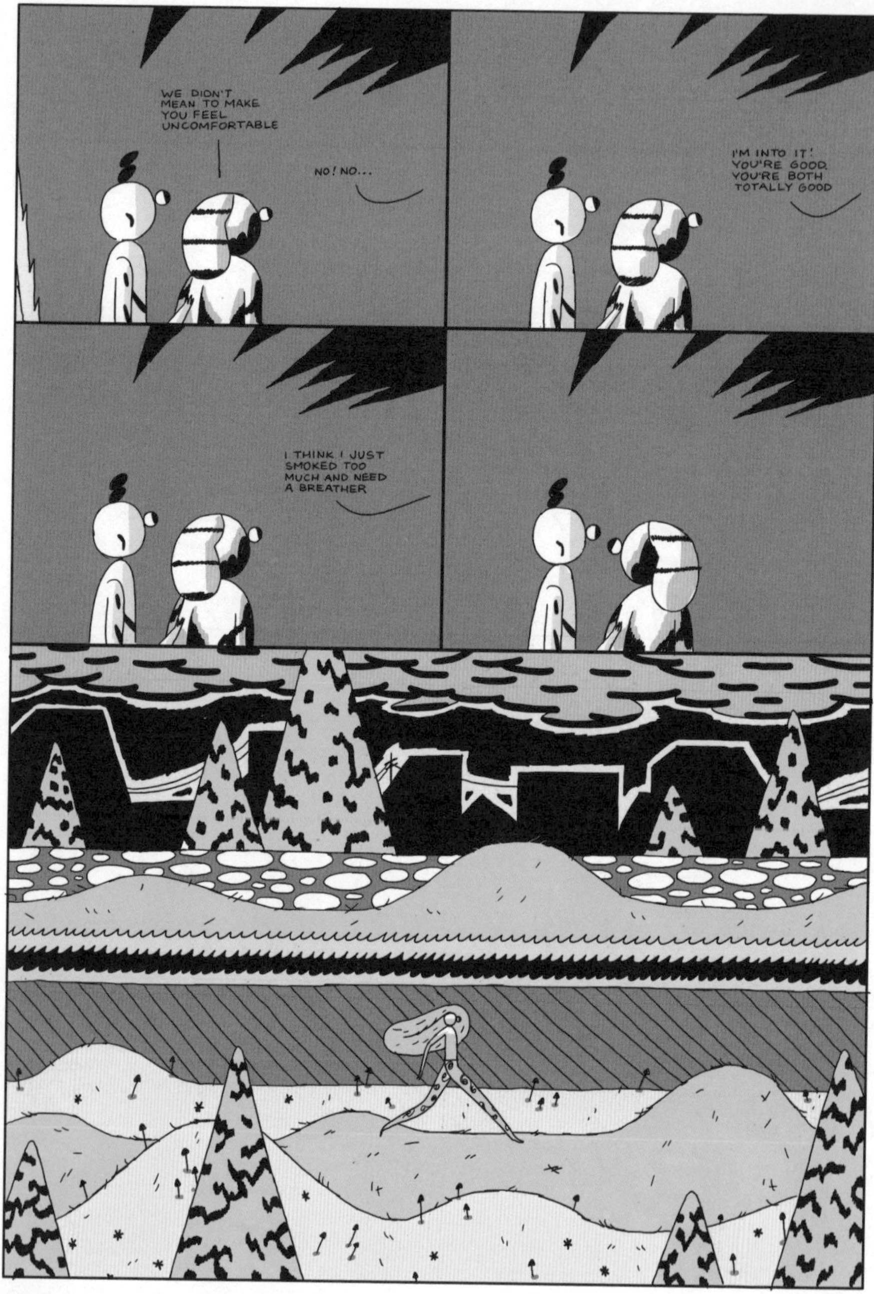
WE DIDN'T MEAN TO MAKE YOU FEEL UNCOMFORTABLE
NO! NO...
I'M INTO IT! YOU'RE GOOD. YOU'RE BOTH TOTALLY GOOD
I THINK I JUST SMOKED TOO MUCH AND NEED A BREATHER

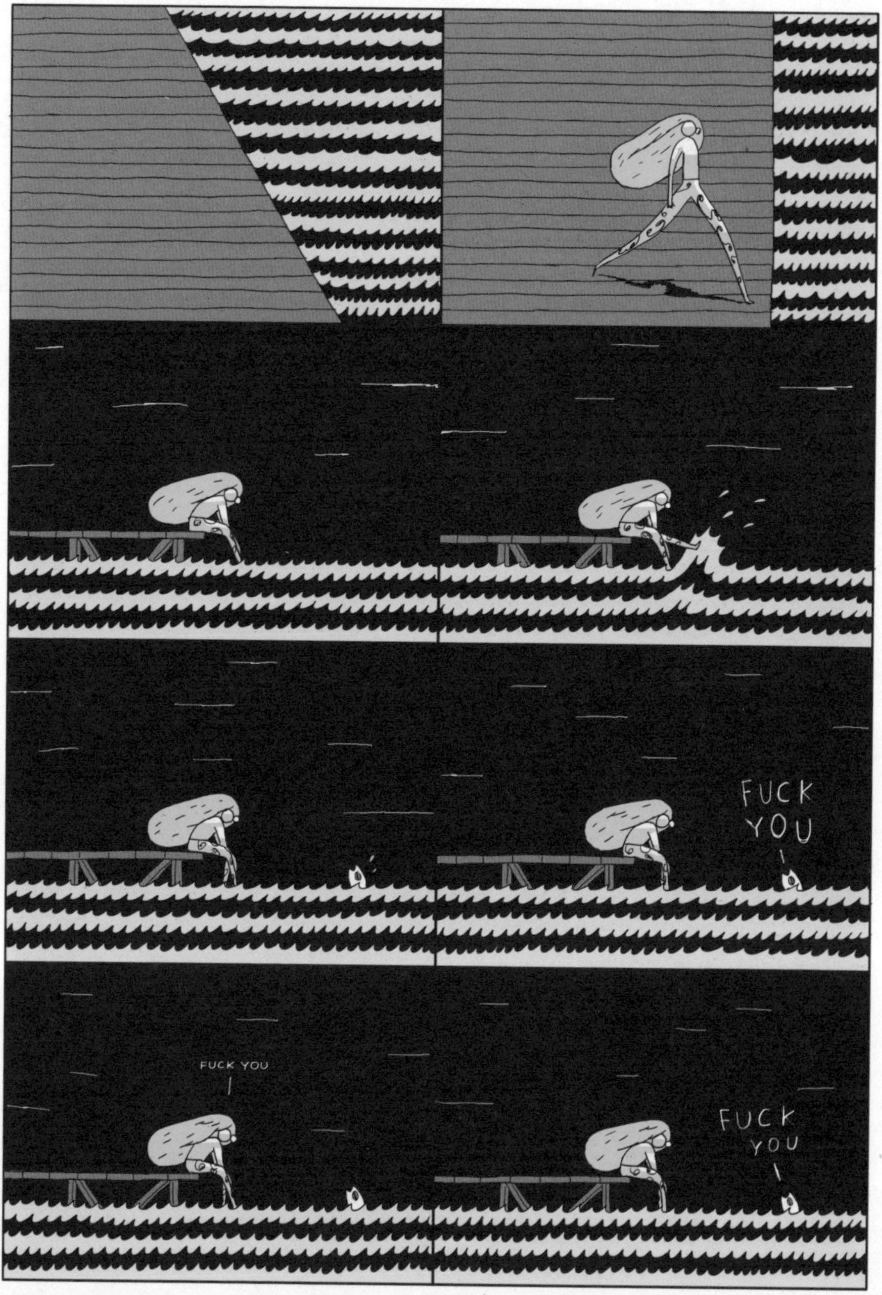
FUCK YOU
FUCK YOU
FUCK YOU

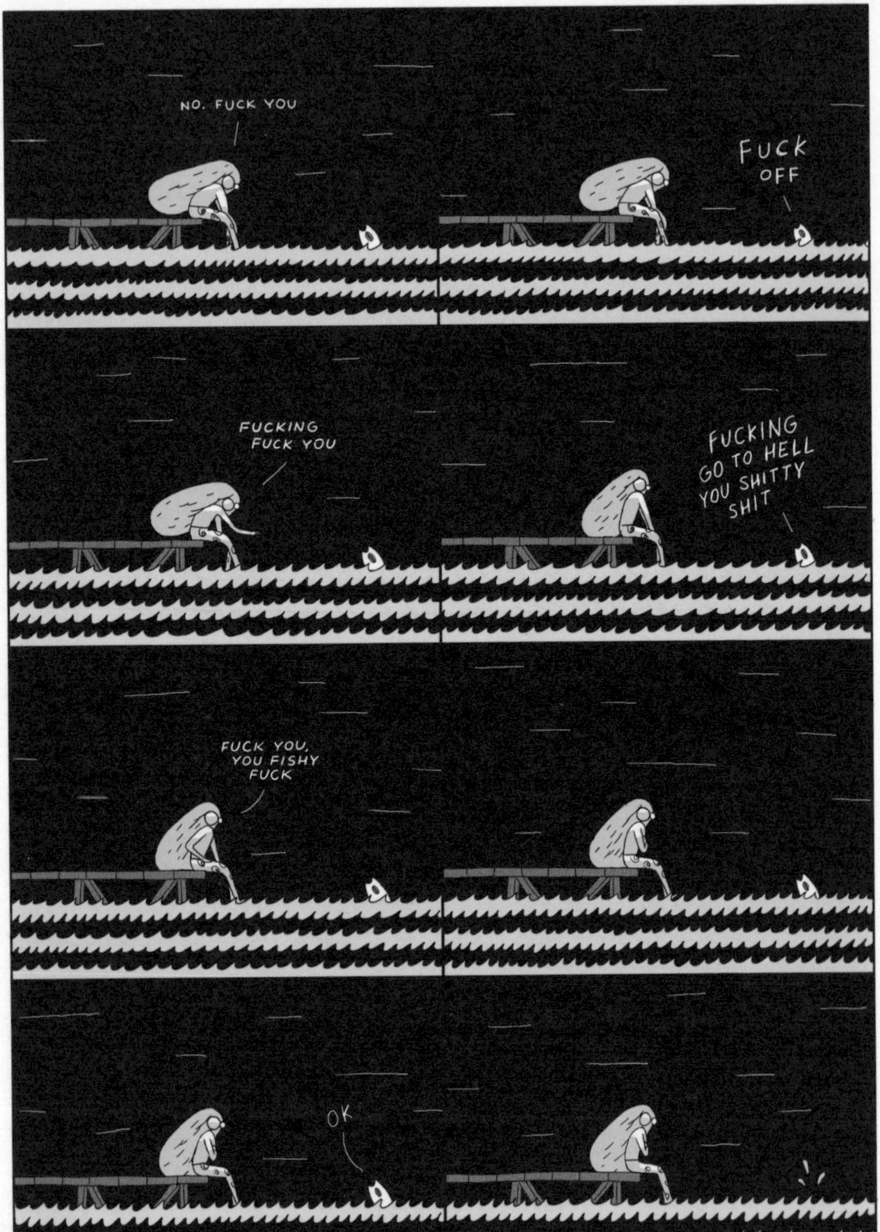
NO. FUCK YOU
FUCK OFF
FUCKING FUCK YOU
FUCKING GO TO HELL YOU SHITTY SHIT
FUCK YOU, YOU FISHY FUCK
OK
!

END

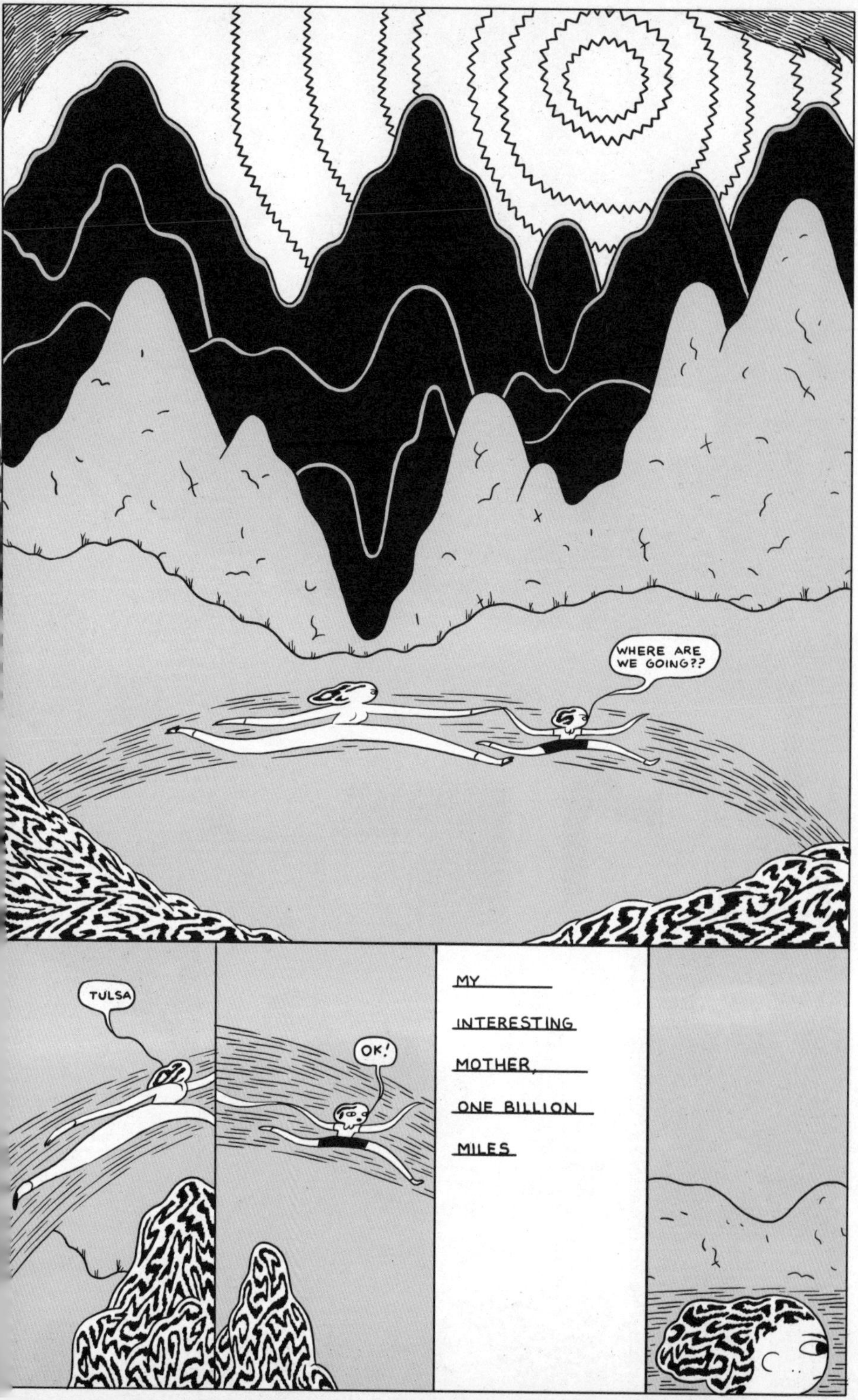
WHERE ARE WE GOING??
TULSA
OK!
MY
INTERESTING
MOTHER,
ONE BILLION
MILES

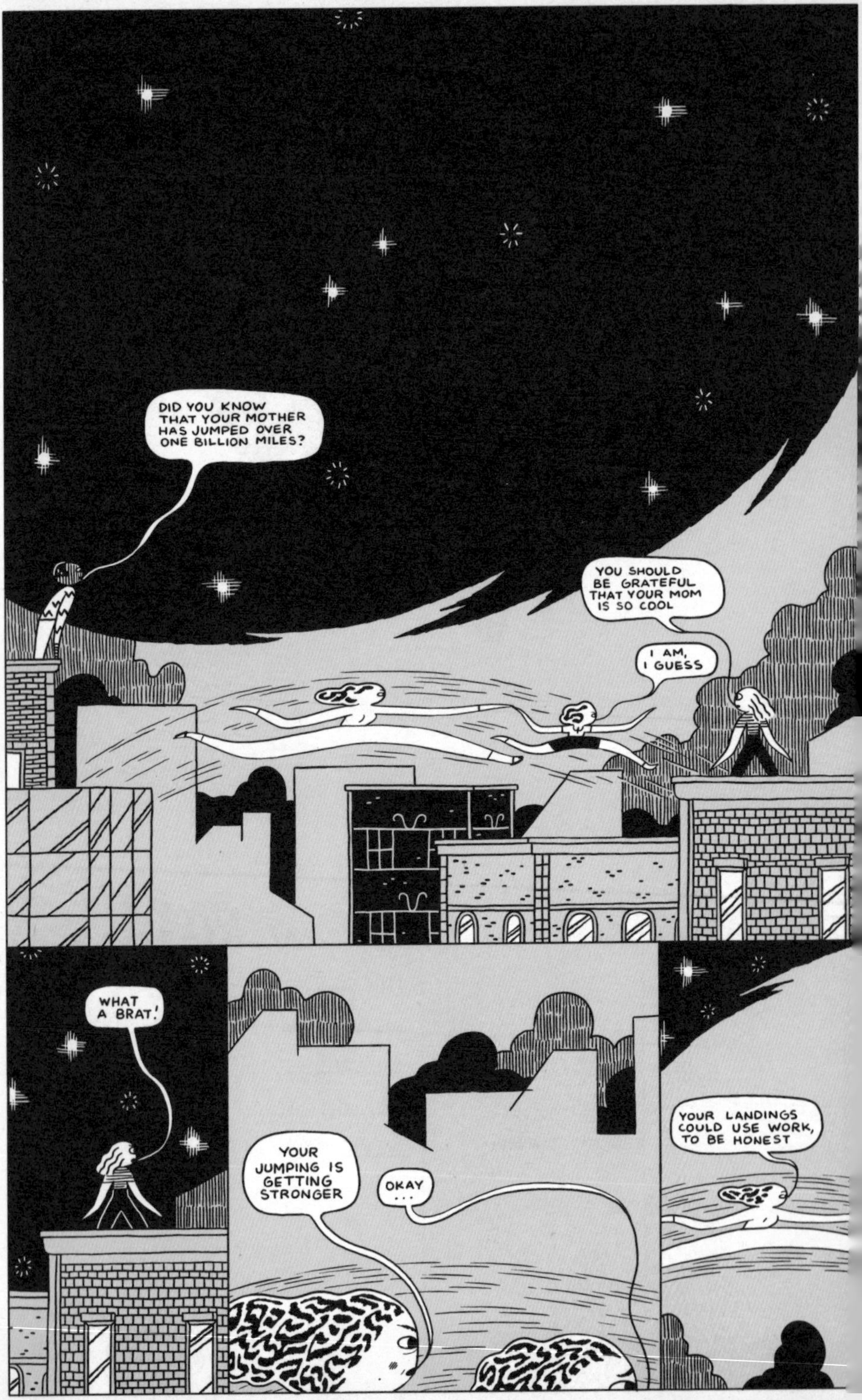
DID YOU KNOW THAT YOUR MOTHER HAS JUMPED OVER ONE BILLION MILES?
YOU SHOULD BE GRATEFUL THAT YOUR MOM IS SO COOL
I AM, I GUESS
WHAT A BRAT!
YOUR JUMPING IS GETTING STRONGER
OKAY...
YOUR LANDINGS COULD USE WORK, TO BE HONEST

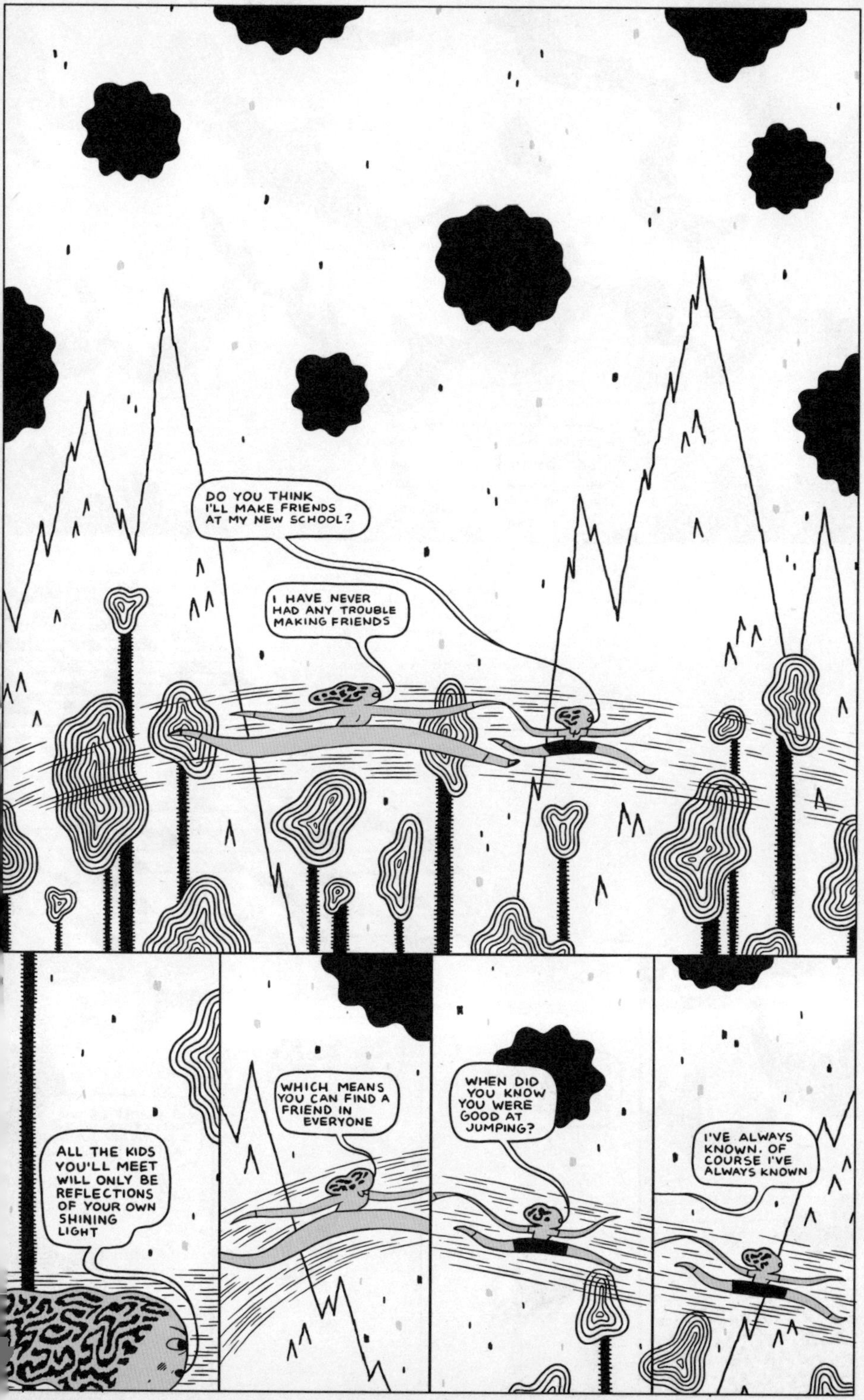
DO YOU THINK I'LL MAKE FRIENDS AT MY NEW SCHOOL?
I HAVE NEVER HAD ANY TROUBLE MAKING FRIENDS
ALL THE KIDS YOU'LL MEET WILL ONLY BE REFLECTIONS OF YOUR OWN SHINING LIGHT
WHICH MEANS YOU CAN FIND A FRIEND IN EVERYONE
WHEN DID YOU KNOW YOU WERE GOOD AT JUMPING?
I'VE ALWAYS KNOWN. OF COURSE I'VE ALWAYS KNOWN

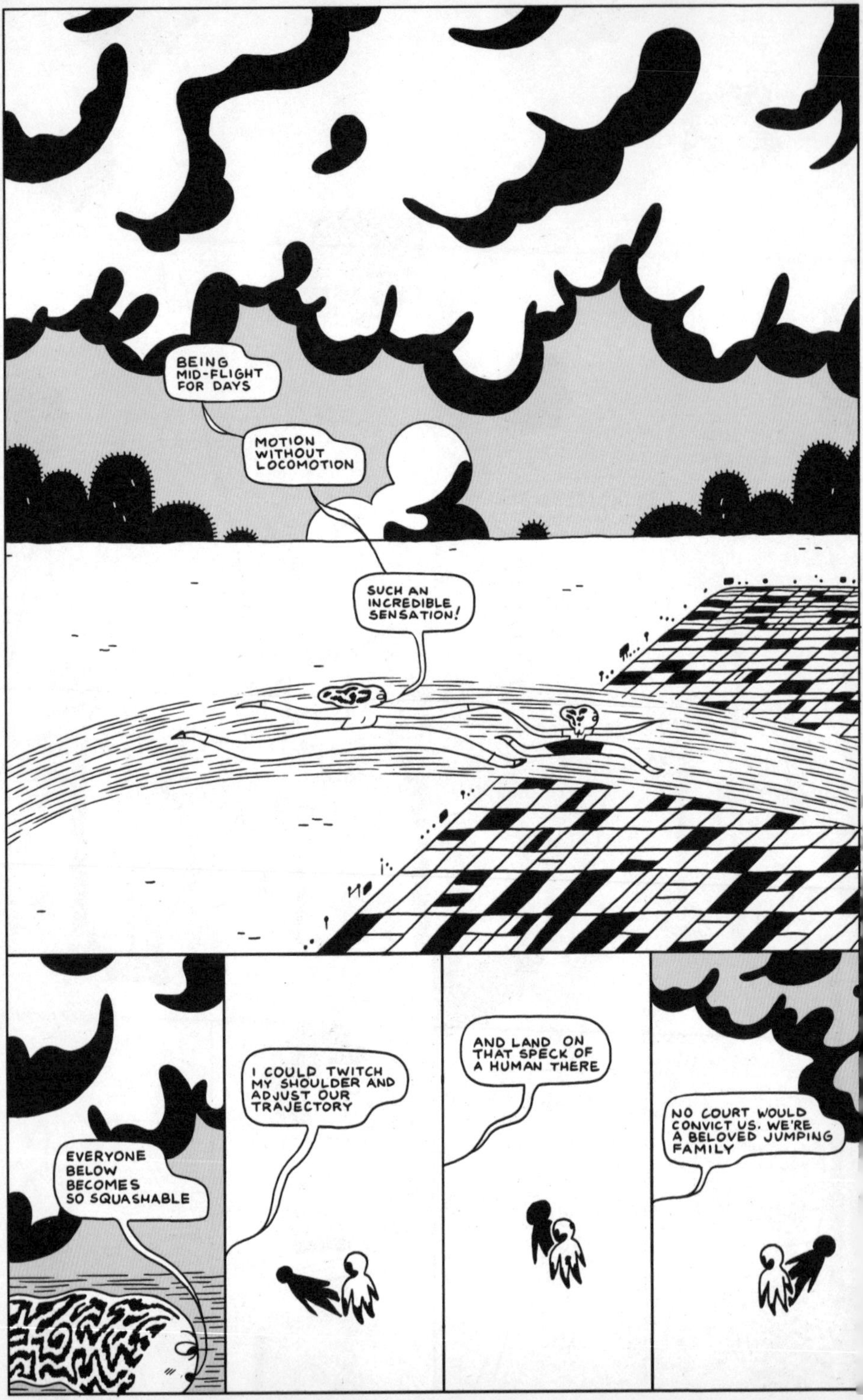
BEING MID-FLIGHT FOR DAYS
MOTION WITHOUT LOCOMOTION
SUCH AN INCREDIBLE SENSATION!
EVERYONE BELOW BECOMES SO SQUASHABLE
I COULD TWITCH MY SHOULDER AND ADJUST OUR TRAJECTORY
AND LAND ON THAT SPECK OF A HUMAN THERE
NO COURT WOULD CONVICT US. WE'RE A BELOVED JUMPING FAMILY

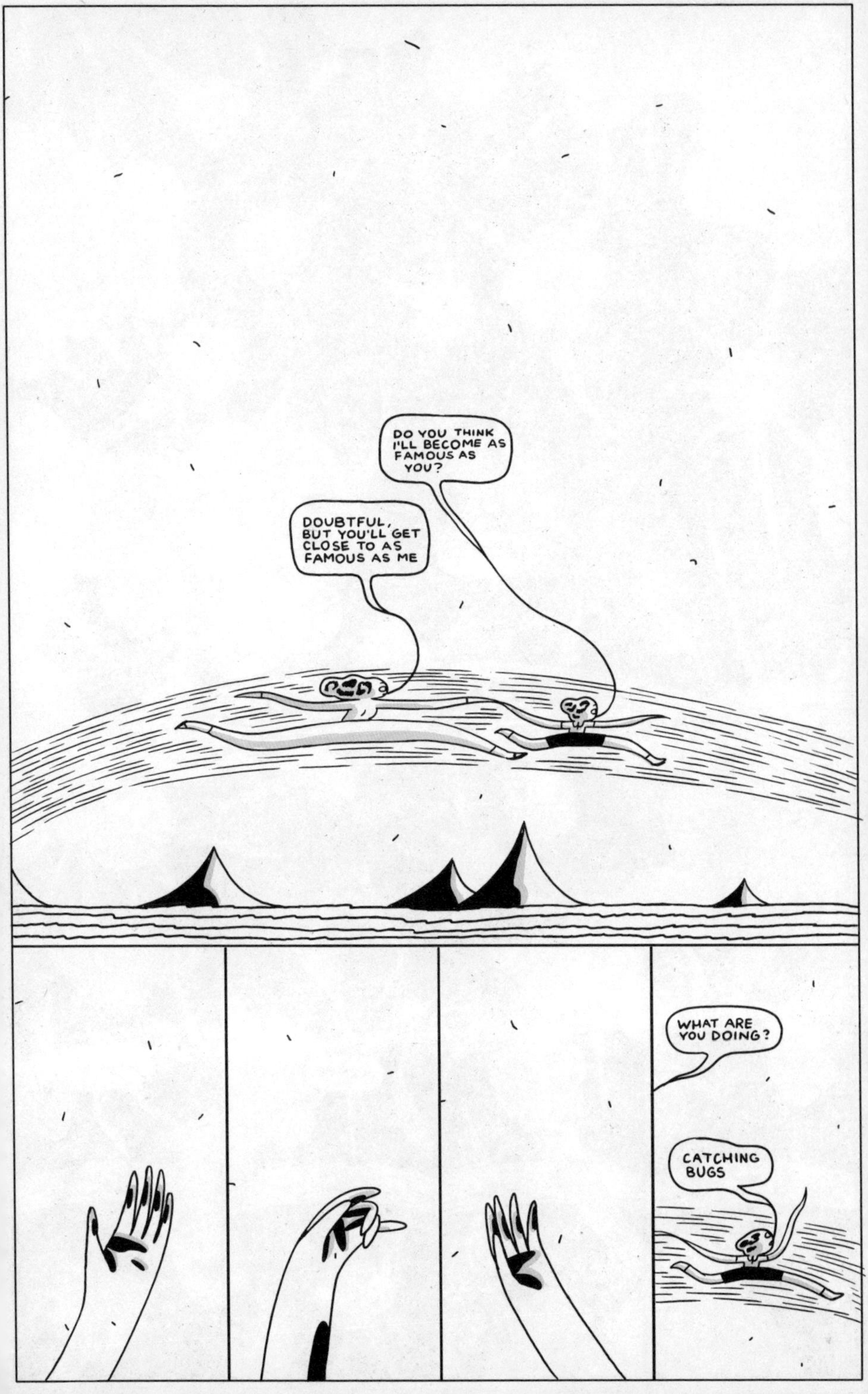
DO YOU THINK I'LL BECOME AS FAMOUS AS YOU?
DOUBTFUL, BUT YOU'LL GET CLOSE TO AS FAMOUS AS ME
WHAT ARE YOU DOING?
CATCHING BUGS

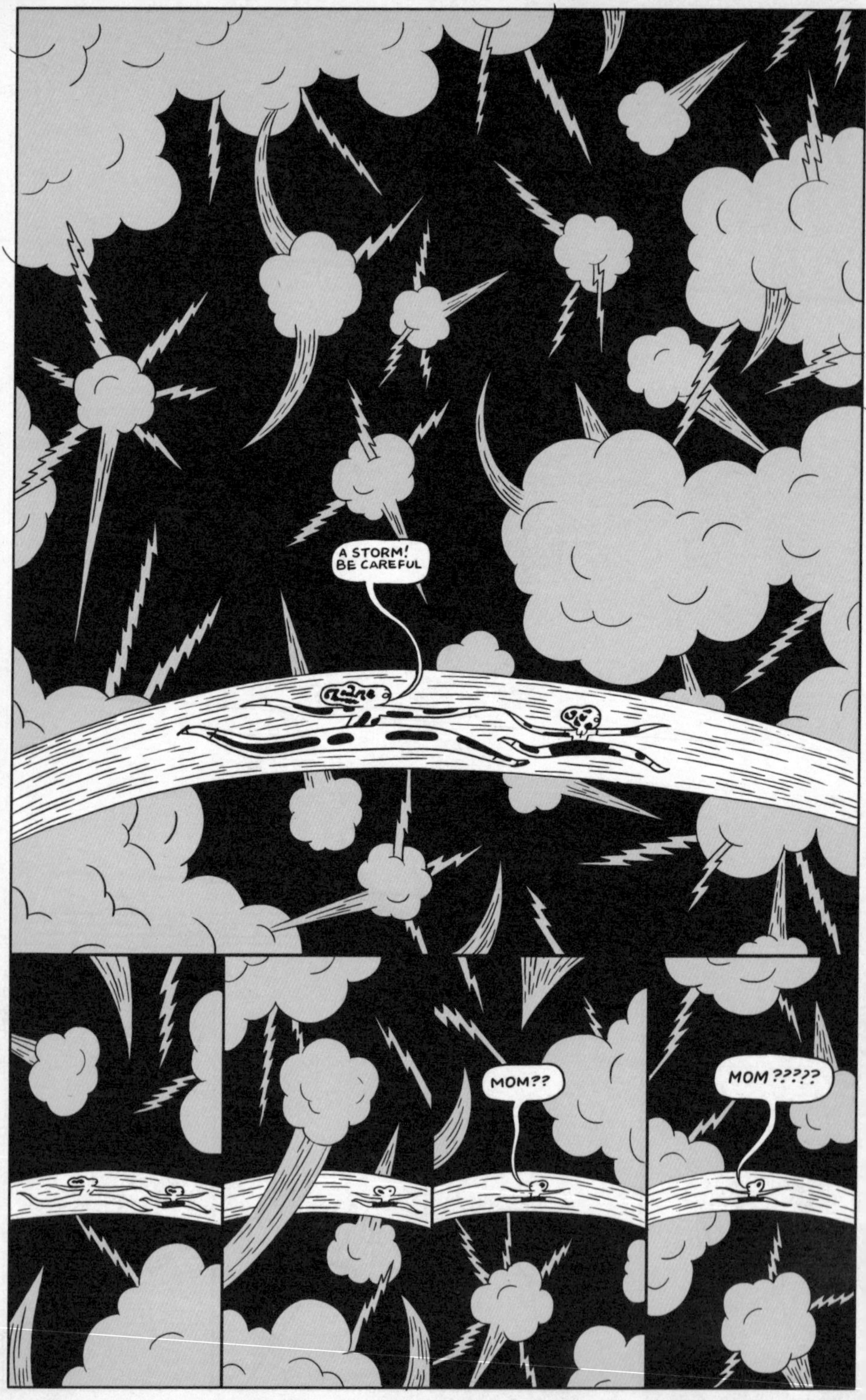
A STORM!
BE CAREFUL
MOM??
MOM?????

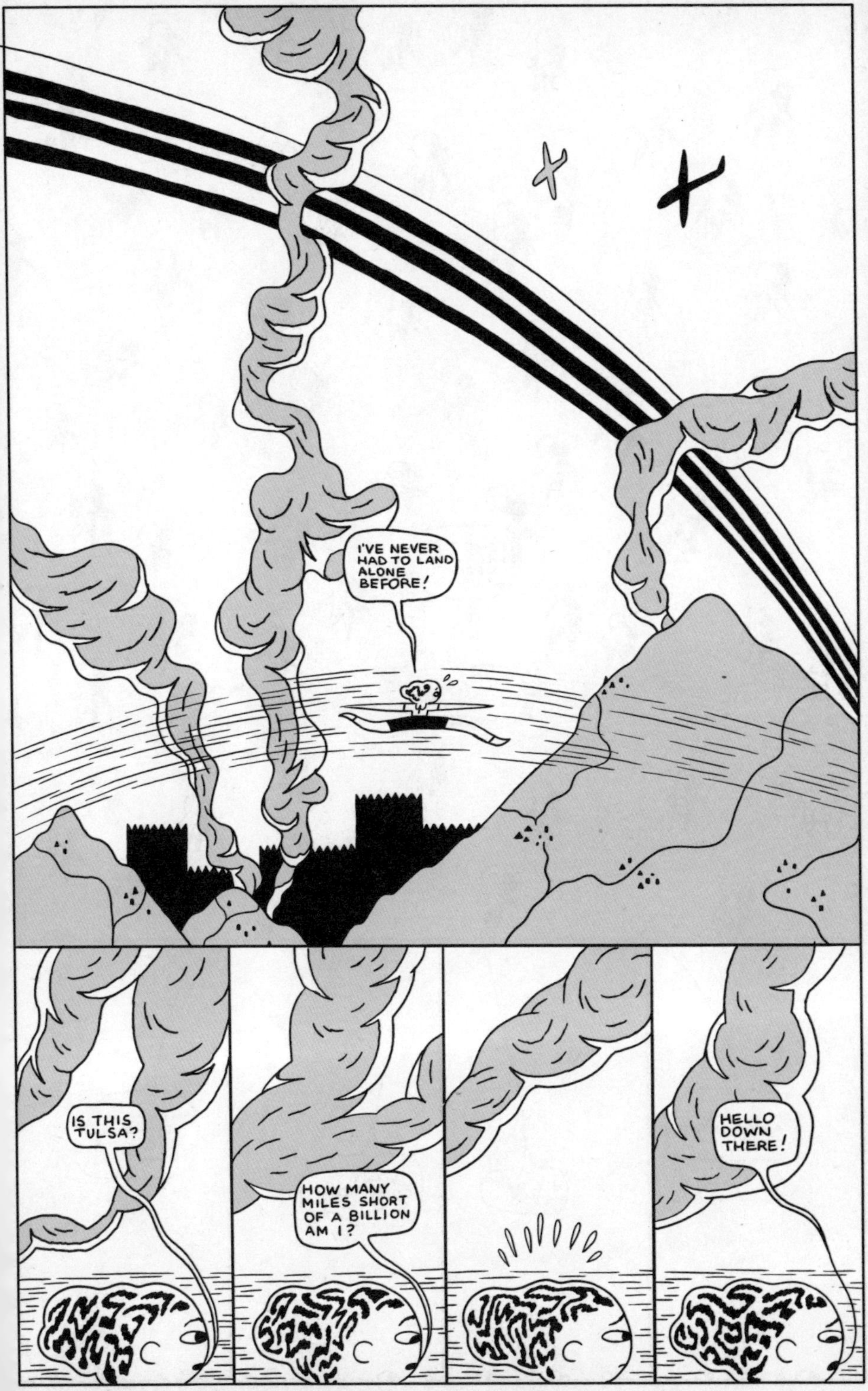
I'VE NEVER HAD TO LAND ALONE BEFORE!
IS THIS TULSA?
HOW MANY MILES SHORT OF A BILLION AM I?
HELLO DOWN THERE!

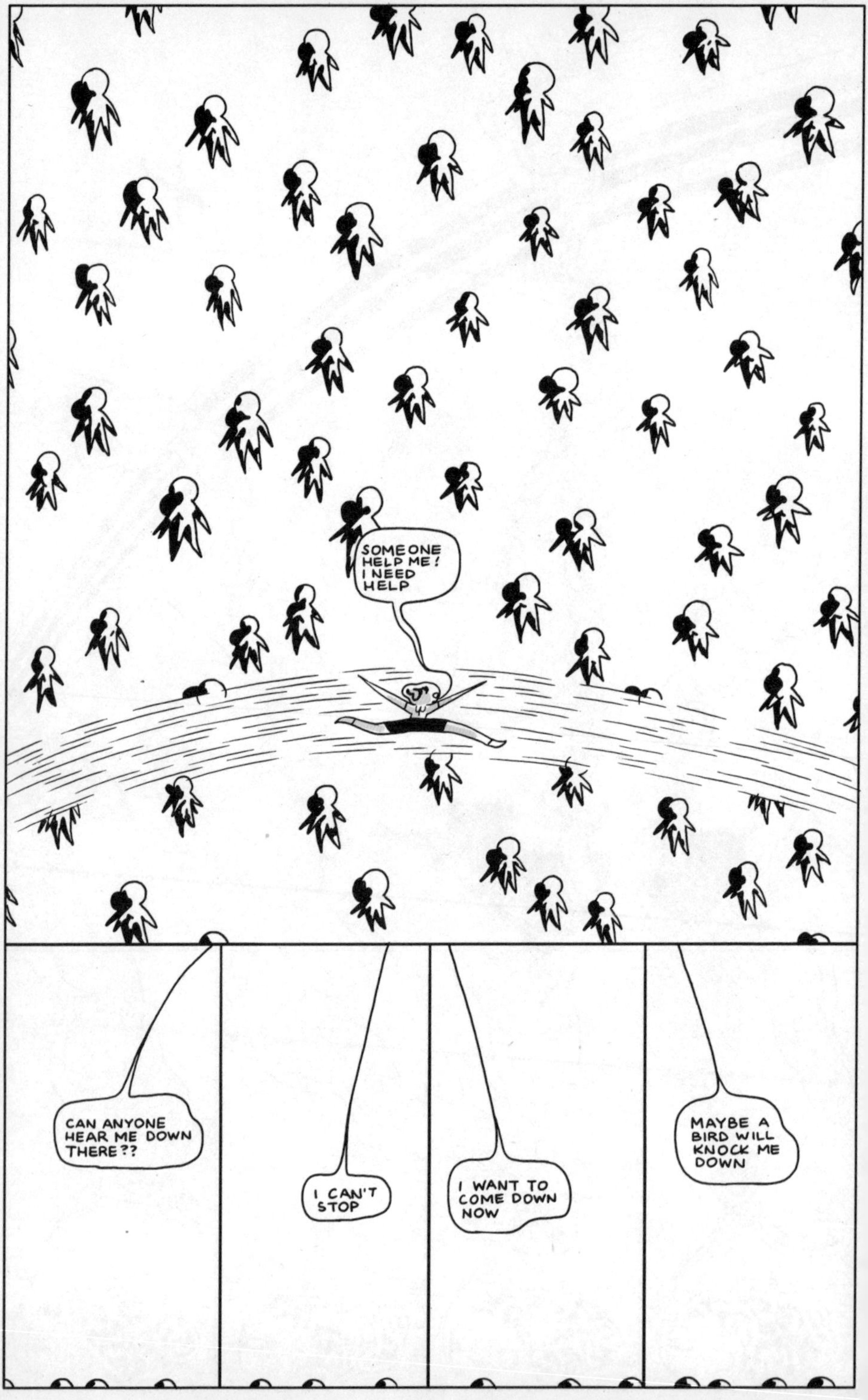
SOMEONE HELP ME! I NEED HELP
CAN ANYONE HEAR ME DOWN THERE??
I CAN'T STOP
I WANT TO COME DOWN NOW
MAYBE A BIRD WILL KNOCK ME DOWN

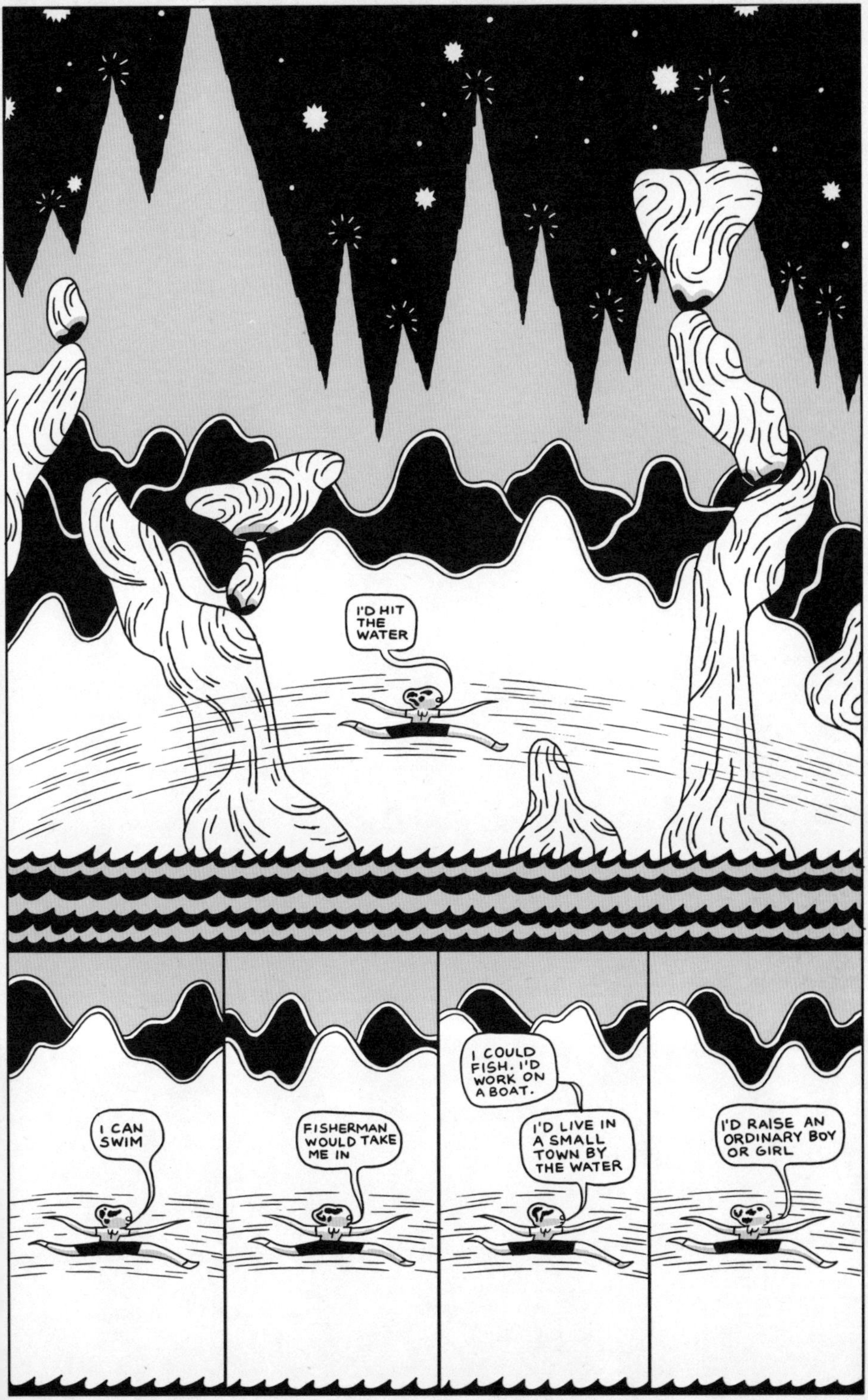
I'D HIT THE WATER
I CAN SWIM
FISHERMAN WOULD TAKE ME IN
I COULD FISH. I'D WORK ON A BOAT.
I'D LIVE IN A SMALL TOWN BY THE WATER
I'D RAISE AN ORDINARY BOY OR GIRL

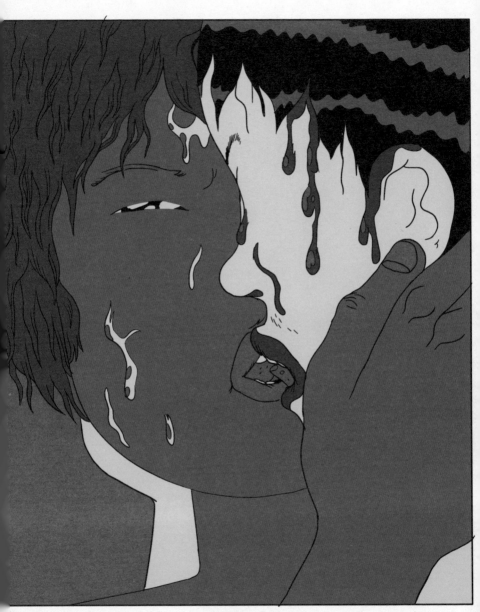

They kissed and Jason tasted his own come. Jason moved his hand down to work on Wattie, but Wattie said that it was okay and that he didn't want to do anything else, even though he was still hard. Jason lit a cigarette and became very self-conscious about the fact that he had been screwing wearing a T-shirt and nothing else—like that term he kept hearing lately, "Winnie the Pooh-ing."

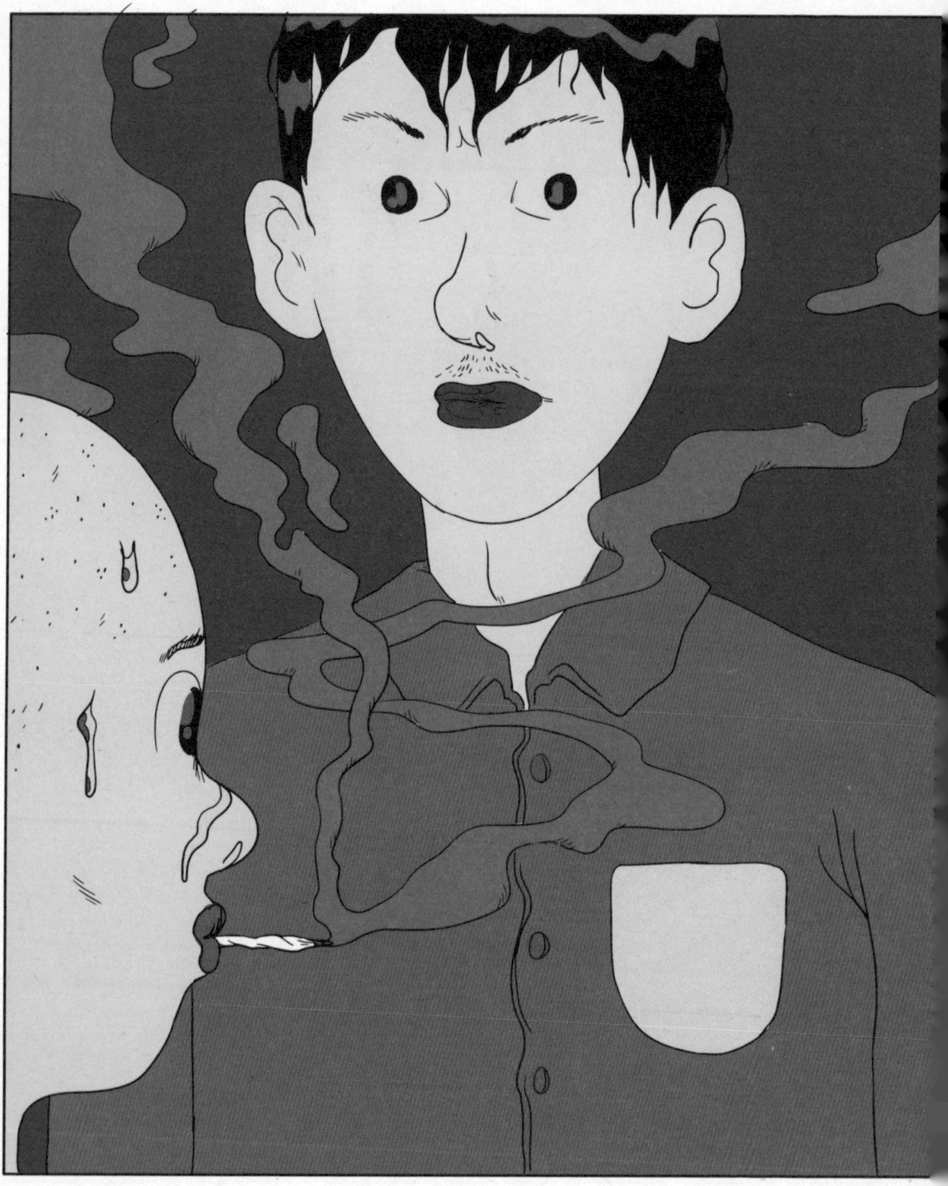

Jason had some pot he'd confiscated from one of his students earlier that day. He felt lousy about it, but he knew he was still seen as the "new" teacher. If he let the kid off the hook, it'd set a bad precedent. On the other hand, he also didn't care enough to want the kid to get into any actual trouble with the principal, who would have done God knows what to him. Confiscating the pot was his little compromise with himself.

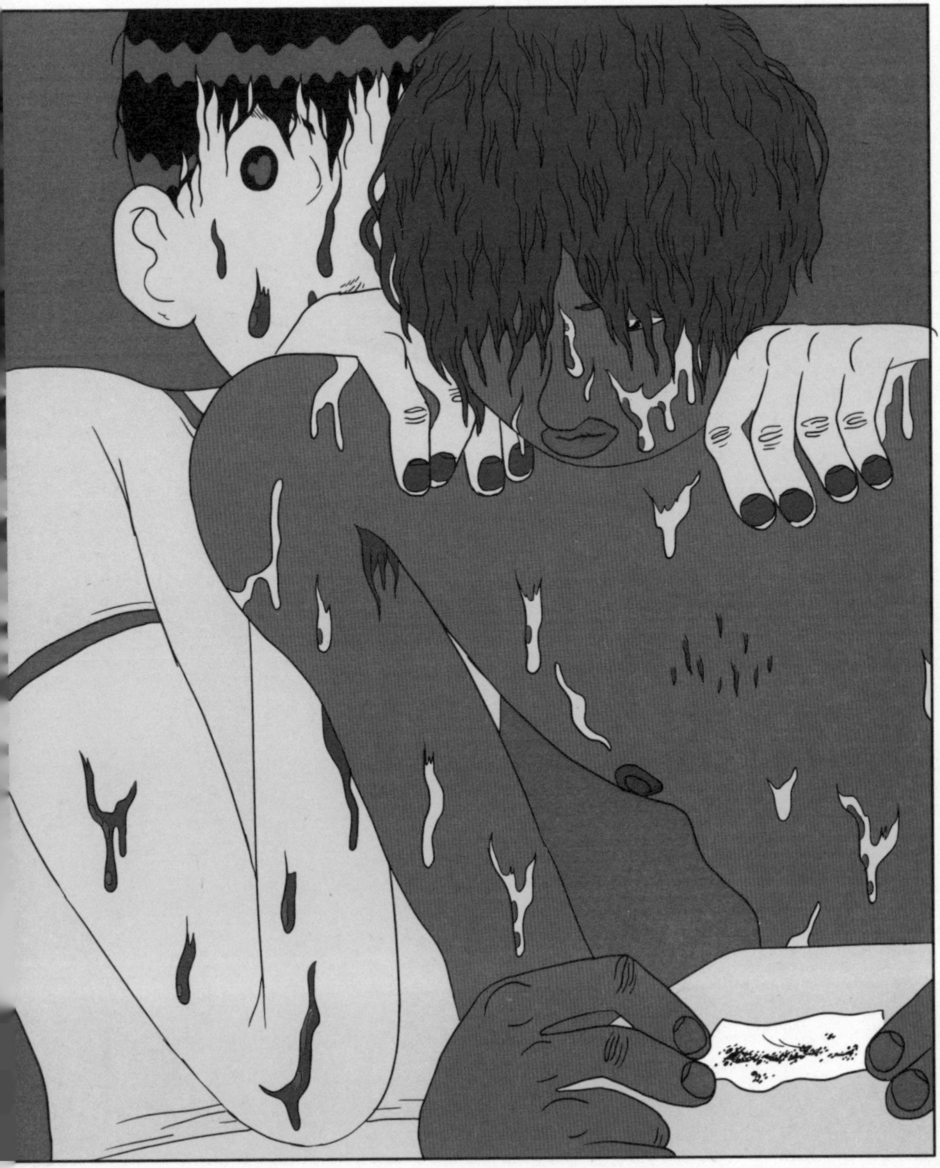

Jason and Wattie, who was still hard, spent a while trying to roll and reroll a proper joint, failing to produce a satisfactory one each time. They remarked on how funny it was that neither of them had ever learned how to roll properly. Jason eventually walked across the street to a corner store to buy some piece-of-shit glass pipe. Wattie would have done it himself—Jason had already went on a booze run earlier in the evening—but he couldn't put on pants yet, because of the erection. So it took them forty minutes to actually get to smoking the pot, which they had a laughing fit about, and when they finally got stoned, they had another fit about that.

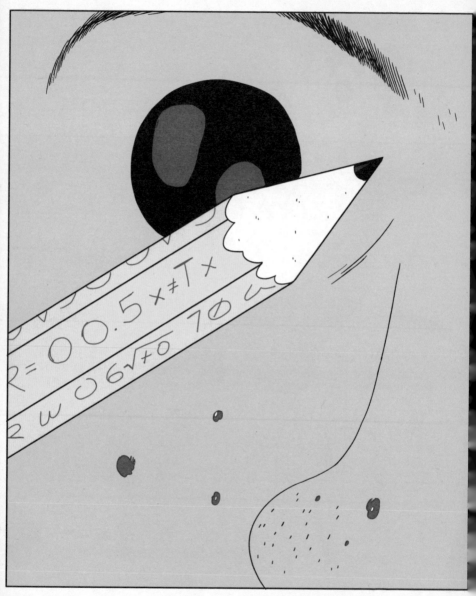

The confiscated weed distinctly reminded Jason of the shitty brick weed he and his friends used to pro-
cure in high school. They'd hang out behind the grocery store's loading dock and try to suck whatever
buzz they could out of some limp, loose thing. Sometimes they'd do it right before an exam, which was a
rush, sort of. Jason, perched on top of a dumpster or whatever, would furtively copy equations onto the
sides of a set of yellow pencils with a very fine pen he'd purchased for the express purpose of using it to
cheat. During the exam itself, he'd extract all the information he needed out of a pencil and then wipe
away his writing with a sweaty thumb.

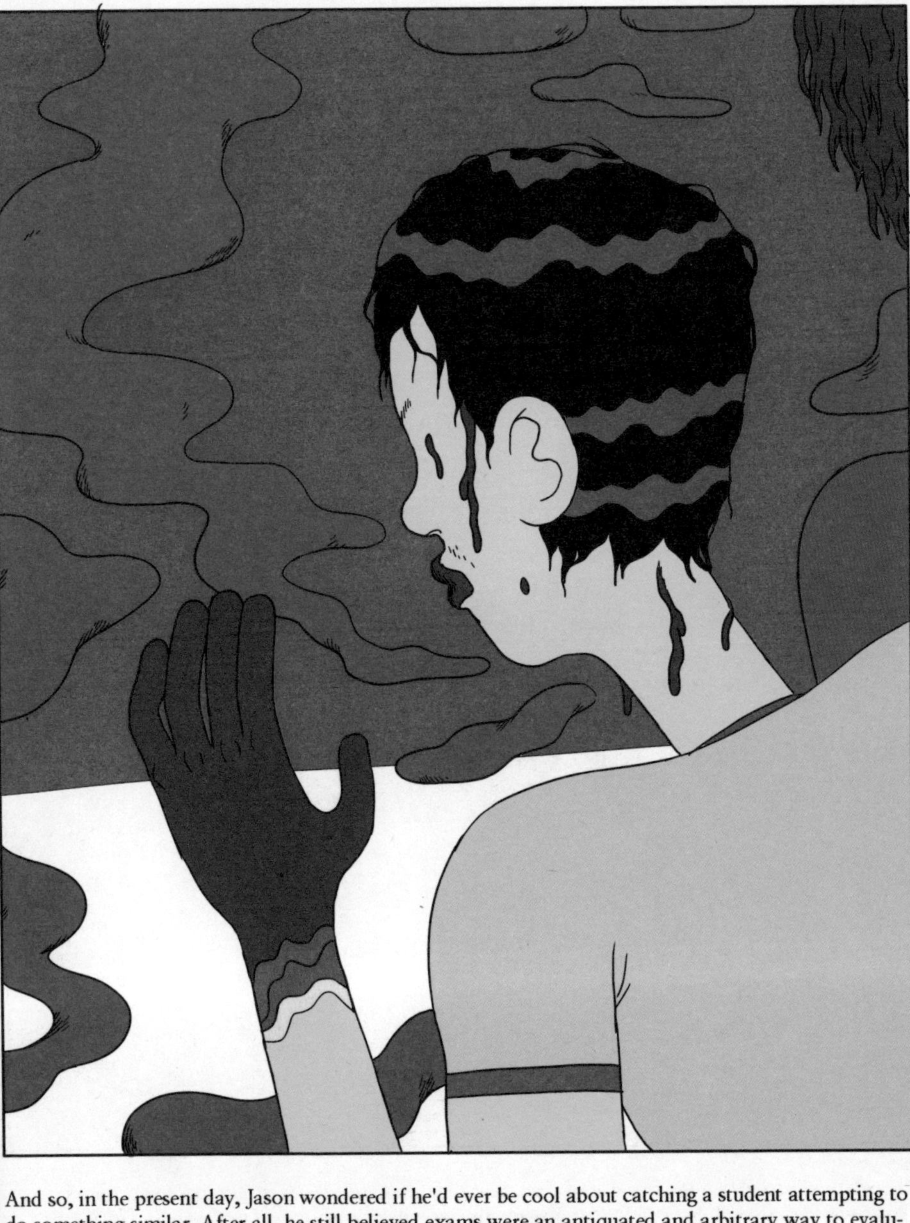

And so, in the present day, Jason wondered if he'd ever be cool about catching a student attempting to do something similar. After all, he still believed exams were an antiquated and arbitrary way to evaluate a child. He felt sad because he was pretty sure he wouldn't be cool about it at all, and was also sad because his fingers felt very swollen and heavy, because of the pot.

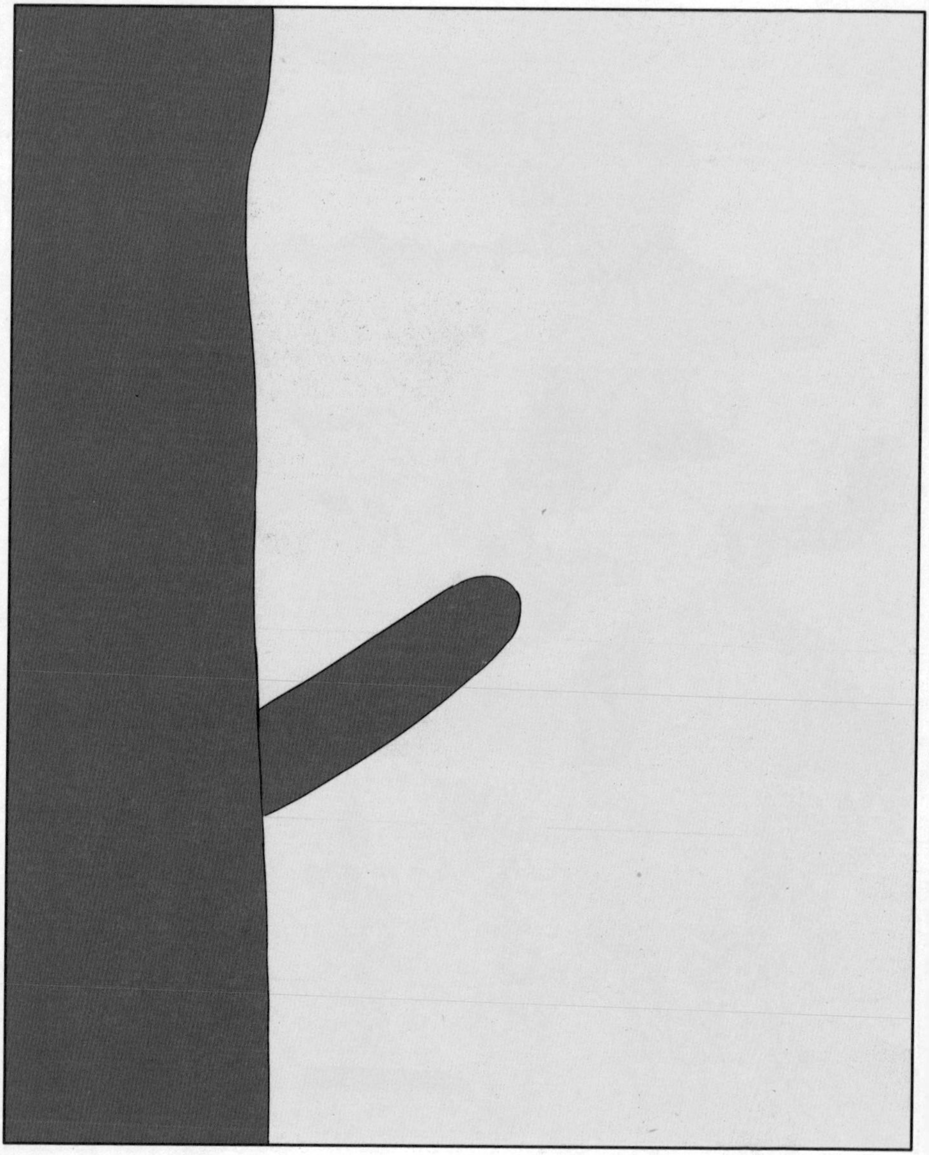

Enough time passed that the two weren't certain if they were still stoned or just in a funny mood (Jason was sad, overall, but still funny). Eventually the conversation turned to the subject of Wattie's erection, which still persisted, and in fact hadn't let up in the slightest.

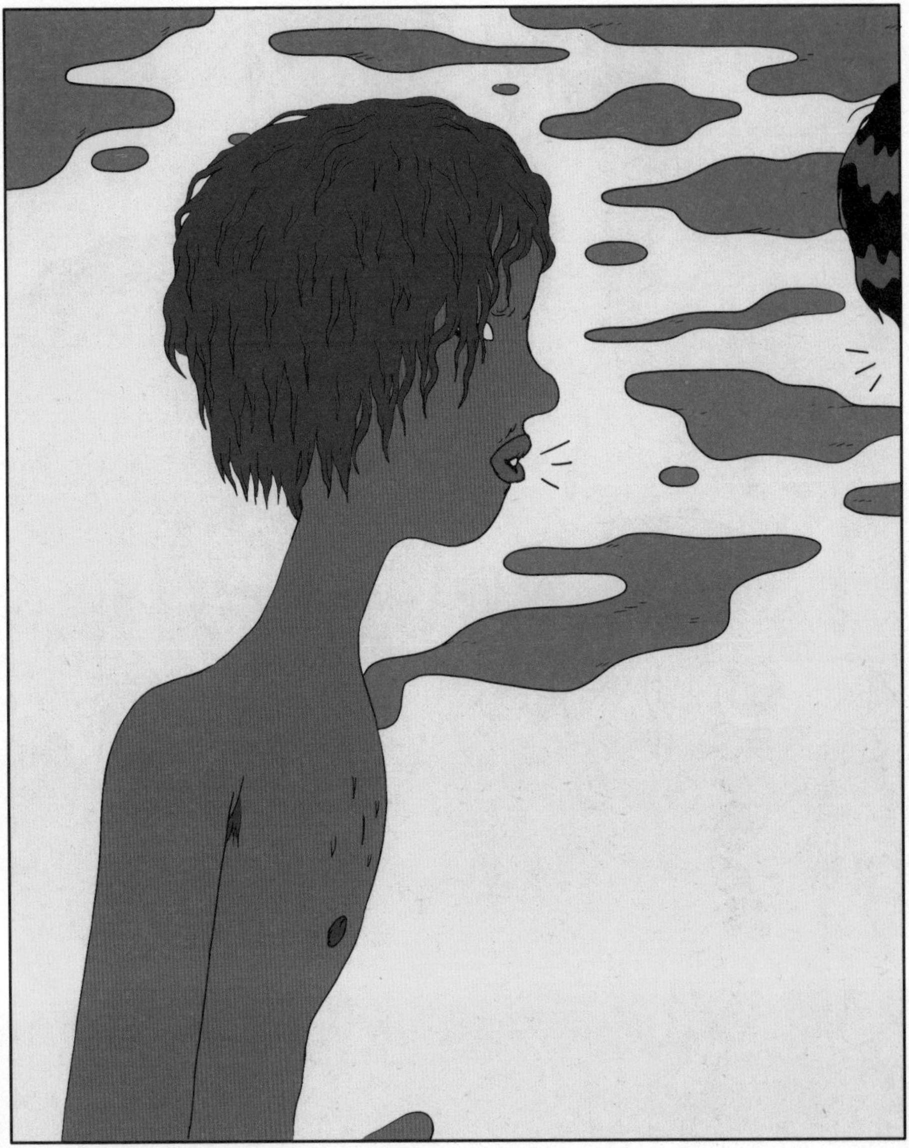

It'd been up for hours at this point, and that couldn't be healthy, and had Wattie taken any drugs to, you know, "help him out" a little, and it's nothing to be ashamed of if he had, but you just have to let me know because I'm starting to get freaked out, and of course I didn't take anything, and how could you even ask me that, and I wish you'd stop bringing up the age thing, and it has nothing to do with your age, etc. After fighting a bit longer and unsuccessfully looking up symptoms and conditions on Wattie's phone, they decided to try to do something about it.

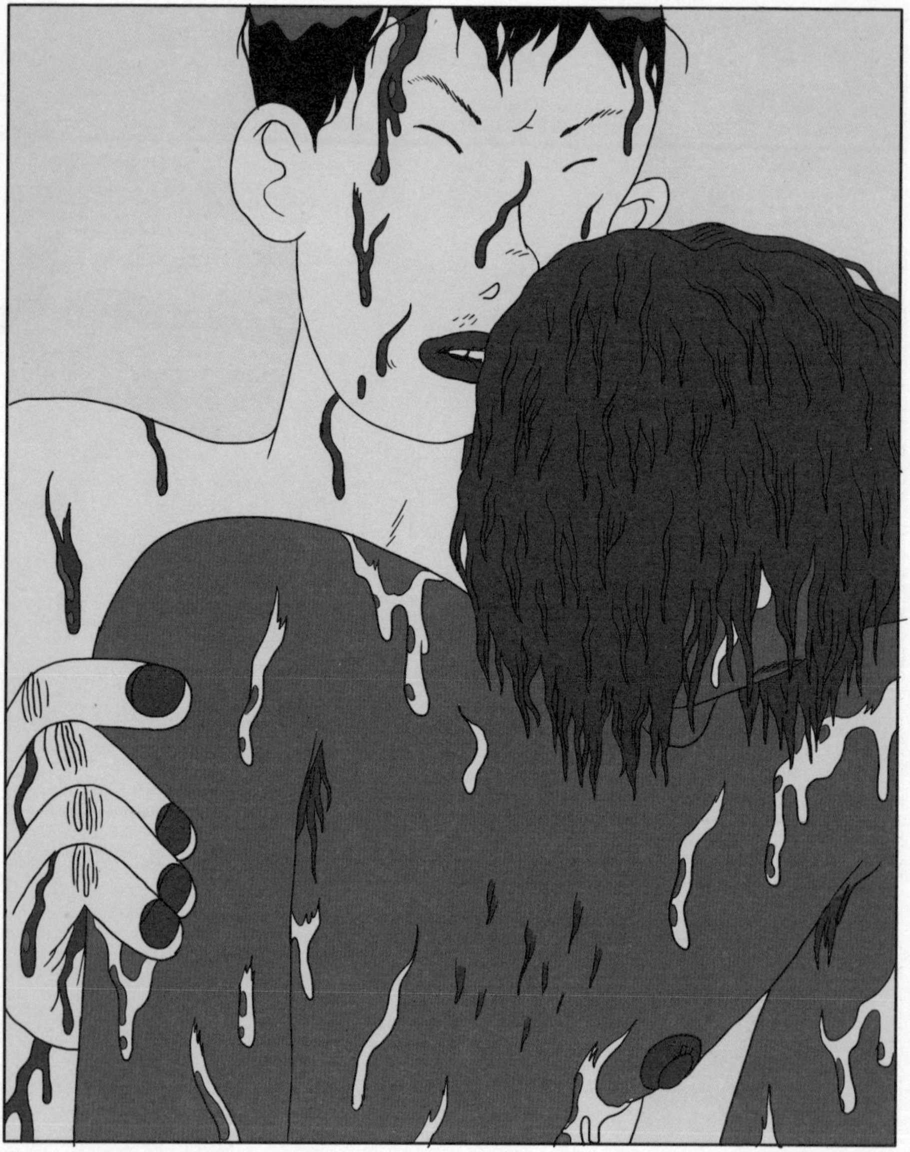

Jason tried jacking Wattie off while intermittently jacking himself off, getting hard and then losing it and then getting hard again. Then Wattie tried jacking off to Jason jacking off. They tried fucking each other in the usual ways, and then in some new ways. Nothing worked.

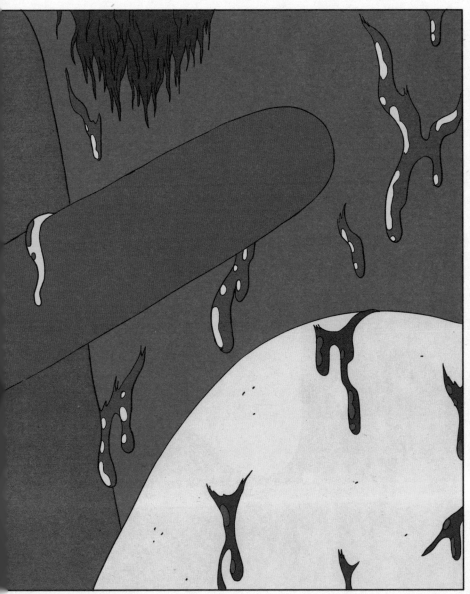

son suggested that maybe Wattie had grown bored with him, and that Jason just couldn't bring him
ere the way he used to. Maybe third parties needed to be introduced. And so third parties were intro-
ced. First men and then eventually women. (Because why not women?) Sometimes Jason would join in,
t not every time. Jason would get off pretty frequently, but he'd always be overwhelmed with this sick,
king guilt in the space between coming and coming back to his senses. It was a space he used to love
t now couldn't, because how could he ever truly enjoy his relief the way he used to when he knew that
attie, this man he adored, was no longer able to enjoy that relief for himself?

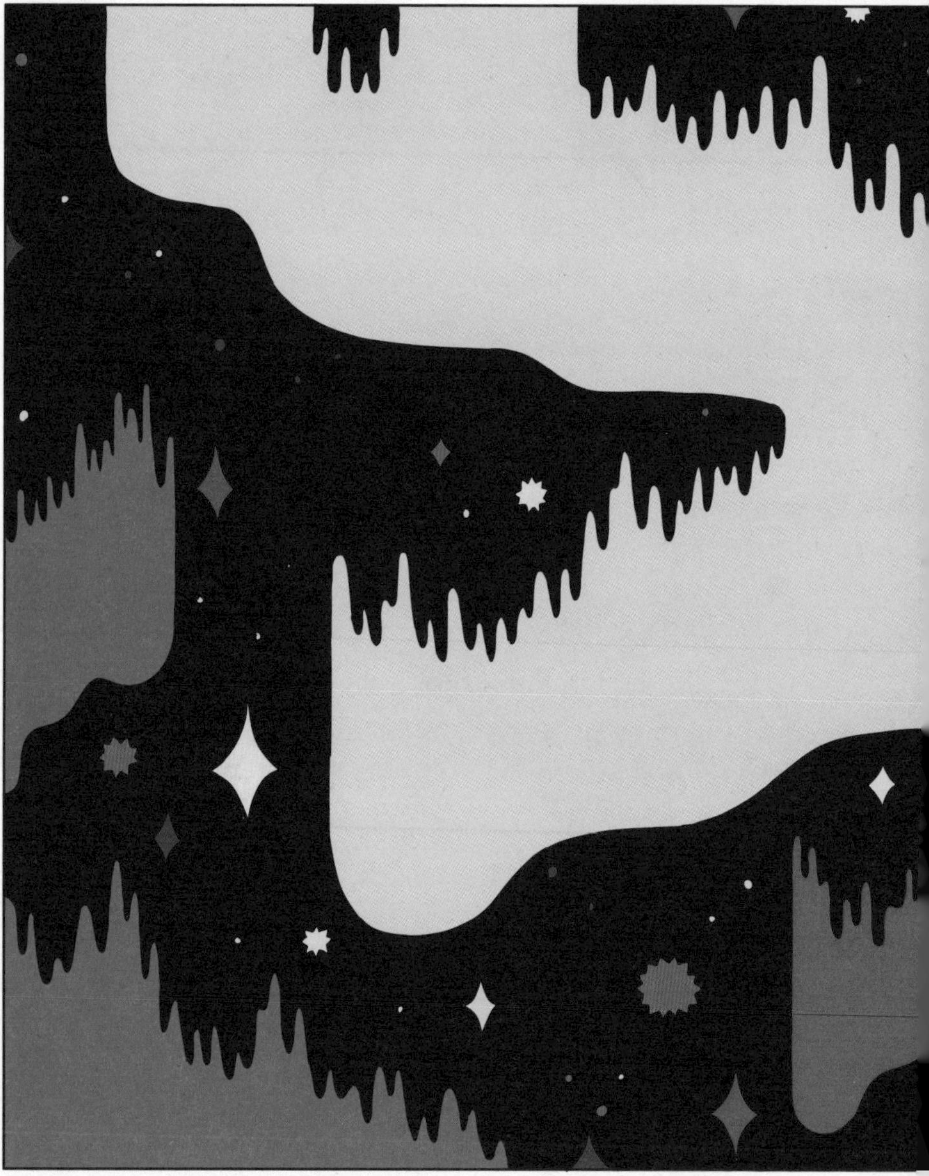

They consulted doctors around the world, fucked the doctors, took drugs, sold drugs, fucked cops in holding cells after bribing and seducing them, had celebrities and dignitaries and once a prime minister pressed up against palatial columns, against museum walls, inside limousines, below racks of firearms, below the Liberty Bell, below the northern lights.

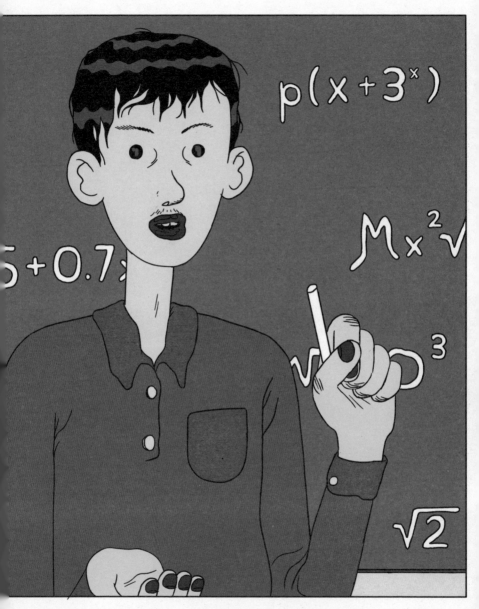

...ason got tired of the parties and the travel, of waking up with strangers and making small talk with ...hose strangers. His job at the school began to feel like his anchor, the one thing stopping his body from ...reaking away into a million pieces. He was torn up about it because he wasn't even sure if he liked his ...ob, and because wasn't Wattie supposed to be his anchor? Because isn't that what a relationship is for, if ...'s for anything at all?

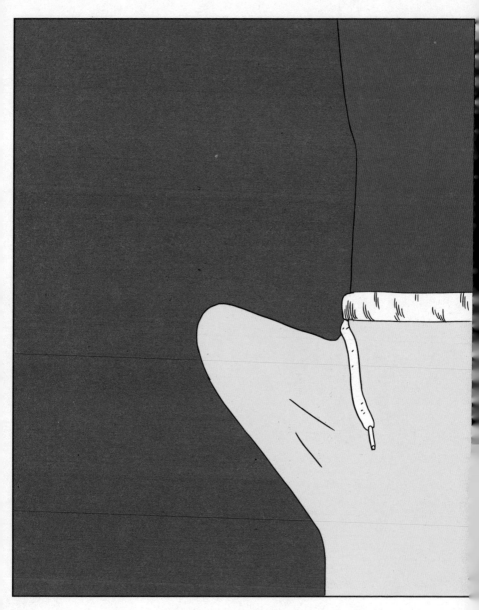

Wattie, on the other hand, had given up completely, but he still went through the motions and tried all the new stuff. He'd long ago abandoned all hope of ever obliterating the erection. But he still pretended, because he thought that's what Jason needed from him, that Wattie's resignation would destroy Jason, and he was right, probably.

So Jason was lying there in bed, fondling his balls with one hand while working Wattie's cock with the other. They'd gone back to just regular jacking off again, because they were really wiped by that point. Jason couldn't tell how long the night had gone on for, and couldn't tell if he was still a little bit stoned after all, even though so many hours had passed since they'd smoked that fucking thing. His fingers still felt fat. He once again thought about high school. He wondered if, as a sixteen-year-old, he'd ever expected to end up as a teacher, settled down and practically married. He wondered if that would have been disappointing information to have at the time. Then Jason wondered if that disappointment would have been softened by the fact that even though he'd washed up as a teacher, he'd been to so many places, screwed so many people and tried so many drugs on his way there.

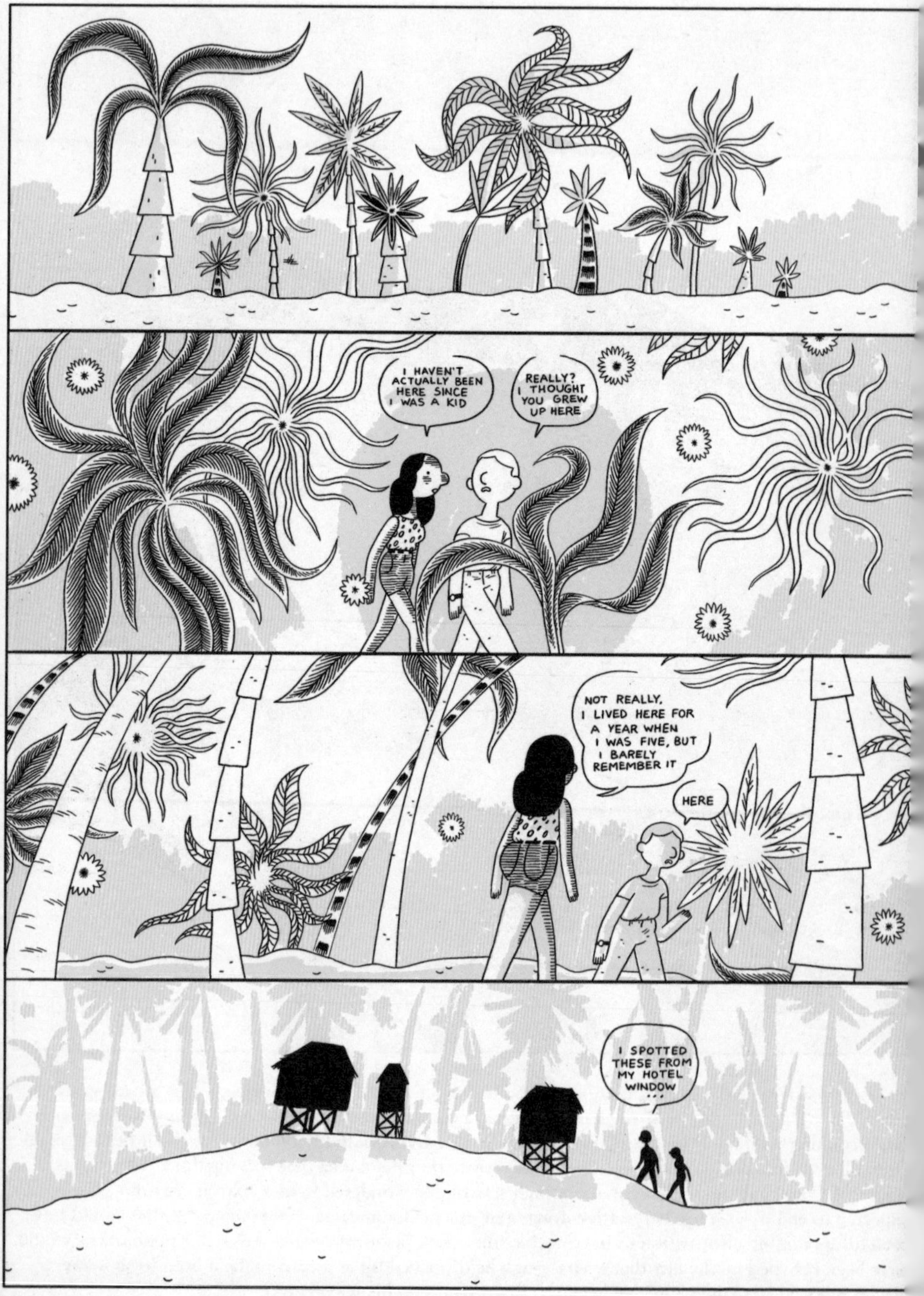
I HAVEN'T ACTUALLY BEEN HERE SINCE I WAS A KID
REALLY? I THOUGHT YOU GREW UP HERE
NOT REALLY, I LIVED HERE FOR A YEAR WHEN I WAS FIVE, BUT I BARELY REMEMBER IT
HERE
I SPOTTED THESE FROM MY HOTEL WINDOW ...

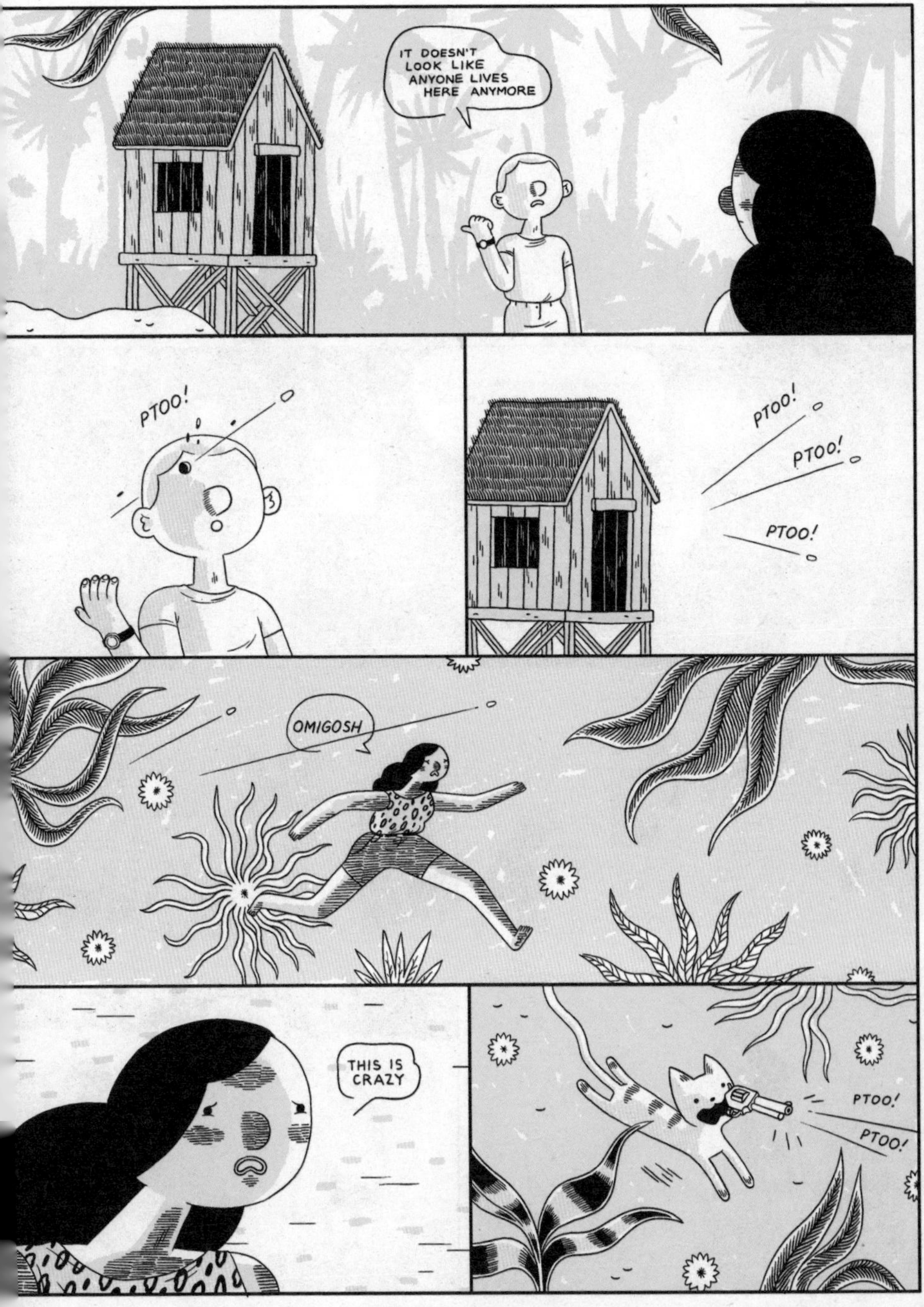
IT DOESN'T LOOK LIKE ANYONE LIVES HERE ANYMORE
PTOO!
PTOO!
PTOO!
PTOO!
OMIGOSH
THIS IS CRAZY
PTOO!
PTOO!

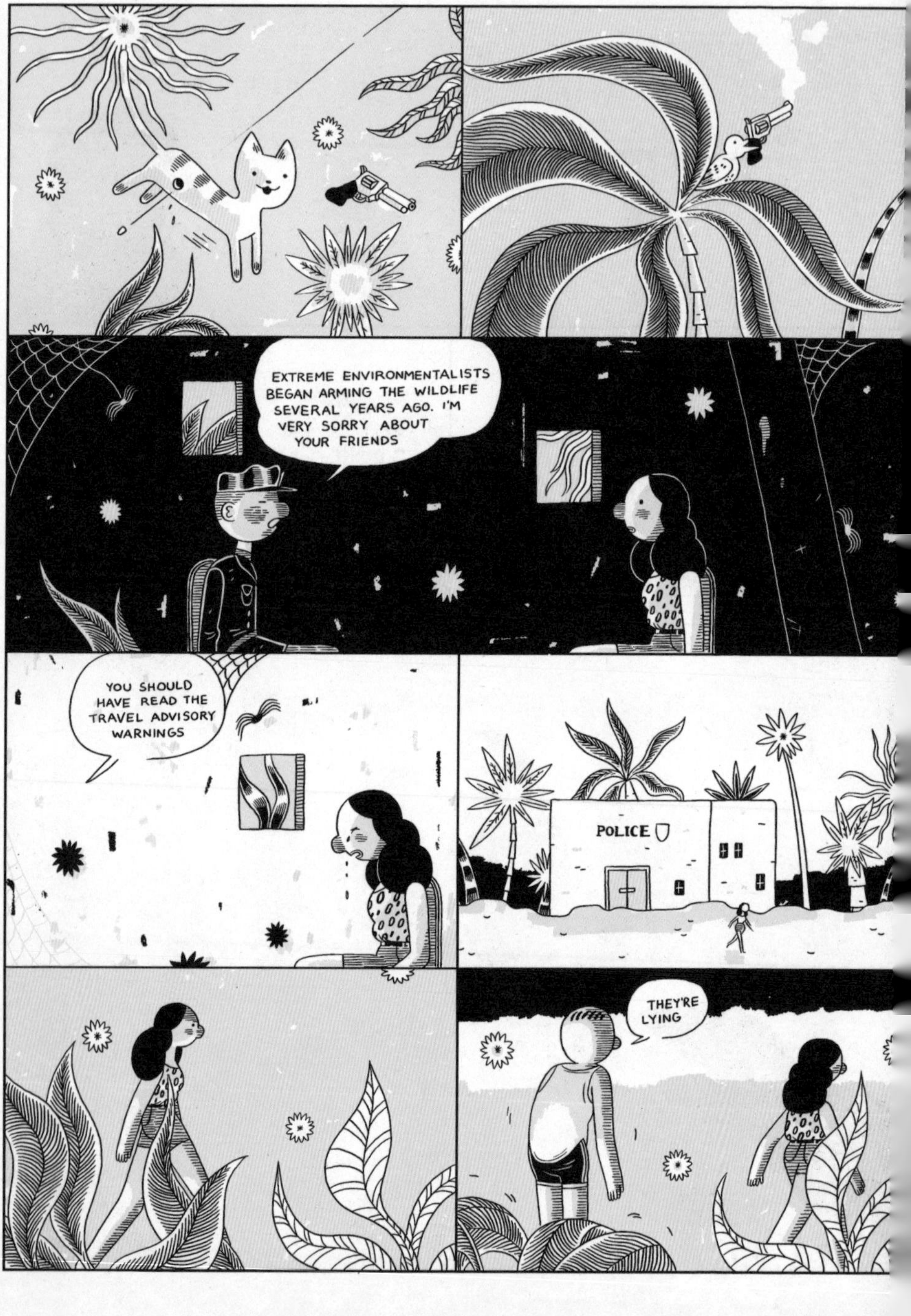
EXTREME ENVIRONMENTALISTS BEGAN ARMING THE WILDLIFE SEVERAL YEARS AGO. I'M VERY SORRY ABOUT YOUR FRIENDS
YOU SHOULD HAVE READ THE TRAVEL ADVISORY WARNINGS
POLICE
THEY'RE LYING

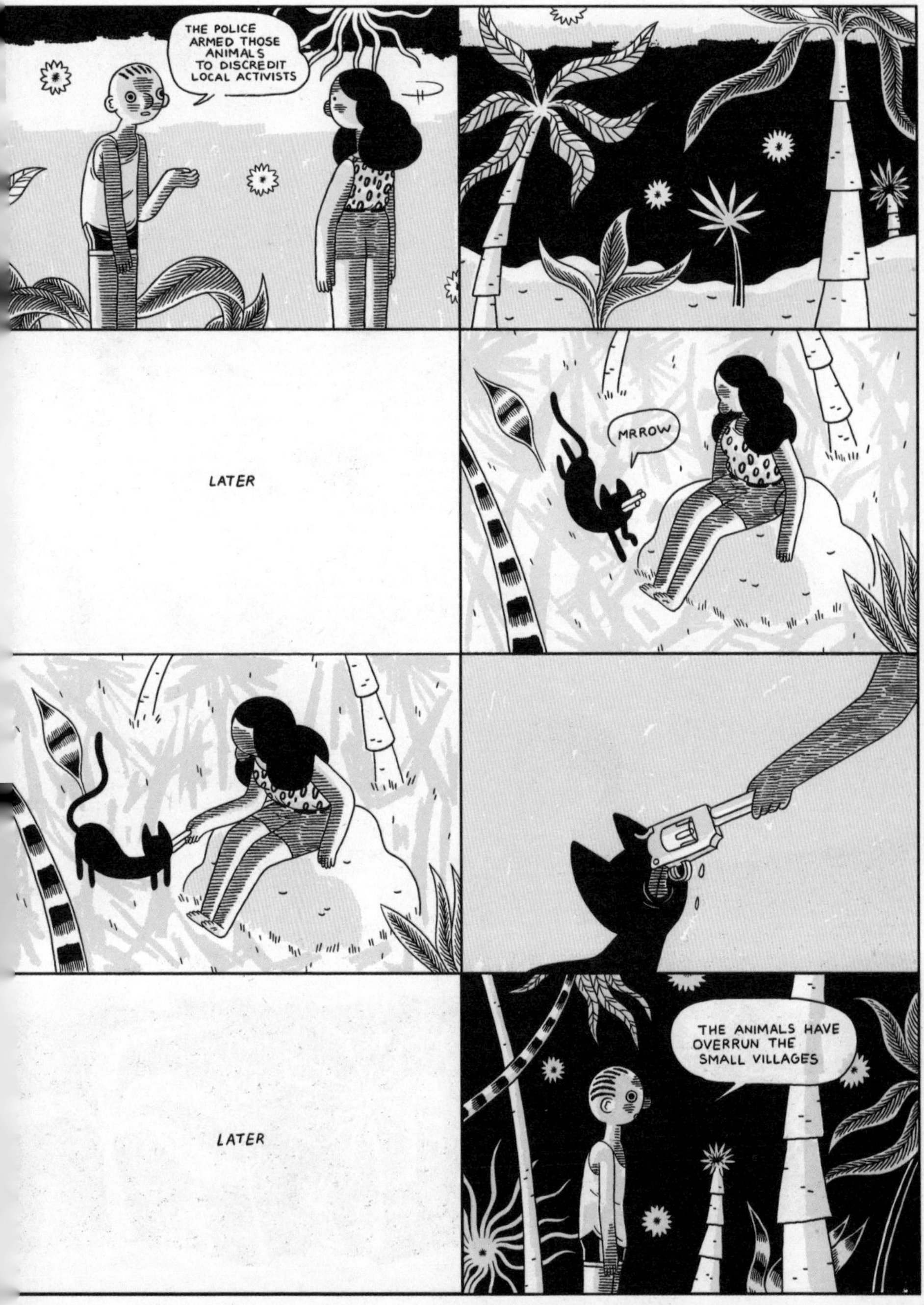
THE POLICE ARMED THOSE ANIMALS TO DISCREDIT LOCAL ACTIVISTS
LATER
MRROW
LATER
THE ANIMALS HAVE OVERRUN THE SMALL VILLAGES

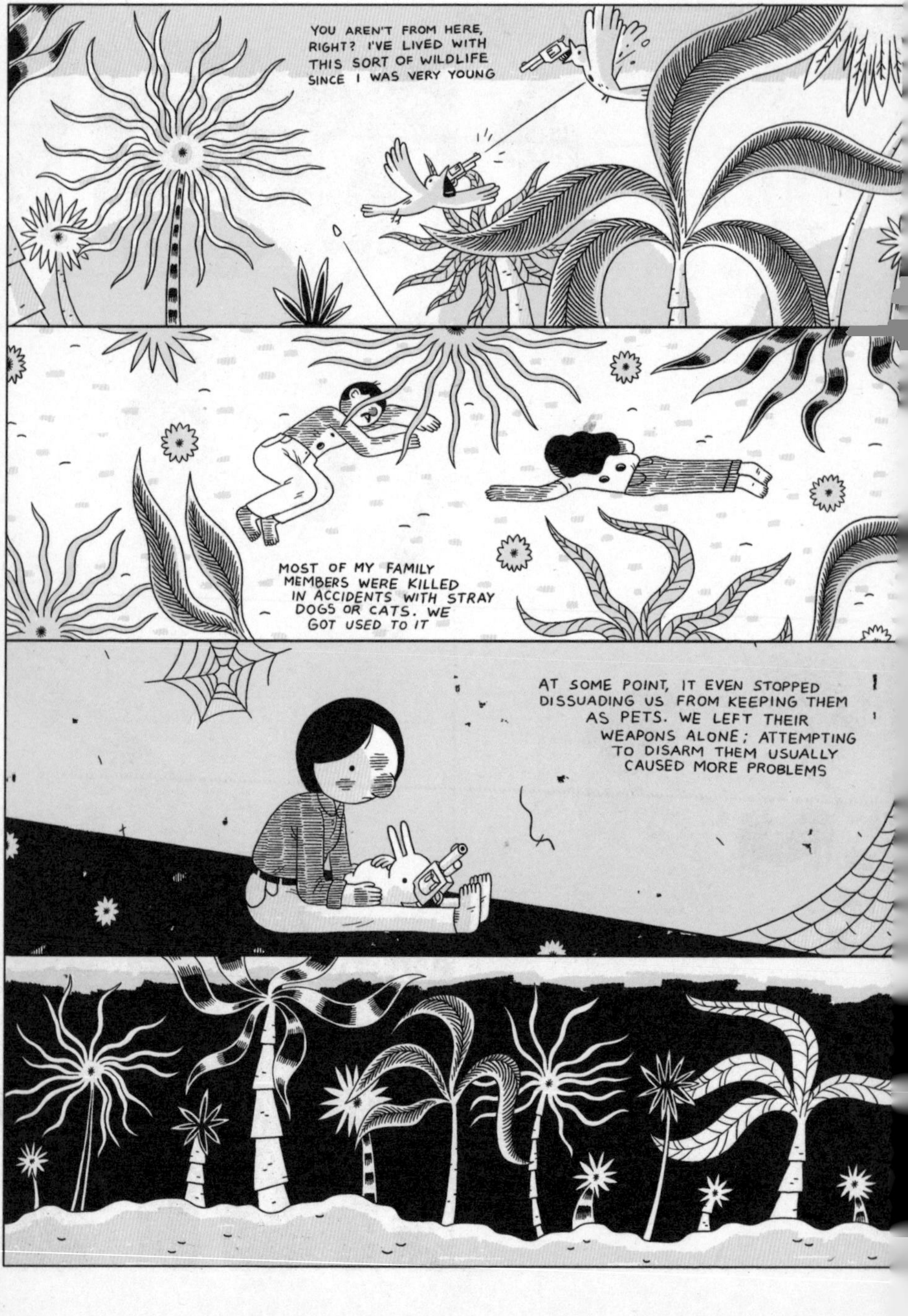
YOU AREN'T FROM HERE, RIGHT? I'VE LIVED WITH THIS SORT OF WILDLIFE SINCE I WAS VERY YOUNG
MOST OF MY FAMILY MEMBERS WERE KILLED IN ACCIDENTS WITH STRAY DOGS OR CATS. WE GOT USED TO IT
AT SOME POINT, IT EVEN STOPPED DISSUADING US FROM KEEPING THEM AS PETS. WE LEFT THEIR WEAPONS ALONE; ATTEMPTING TO DISARM THEM USUALLY CAUSED MORE PROBLEMS

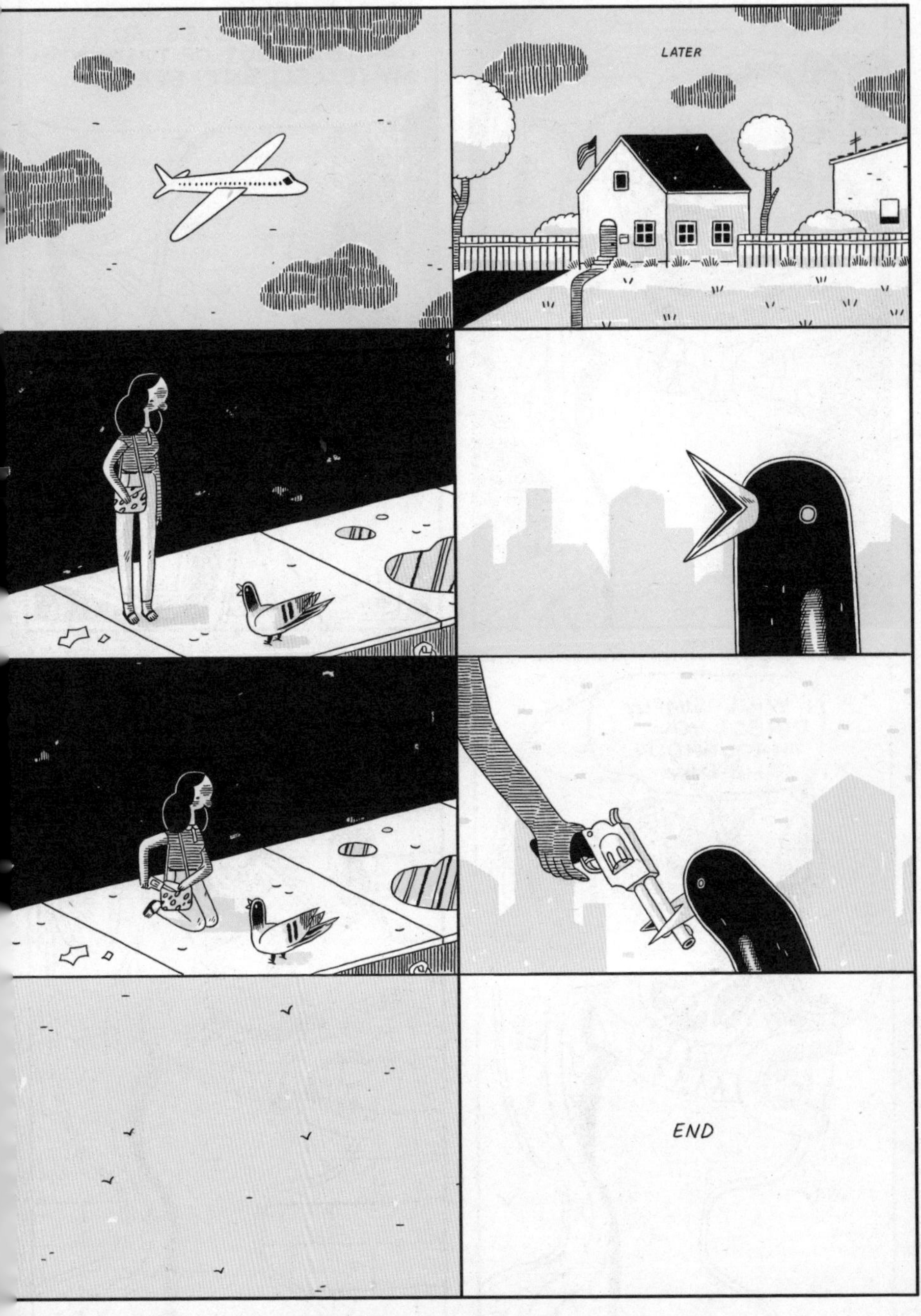
LATER
END

TINY OPHTHALMOLOGIST

WHAT KIND OF OPHTHALMOLOGIST ARE YOU
THE TINY KIND. I DRILLED SMALL HOLES THROUGH YOUR FAULTY EYES SO I CAN LOOK OUT OF THEM WITH MY (EXCELLENT) EYES
I WILL SIMPLY DIRECT YOU THROUGHOUT THE DAY
TAKE THREE STEPS FORWARD

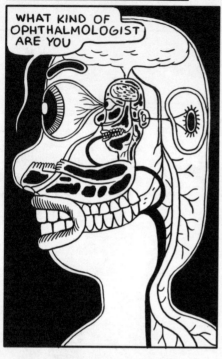

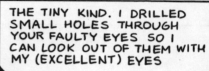

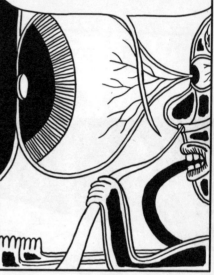

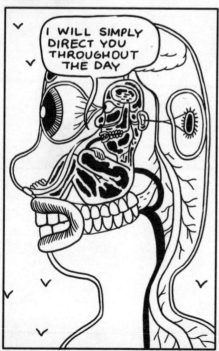

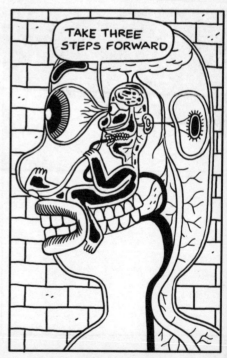

TURN RIGHT
OK STOP
DO YOU SEE THAT GIRL?
YEAH
TALK TO HER

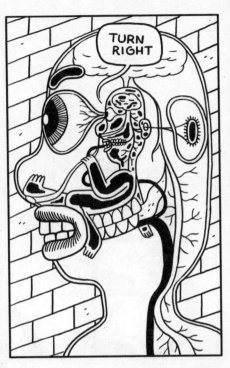

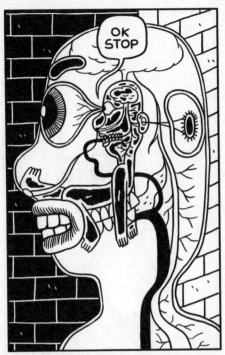

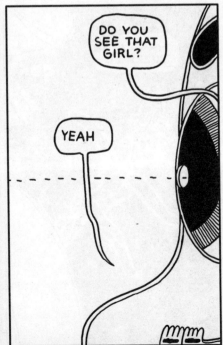

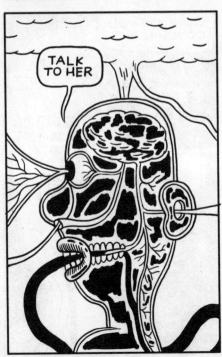

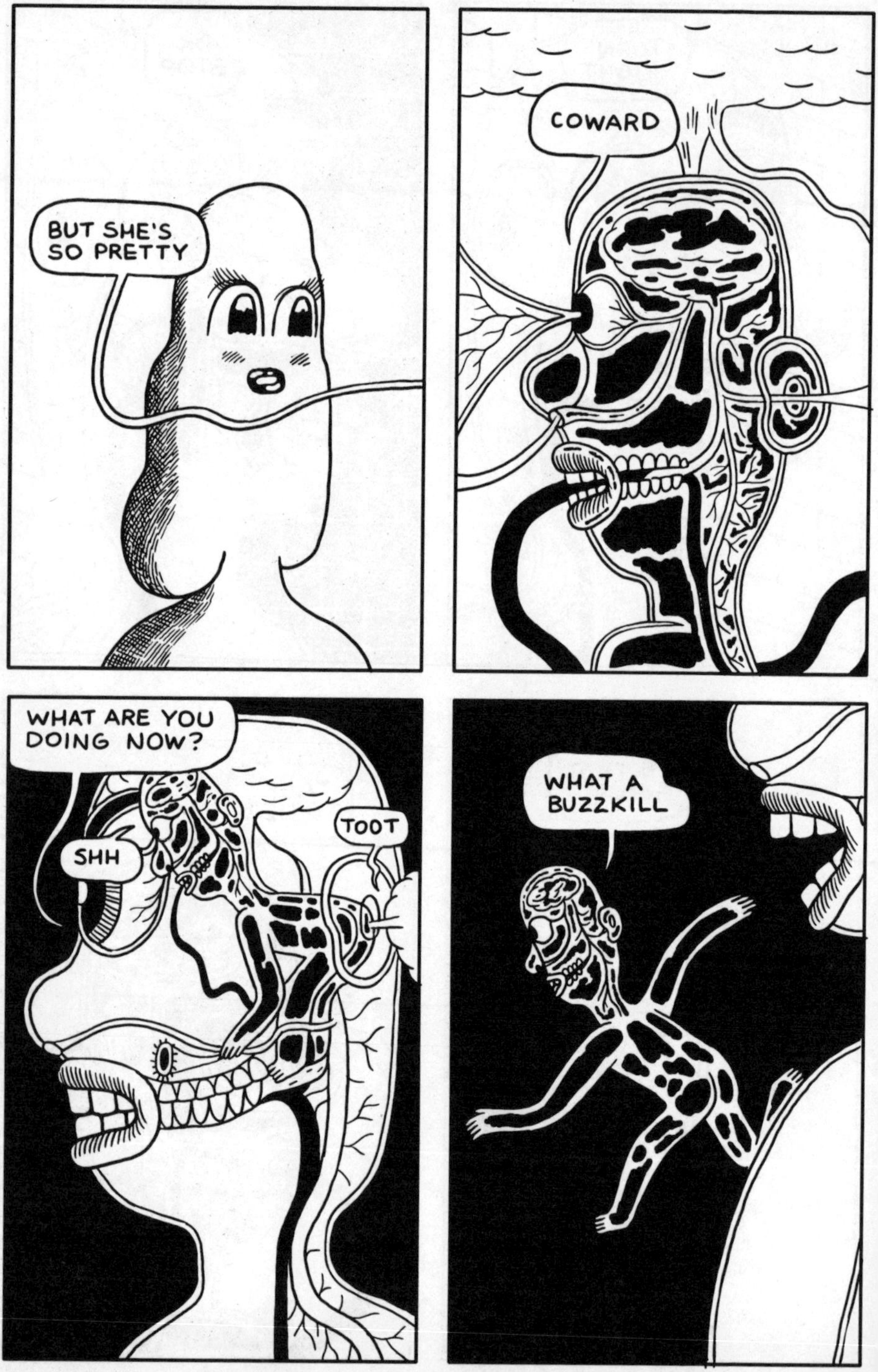
BUT SHE'S SO PRETTY
COWARD
WHAT ARE YOU DOING NOW?
SHH
TOOT
WHAT A BUZZKILL

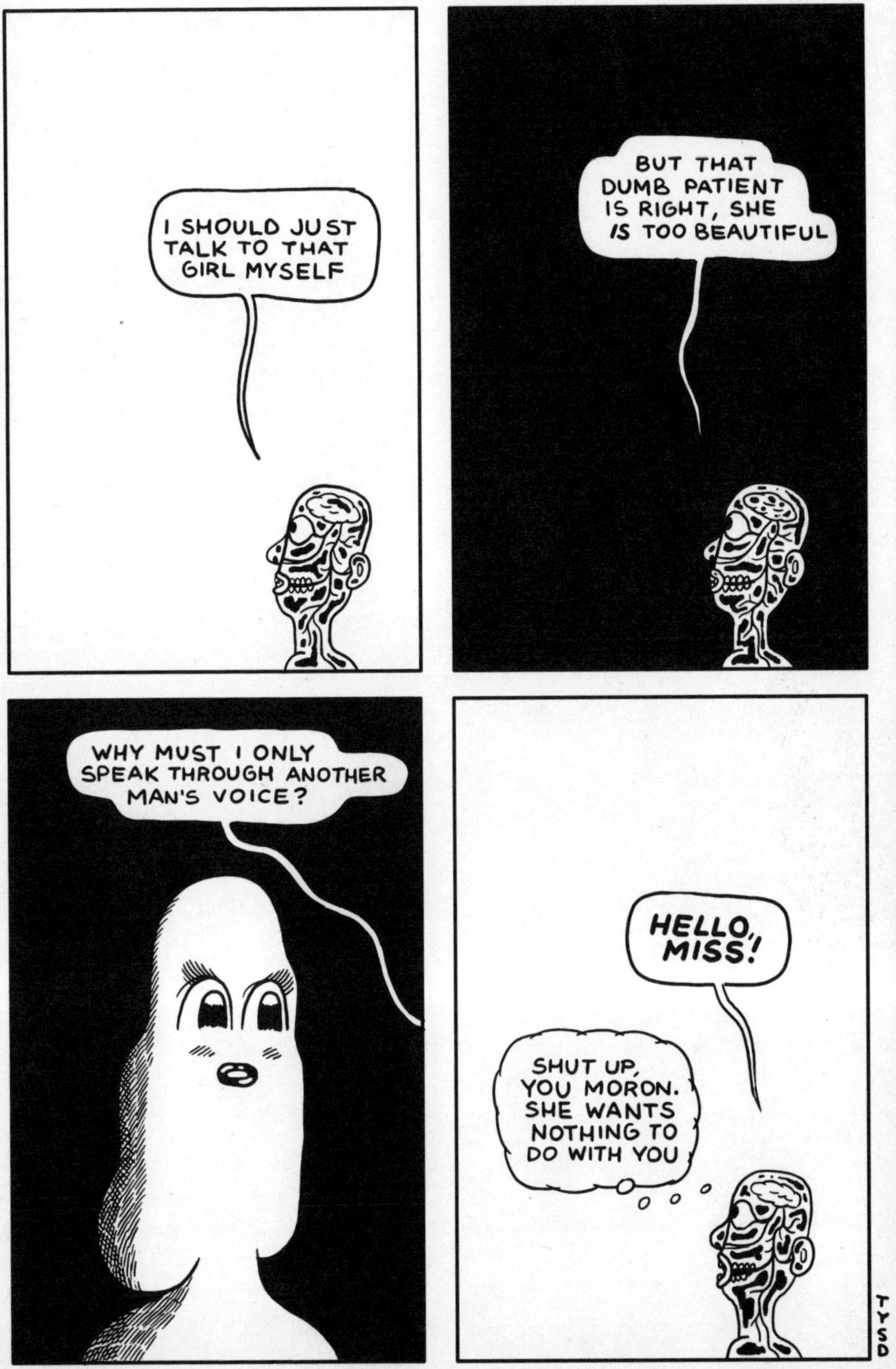
I SHOULD JUST TALK TO THAT GIRL MYSELF
BUT THAT DUMB PATIENT IS RIGHT, SHE *IS* TOO BEAUTIFUL
WHY MUST I ONLY SPEAK THROUGH ANOTHER MAN'S VOICE?
HELLO, MISS!
SHUT UP, YOU MORON. SHE WANTS NOTHING TO DO WITH YOU
TYSD

ALL OF MY FRIENDS, UP HIGH, IN A JUMBO JET

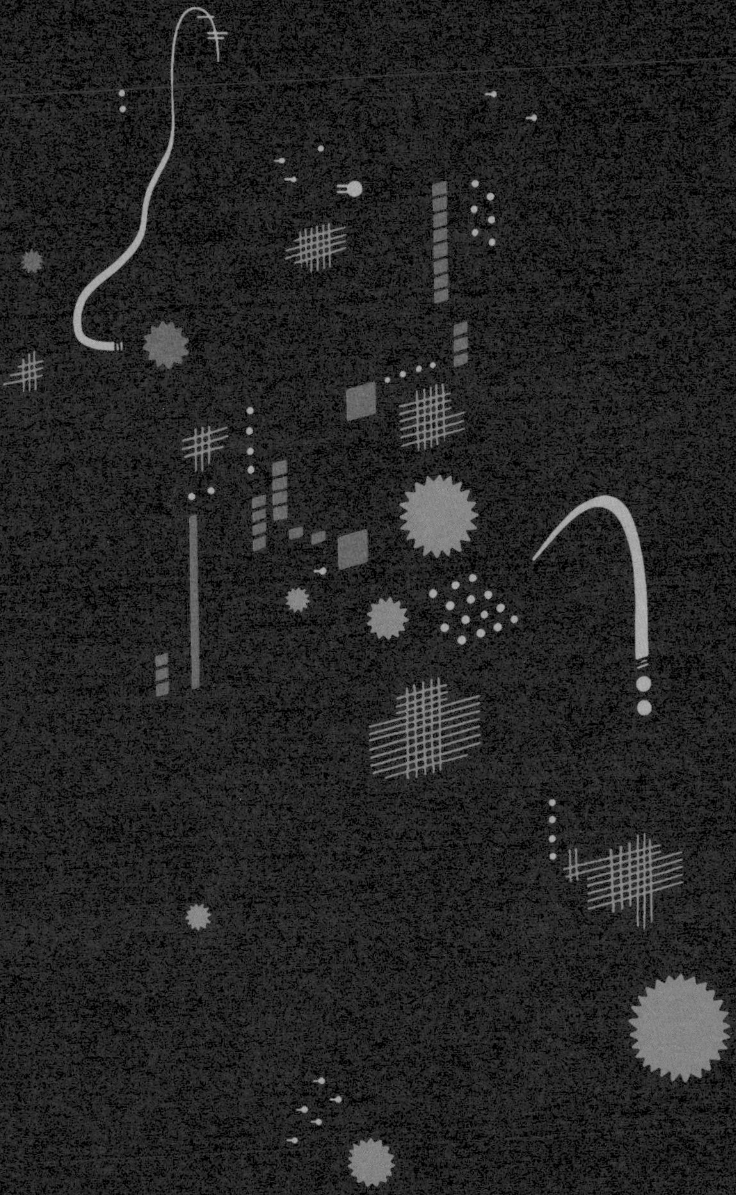

(Flying through a cloud)

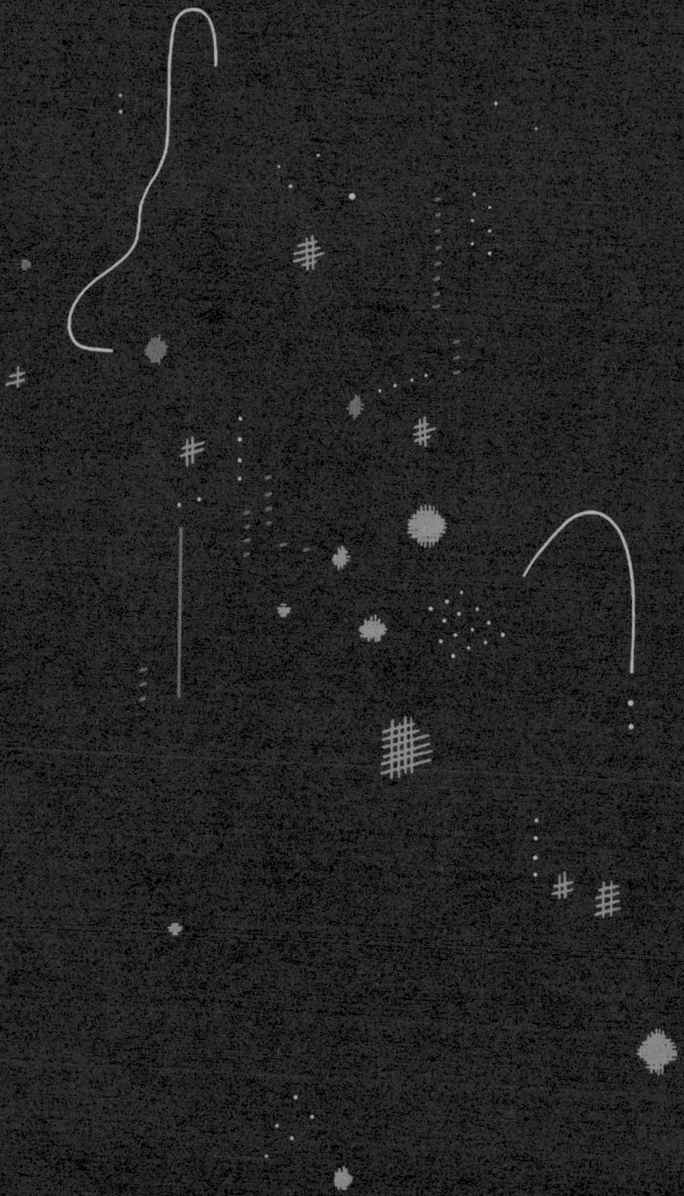

Since we stole the thing, we had to spend the first few years circling the globe so cops wouldn't find us. After that, we'd find places that seemed okay or interesting and just sort of hover over there for a while? The pilot died, by the way, a decade later.

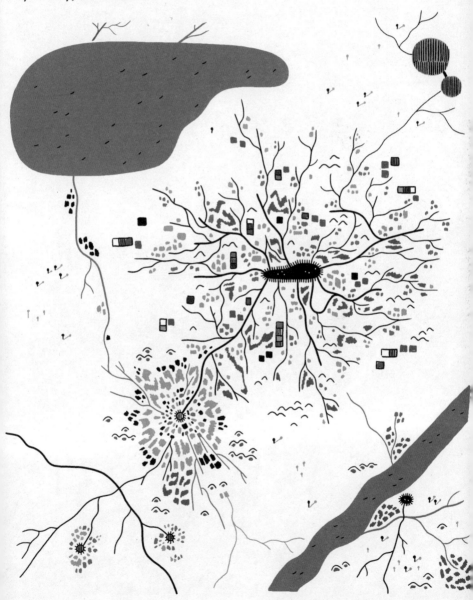

Moss covered him and covered his chair until they didn't look like a person or a chair at all, but then the moss collapsed in on itself and it became a chair again.

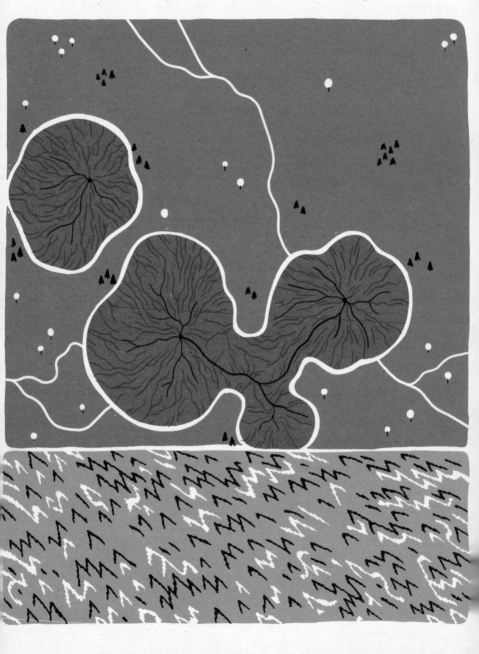

It wasn't a big deal. We had already run out of fuel at that point. We were letting air currents keep us afloat.

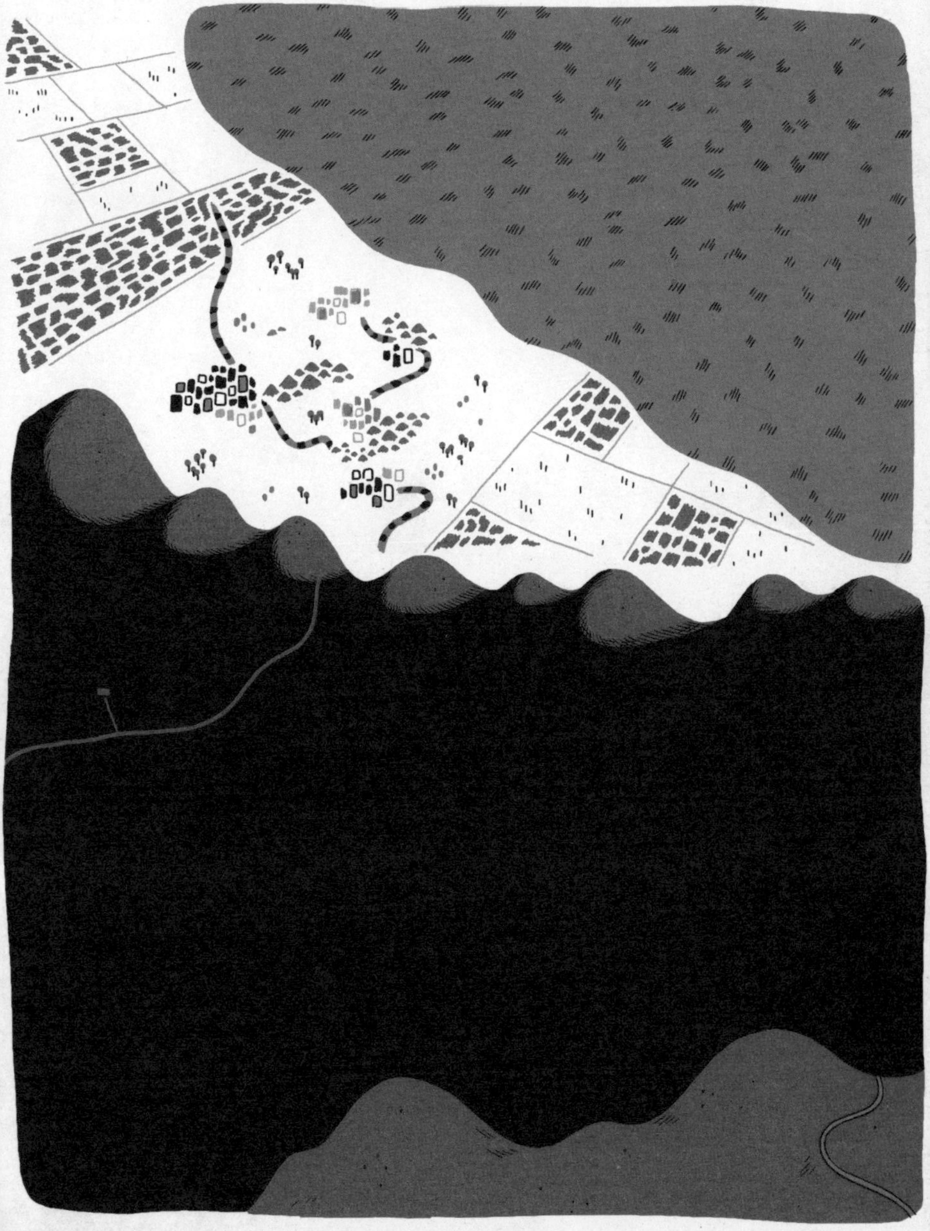

We punched holes through the windows and caught birds for eating and sometimes for pets.

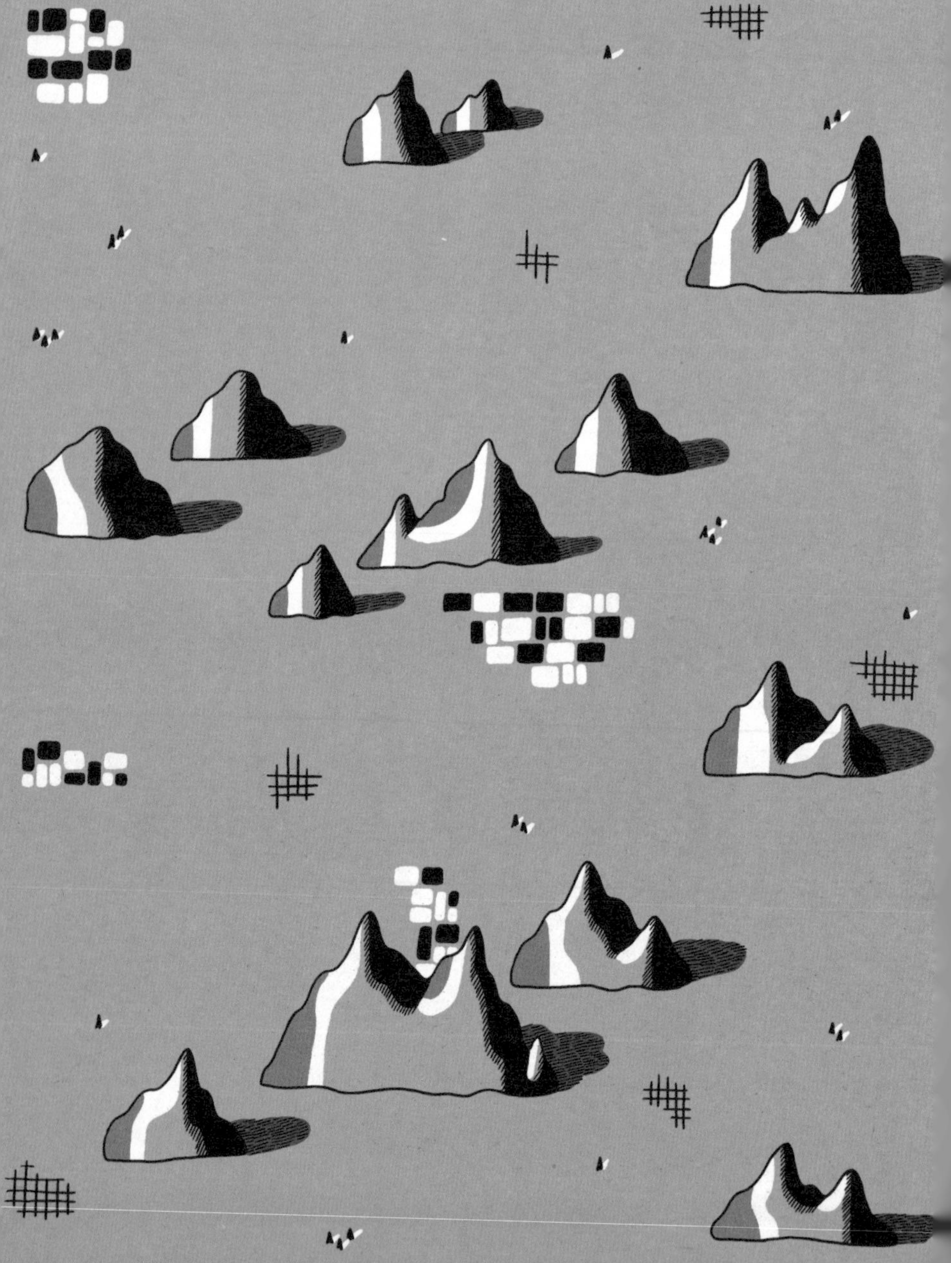

Nobody ever brought up landing.

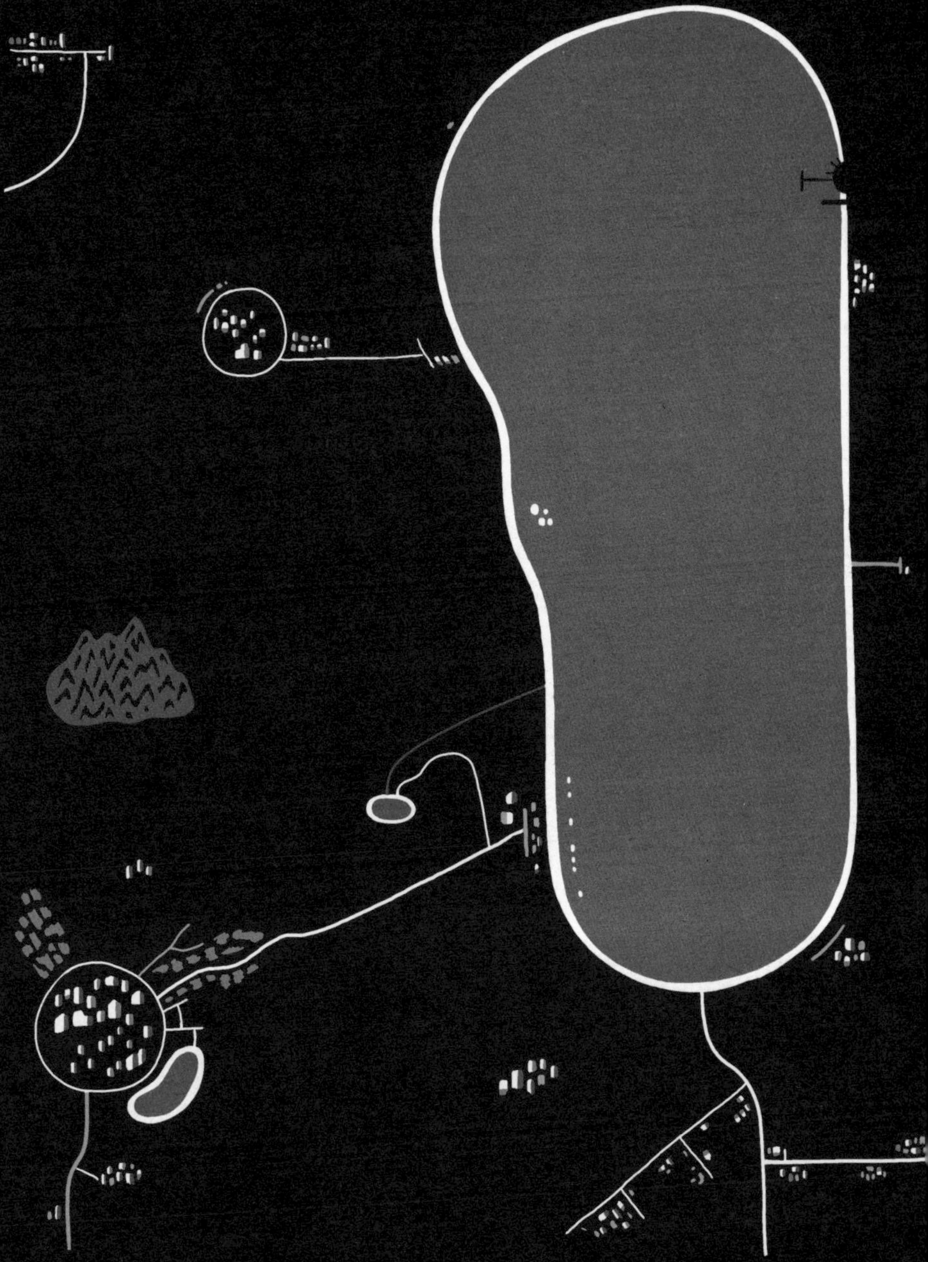

One million years passed

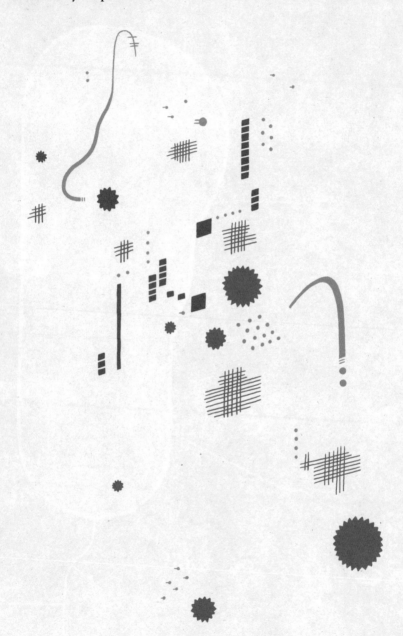

FOR R+J

MICHAEL DEFORGE DRAWS COMIC BOOKS IN TORONTO

THANKS: ANNE, RYAN, PATRICK, GINETTE, ROBIN, PHIL, JILLIAN, LALA, RYAN, SADIE,
ALVIN, JANE, MICKEY, FRANK, LESLIE, NOEL, SIMON, THE BEGUILING AND MY FAMILY

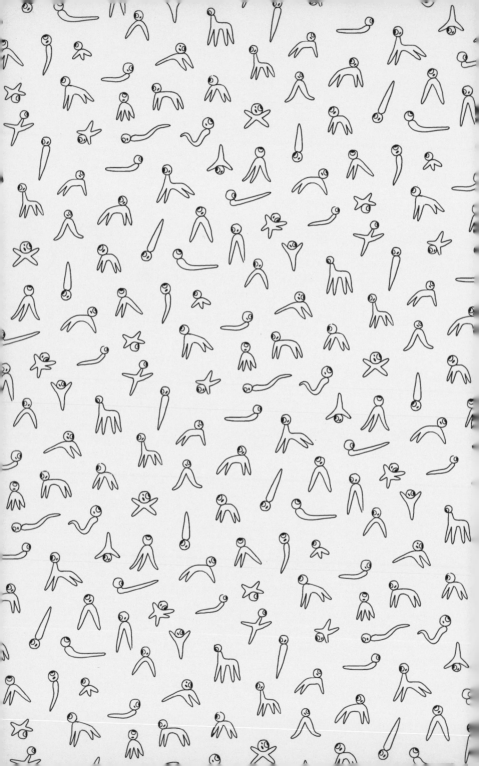